ECO-ARCHITECTURE
1000 Ideas by 100 Architects

ECO-ARCHITECTURE
1000 Ideas by 100 Architects

Edited by **Marta Serrats**

ECO-ARCHITECTURE
1000 Ideas by 100 Architects

Editorial coordinator: Aitana Lleonart Triquell
Editor: Marta Serrats
Art director: Mireia Casanovas Soley
Design and layout coordination: Claudia Martínez Alonso
Layout: Cristina Simó Perales
Cover layout: María Eugenia Castell Carballo
Translation: Cillero & de Motta

Cover drawing: © LOLA LANDSCAPE ARCHITECTS

PROMOPRESS is a brand of:
PROMOTORA DE PRENSA INTERNACIONAL, S. A.
Ausiàs March, 124
08013 Barcelona
Spain
Tel.: +34 93 245 14 64
Fax: +34 93 265 48 83
E-mail: info@promopress.es
www.promopress.es
www.promopresseditions.com

First published in English: 2012

ISBN: 978-84-92810-45-1

Printed in Spain

Contents

Introduction 6
0 to 1 8
Amunt Architekten Martenson und Nagel Theissen 10
Andrea Tognon Architecture 14
Andrew Maynard Architects pty ltd 18
Architectenbureau Paul de Ruiter bv 22
Arkitekstudio Widjedal Racki 26
Architekturbüro Reinberg ZT GmbH 28
Arconiko Architecten (Frido van Nieuwamerongen, Roswitha Abraham) 30
Arkin Tilt Architects. Ecological Planning & Design 34
Atelier Riri (Novriansyah Yakub) 38
Atelier RVL Architectes 40
Baumraum (Andreas Wenning) 44
Beals–Lyon Architects 48
Bipolaire Arquitectos (Miguel Arraiz García) 52
BNIM 54
Bourne Blue Architecture 58
Casagrande Laboratory 60
Center for Design Research, University of Kansas 64
Christina Zerva Architects 68
Correia/Ragazzi Arquitectos 72
Coste Architectures 76
Designs Northwest Architects 80
Despang Architekten 84
Dick van Gameren Architekten 86
Djuric Tardio Architectes 88
Dorte Mandrup Arkitekter ApS 92
Ecospace® Ltd. 94
Ecosistema Urbano 96
FLOAT architectural research and design (Erin Moore) 100
Francisco Portugal e Gomes, Arquitecto 104
François Perrin 108
Garrison Architects 110
Green Dwellings/Leger Wanaselja Architecture 112
GROUP A Architects 114
Gudmundur Jonsson Arkitektkontor 118
Guz Architects 120
Harquitectes 122
H2o Architects 126
Heliotrope Architects 130
Hiroshi Nakamura & NAP Architects 134
HOK 136
House + House Architects 138
Huttunen-Lipasti-Pakkanen Oy/Ltd 142
I-Beam Design 144
Iredale Pedersen Hook Architects 146
J. Mayer H. Architects 150
Johnsen Schmaling Architects 152
Kendle Design Collaborative 156
Kirkland Fraser Moor 160
Living Homes 162
LMN 164
Luis de Garrido 168
Manasaram Architects (Neelam Manjunath) 172
Mario Cucinella Architects srl. 174
Mark Kingsley Architects 176
Mark Merer 180
Max Pritchard Architect 182
Leddy Maytum Stacy Architects 186
Michael Jantzen 188
Minarc 190
MVRDV 194
Nicholas Burns Associates 198
OFIS Arhitekti 202
Office of Mobile Design by Jennifer Siegal 206
OLGGA architectes 208
Paratelier (Leonardo Paiella, Monica Ravazzolo) 212
Paterson Architects 216
Patrick Nadeau 218
Paul McKean Architecture Llc. 220
Paul Morgan Architects 224
Peter Kuczia 226
PopovBass Architects 230
ProdesilDomesi 232
R&Sie(n) 236
Ray Kappe 240
Resolution: 4 Architecture 242
Rintala Eggertsson Architects 246
Rob Paulus Architects 248
Rongen Architekten GmbH 250
SAAI. Sustainable Architecture Advisors International 254
Samyn and Partners, Architects & Engineers 258
Sander Architects, LLC 262
Sau, Taller d'Arquitectura S. L. 264
Schlyter / Gezelius Arkitektkontor AB 268
Simon Winstanley Architects 272
SPGArchitects 276
Stuart Tanner Architects 280
Studio 804, Inc. (Dan Rockhill) 282
Studio of Environmental Architecture (David Hertz) 284
Studio Negri 288
Suppose Design Office 292
Taalman Koch Architecture 294
Theis and Khan Architects Ltd. 298
TYIN Tegnestue Architects 300
UCARCHITECT 302
UdA, Architetti Associati 306
Vincent Snyder Architects 308
WD Architects 310
Werner Sobek Stuttgart GmbH & Co. KG 314
ZeroEnergy Design 316

Introduction

First of all, we would like to highlight what has been the main intention of this book, which like the other volumes already published in this series, gives the leading role to the participating architects. The book aims to reveal the trends in sustainable architecture in the most practical manner, and this is what we asked to architects who have worked on the final content and who have contributed through their ideas to the basics of sustainable architecture.

During the preparation of the content, we should mention that the involvement has been difficult for the architects, many of whom refused to participate due to lack of time and workload, even though the field of architecture has been one of the hardest-hit sectors by the current construction crisis.

For several decades now, the concepts of ecology and sustainability have generated highly influential currents of opinion in our society, invading all areas of our life. Nowadays no one goes against the theories of global warming or the ever more pressing need to reduce greenhouse gas emissions. In the field of architecture, significant changes and developments are evolving. However, reality tells us that we still have a way to go. The percentage of sustainable buildings is still very low and in open conflict with the increase in building projects all over the world. In the field of residential architecture alone, there is now an increase in the number of homes as a result of the growth in population. This, in turn, leads to greater consumption of raw materials and rising environmental costs for their transportation.

Much more participation is still required on the part of everyone involved, from architects and building contractors to manufacturers of materials and end customers, if we hope to achieve a quality building that is also environmentally friendly and sustainable at the same time.

The 100 architects involved in this book present the main guidelines for responsible architecture. Among the participating architects, some have presented a brief explanation of the basics of eco-construction and green criteria applied in their work, others have expressed by using basic concepts the building process of a healthy home with green, renewable materials, heated with solar and geothermal energy and naturally lit. Some have opted to describe the project, and from their personal experience, publicize the use of new materials or strategies to achieve a self-sufficient architecture.

We appreciate the complicity of these 100 architects, who, through their expertise, offer us a brief introduction to the most common terms of ecological architecture. We would like to thank them all.

Marta Serrats

0 to 1

4 Lexington Avenue #2M
New York, NY 10010, USA
Tel.: +1 646 279 9387
www.0-to-1.com

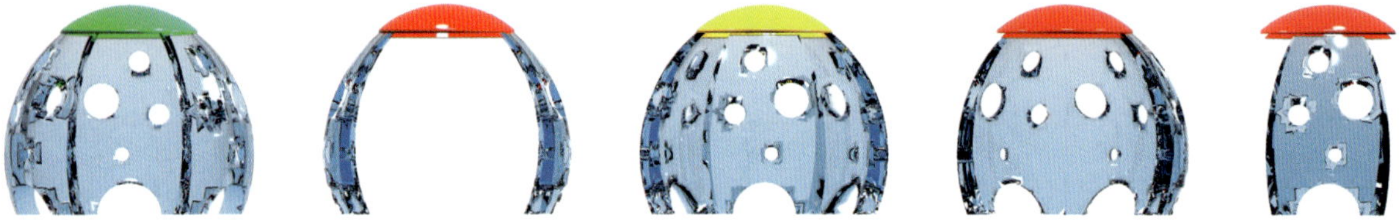

0003 ▼
Artist Retreat
Create an efficient thermal envelope, while providing optimal natural light. The highly insulated envelope offsets the harsh winters. The triple-paned north-facing windows provide soft natural lighting for artist to work.

0001 ▲
Street vendor tent
Modular design. A single form can be arranged in various configurations to meet the needs of the vendor.

0002 ▼
Street vendor tent
Explore alternative methods. Ice as material object will melt away at the end of its required time span.

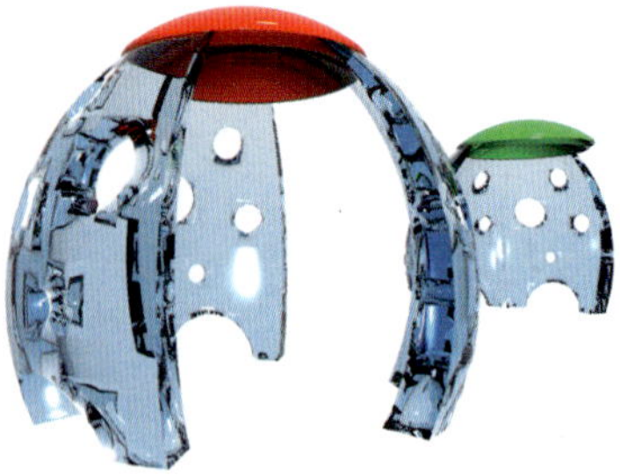

◄ 0004
Artist Retreat
Efficiently designed spaces require less energy. A single space that ascends in height, from outdoor terrace, to work space, to a small utility cube that doubles as a sleeping loft.

◄ 0006
Star table
Geometry allows the use of thin material. Four lightweight, 2.4-in thick, interlocking planes create a strong stable base.

0007 ►
Star table
Rapidly renewable material. Bamboo plywood planes pack flat to minimize shipping size.

◄ 0009
Townhouse renovation glass
Meet contemporary needs while honoring existing architecture.
Glass walls merge with existing historic moldings. Natural light permeates to spaces without windows, reducing the energy needs for artificial lighting.

◄ 0008
Townhouse renovation stair
Balance design aesthetics with embodied energy. A transparent stair was engineering to minimize the material and maximize the capacity of its strength.

0010 ▲
W House exterior
Form is inspired by the natural site. A three-storey split level house follows the slope of the site. During warm weather the three-storey stair space allows air to naturally move through the house from low to high, providing natural cooling and ventilation.

0005 ►
W House interior
A hearth rethought. At the center of the house we find a fireplace and a staircase. The fireplace touches all spaces, providing a gathering place, acting as structural support, and distributing radiant heat to all the floors.

Amunt Architekten Martenson und Nagel Theissen

Schervierstraße 66
52066 Aachen, Germany
Tel.: +49 711 8496341
www.amunt.info

0011 ➤
Thinking from scratch helps to break new ground/question standards. Instead of reducing the design merely on one function, one condition or one task, JustK is the result of a multiplicity of design aspects that were amalgamated in the architecture of the building.

0013 ▼
Small and simple: use low tec and low energy solutions. The staggered main living space creates various room heights which zone the ground floor and automatically create different climate areas in winter. Cold air from the ouside remains trapped in the lower entrance area while moderate temperatures prevail in the kitchen-living room and the sitting room higher up is warmer.

◄ 0012
Optimize rather than maximize. Clever overlapping means that the ceiling of the bathroom acts as a sleeping loft for the neighboring children's bedroom.

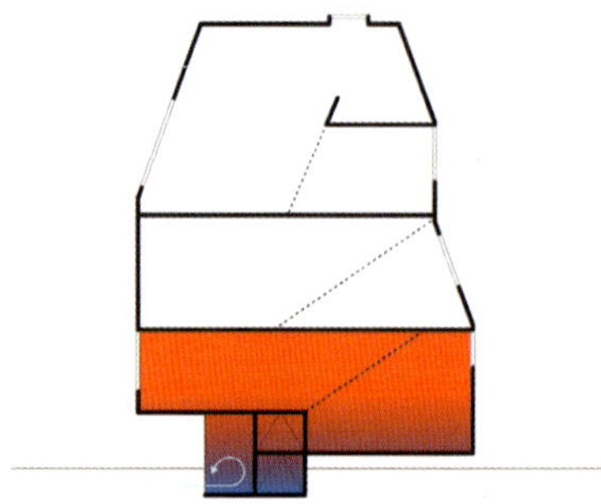

◄ 0014
Use and value renewable resources and services. Wood is the main material to be used consistently throughout the structure and interior surfaces; as a renewable raw material it was chosen not least for its favorable energy balance.

0015 ▼
(It is helpful to) integrate and evolve the existing. The dark red clinker façade of the original building interlocks with the red-brown unplastered pumice and light-weight concrete bricks of the extension; it interprets the existing material in a contemporary manner and combines with the original in color to form a new compact building volume (1 + 1 = 1).

0017 ➤

Use and value diversity, diversity creates potentials. In the warmer months of the year, this living space can be extended by the 129-sq-ft balcony and the 248-sq-ft forecourt.

0016 ▼

Appropriable spaces and spaces of opportunity make a building long-lasting. The living-room hall at the top floor provides room for retreat and serves as a reading and television area. In case of splitting the house, there is an optional build-in kitchen.

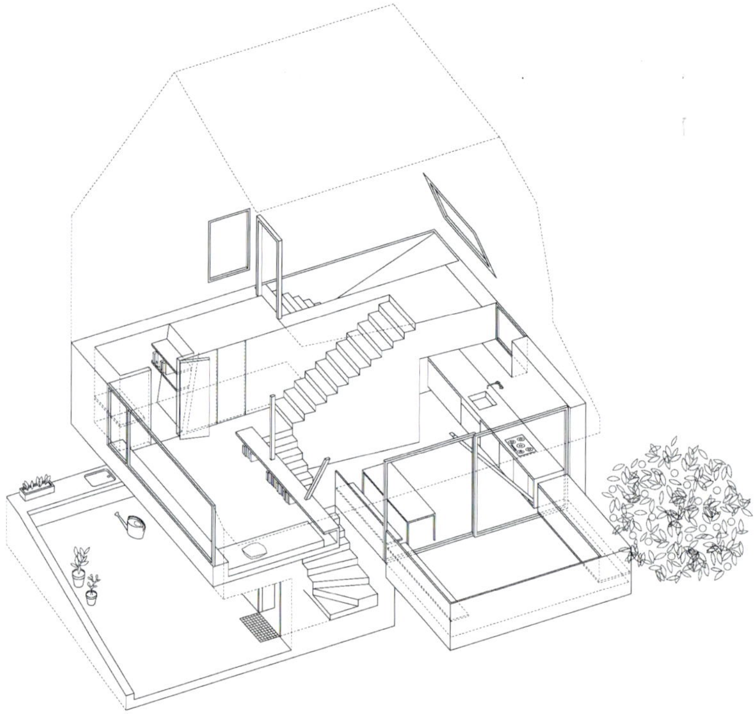

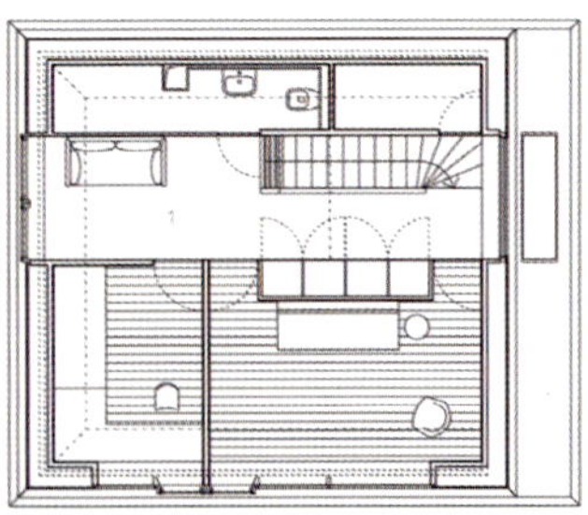

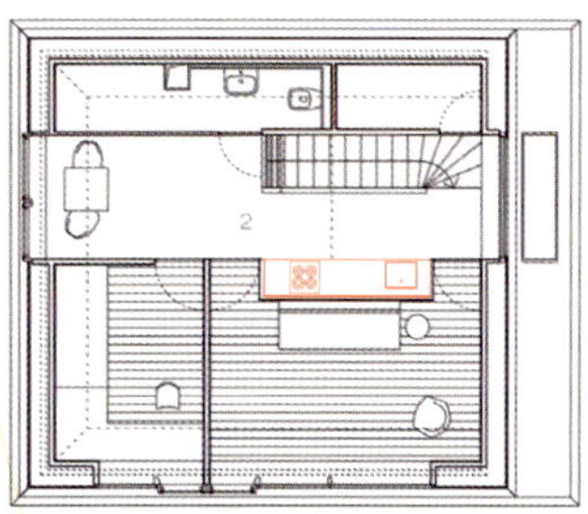

0018 ▼

Use creativity and respond to change sustainable and flexible. The house can be split into two living units with separate entrances without much effort should the family situation change to require that. The total area of the house is 1,485 sq ft; one unit would measure 872 sq ft, and the other 613 sq ft.

◄ 0019

Activate existing potentials. Extending the house towards the garden, opening up the staircase to the upper floor and the new wall panelling of the stairs with integrated balustrade have transformed the role of the old wooden staircase.

0020 ▼

Building is not always the answer.

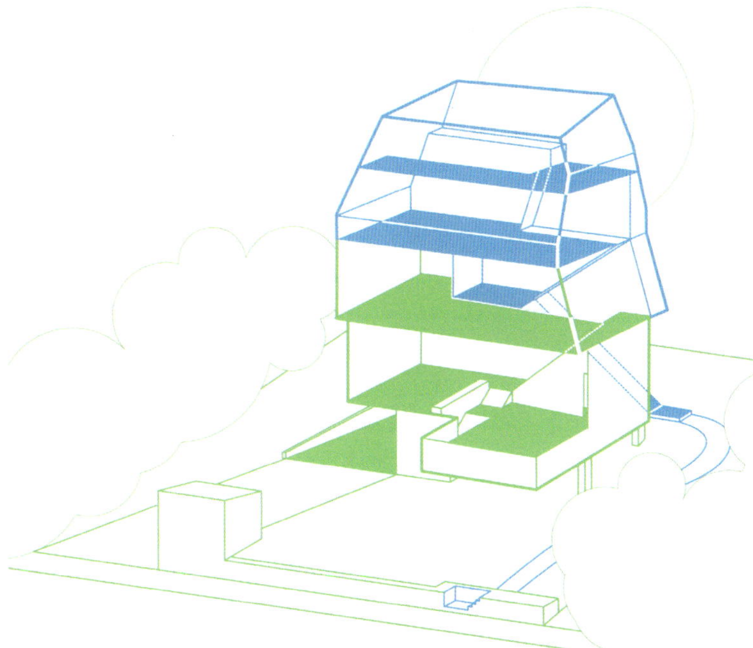

Andrea Tognon Architecture

Via Pericle 14
20126 Milano, Italy
Tel.: +39 348 5809677
www.atognon.com

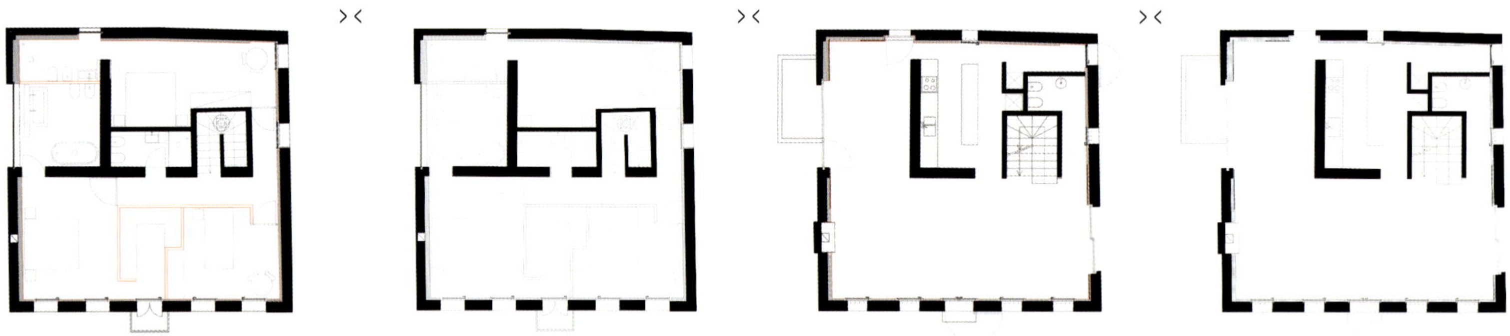

0021

Called Residence O, the project also involved replacing the existing overhanging roof with one that sits flush with the edges of exterior walls and a complete redesign of the interior.

0022

The building we were call to refurbish was built in the 1970s as imitation of vernacular architecture of the Veneto countryside area. It looked pretty fake. The floor plan was a square were a corner was missing (so was an L shape).

0023
The roof was a concrete slab jutting out in a very inelegant and bad proportionated way. So we decide to add the corner that was missing to complete the square floor plane.

0024
Because of the total redefinition of the insulation parameter, we reshaped the profile of the building cutting the old roof edge and redesigning the junction between the roof and the perimetrical walls.

0025 ➤
All of the walls and ceilings were insulated with Styrodur panels. This material reduces CO_2 emissions, as the foam cells contain nothing other than air, and the foam itself is made from extruded polystyrene foam (XPS), which is free if CFSs, HCFCs and HFCs.

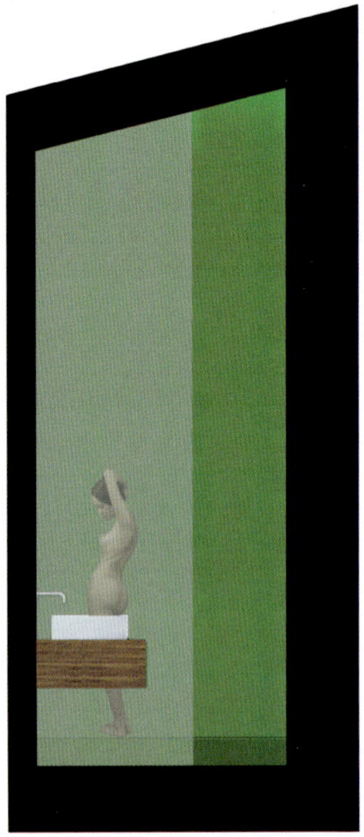

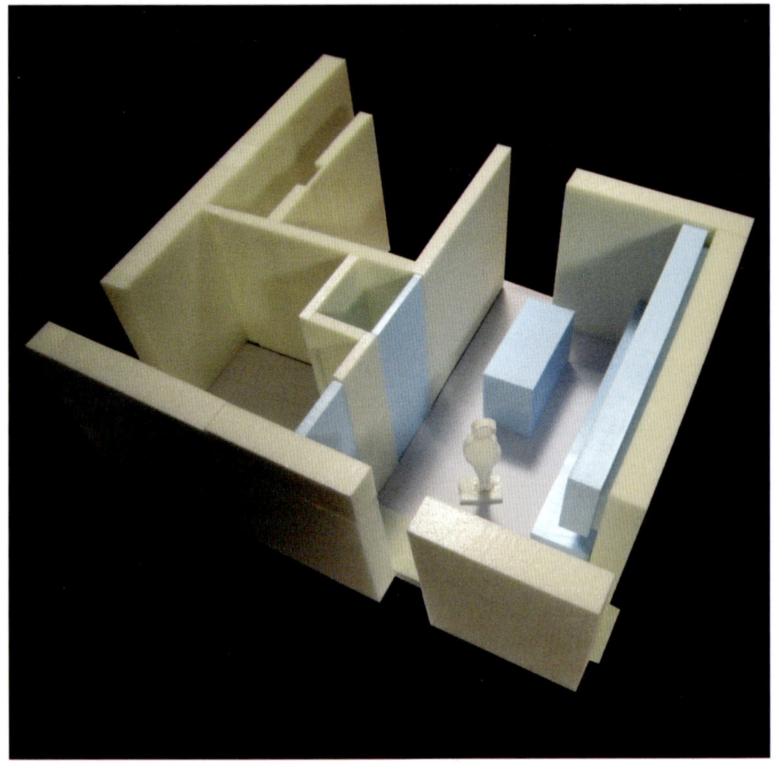

0026 ▲
The remodeling of the residence improved both its appearance and the sustainable aspects of its architecture.

0027 ▲
The whole interior layout was redesigned, all the walls and roof were insulated, and the heating system was switched to solar energy.

◄ 0028
Window glass and frames were replaced with insulated versions.

0029 ➤
The new wall and ceiling panels increase the thermal insulation of the house, reducing the need for heating, which is from solar power.

◄ 0030
Large insulated expanses of glass let in more daylight while retaining heat inside.

Andrew Maynard Architects pty ltd

551 Brunswick Street
North Fitzroy, Melbourne, VIC 3068, Australia
Tel.: +61 (3)9481 5110
www.maynardarchitects.com

0031

The approach taken for the Mash House is one which, despite first impressions, celebrates the backyard. Or perhaps less so the traditional notion of the backyard, and, more so just plain, outdoor space. The original deep and dark, double-fronted Victorian house offered a plethora of challenges, not least of all, its lack of solar access.

© Kevin Hui

0032

Our response was a series of finely-crafted timber boxes nestled around the bulk of the existing house. The bedroom addition opens up the northern façade of the house to the rugged bush block, doing double duty, as the roof becomes an expansive deck extending the living space out into the treetops.

© Peter Bennets

© Peter Bennets

0033

More frequently, holiday homes are becoming little more than transplanted suburban ugliness. The great Australian tradition of the shack is in danger of being superseded by bloated mansions. With this project we wanted to celebrate the shack, and we kept close to the original building's footprint to avoid taking over the rugged coastal block.

0034

Overall, the design is an experimentation of form and color, albeit simple solution to a rather challenging suburban site. The concept was driven by obtaining passive efficiency, via shrewd siting and orientation. Quality insulation, ample double-glazing and in-slab heating, all combine to make this home a retro-futuristic sustainable modern house renovation.

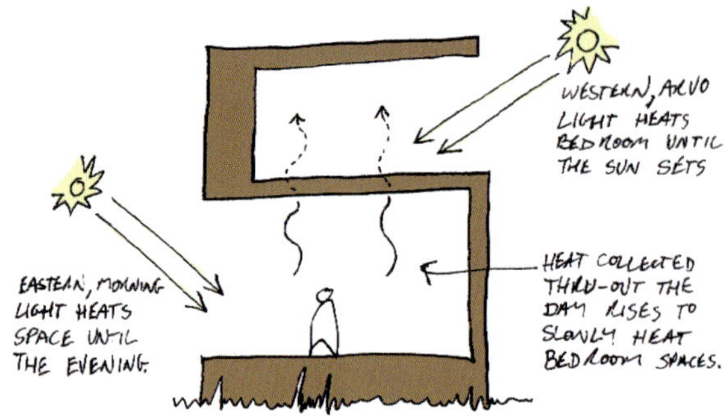

0035 ▲

The Vader House is an extension to a Victorian terrace in the dense inner-city. The high boundary walls, built in disregard of existing height regulations long before such rules were created, permitted a non-standard height along the northern boundary.

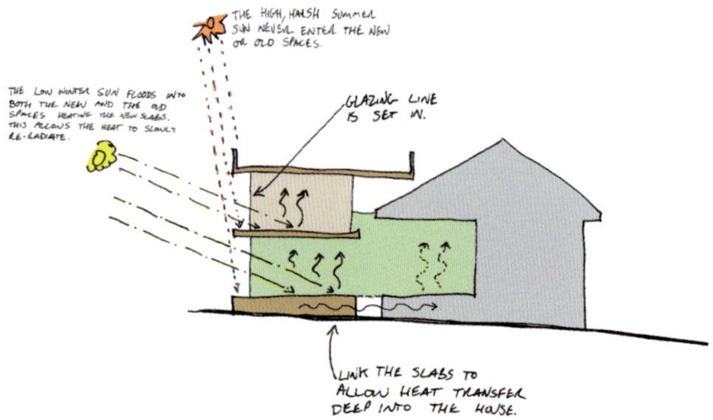

◄ 0036

The roofline then abruptly turns to follow the dictated setback lines, resulting in a playful and telling interpretation of planning rules.

◄ 0037

The refined palate of materials is revealed where volumes are removed to show the flesh inside - colored bright red with glass tiles and joinery.

0038 ➤
Recycled grey ironbark battens on the doors shade the interior from the high summer sun while allowing the lower winter rays to penetrate.

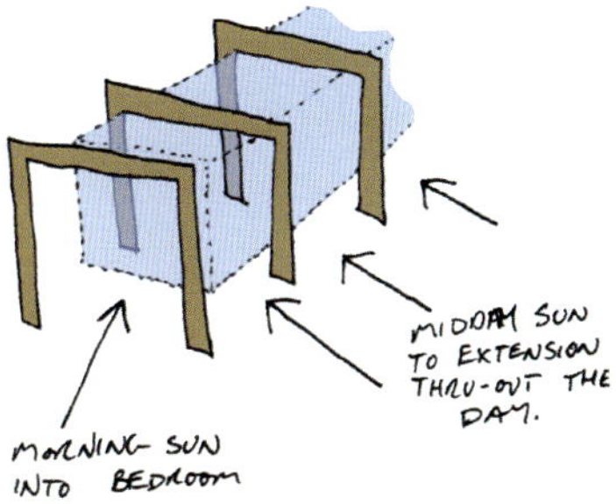

0039 ➤
Council requirements regarding overlooking, which dictate a 75% opacity to second-storey spaces, are resolved by UV stable stickers rather than expensive and elaborate screening.

0040 ➤
Traditional walls were replaced by bi-fold garage doors, which open the interior spaces to the long backyard, blurring the distinction between inside and outside.

© Peter Bennets

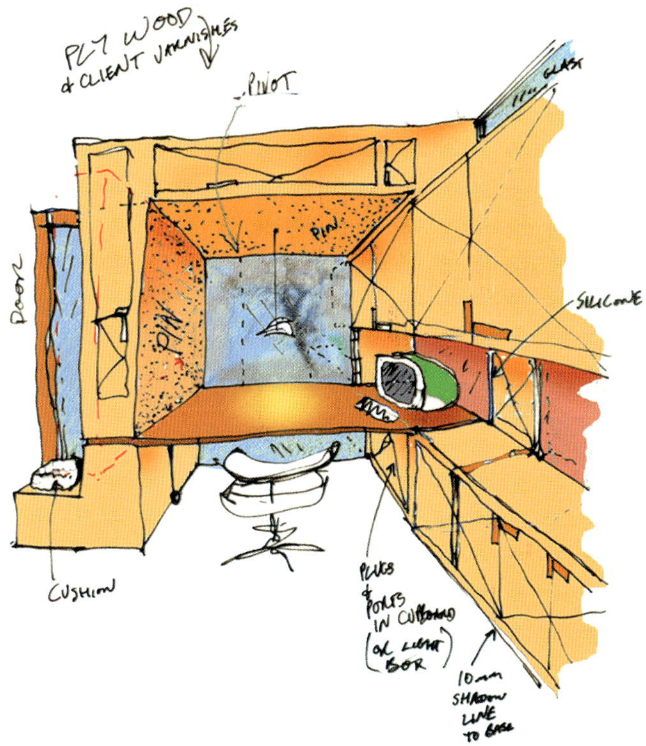

Architectentbureau Paul de Ruiter bv

Valschermkade 36 D
1059 CD Amsterdam, The Netherlands
Tel.: +31 20 626 32 44
www.paulderuiter.nl
twitter.com/pdrarchitects

© Pieter Kers

© Pieter Kers

0041
The Kroeten Eiland is an artificial island with excavated waterways in the agricultural landscape. One result of this collaboration was the collective purchase of a wind turbine, which was erected 3 miles away at the power station in Breda.

© Pieter Kers

0042
To identify the specific wishes of all the users and integrate them into the design and to give the users a good idea of the architectural possibilities, several workshops were held during the design stage of the Bijlmer Parktheater in Amsterdam. One requirement that was specifically identified during the workshops was the need for daylight in the main auditorium.

0043 ➤
Villa Deys is a house for a senior couple in Rhenen, The Netherlands. The water in the integrated swimming pool has a constant temperature of 80,6 °F, which of course needs energy. However, by linking the pool heating system with the low-temperature heating system of the house, in combination with a water pump, the pool area re-emits the energy it has absorbed and becomes part of the energy-saving climate system in the house.

© Rien van Rijthoven

© Rien van Rijthoven

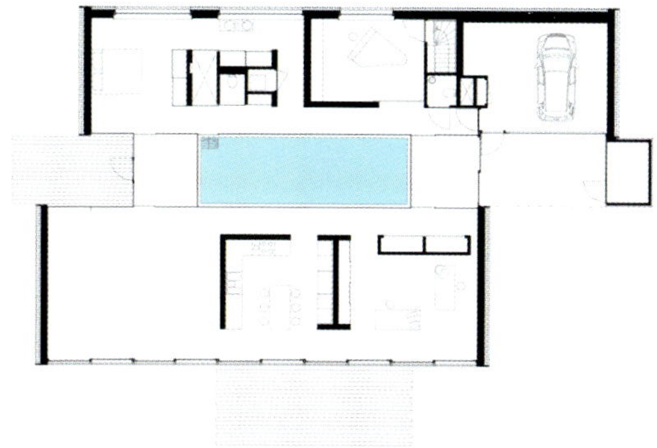

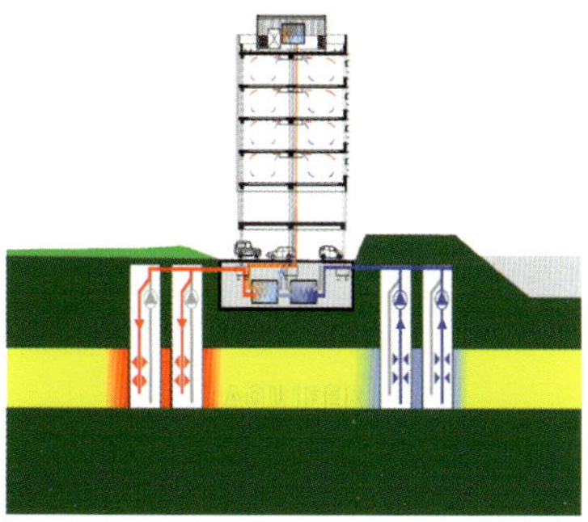

© Rob 't Hart

0044 ➤
For the Rijkswaterstaat Zeeland premises in Middelburg, The Netherlands, existing techniques are used in an innovative manner to create a low-energy building, without sacrificing its economic viability or its architectural quality. The use of "active concrete" in combination with underground cold/heat storage creates a constant and comfortable working climate and results into an energy saving of 40% to 50% over traditional cooling and heating methods.

0045 ➤

All the green electricity in the TNT Center in Hoofddorp, The Netherlands is supplied by its "green machine." The bio-cogeneration plant required for this process runs on organic residual waste, among other things. Periodic power surpluses are directed to the main network, to heat the buildings in the immediate vicinity of the TNT Center, while periodic shortages are met by taking (green) electricity from the network.

0046 ➤

The first sustainable decision for our new office building in Valschermkade was to renovate an existing one. Recycled materials were used during the renovation and the furniture too has been recycled, entirely in keeping with the C2C principle. A geothermal storage system saves 20 to 30% of energy. The adjustable façade serves as a sunshade during the day and as an anti-burglary screen at night.

➤ 0047

TransPort, located in Schiphol, is the first building in The Netherlands to gain LEED Platinum and BREEAM certifications for its sustainability. Energy-efficient technology, such as thermal storage and concrete core activation, will enhance the building's sustainability. A grass-sedum vegetation roof over the lower building provides an additional insulation layer that inhibits heat transfer.

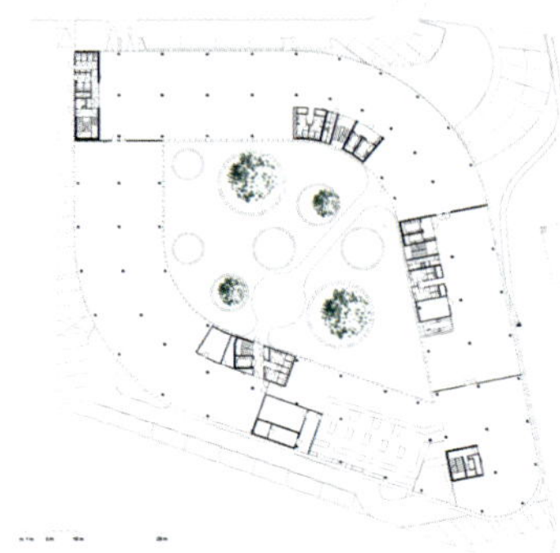

0048 ➤
In the Veranda parking garage, in Rotterdam, the primary function of the central open area, measuring 52.5 x 72 sq ft, is to allow more light and air to penetrate into the car park, to improve the ambience of the underground levels. In four exhaust tubes the back pressure fans are positioned, which ensure that the polluted air from cars is extracted from the building.

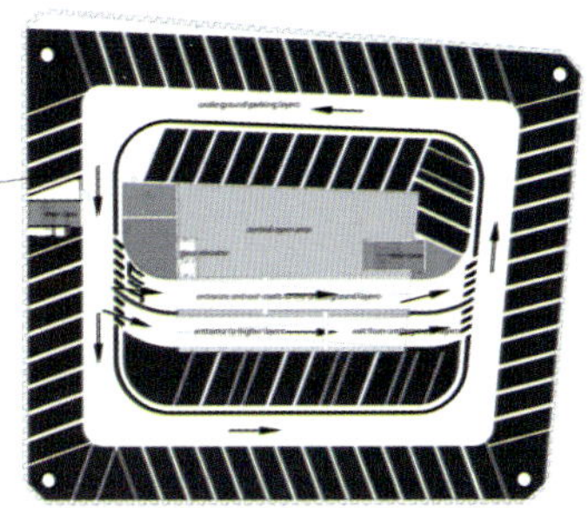

0049 ➤
De Zuidkas is an imaginary building in Amsterdam of over 118,403 sq ft with a functional mix that is far from ordinary: homes, offices, a school, parking facilities, retail, restaurants, a park and a biogas electrical plant. The objective is to make an intelligent autarkic building where energy and CO_2 flows can be interchanged and waste flows can be converted into heat and energy.

◄ 0050
Get inspired by sustainability.

Arkitekstudio Widjedal Racki

Artillerigatan 28
SE-114 51 Stockholm, Sweden
Tel.: +46 73 994 98 57
www.wrark.se

0051 ➤
The Bhouse can be joined together to form a cluster for larger camps in hostile environments.

0052 ▼
Each Bhouse is individualized by choosing the perfect types of "add-ons" for each location an client.

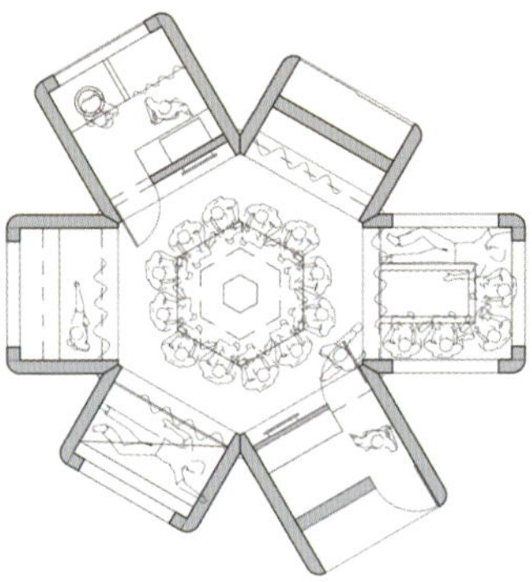

0054 ➤
Each Bhouse contains a floor and a roof plate. The floor plate contains most of the technical installations. These plates connect the "add-ons" and hold the building together. The building is a lightweight patent concrete building with waterproof surface and joints as part of the system. "Add-ons" and base plates are mounted on site.

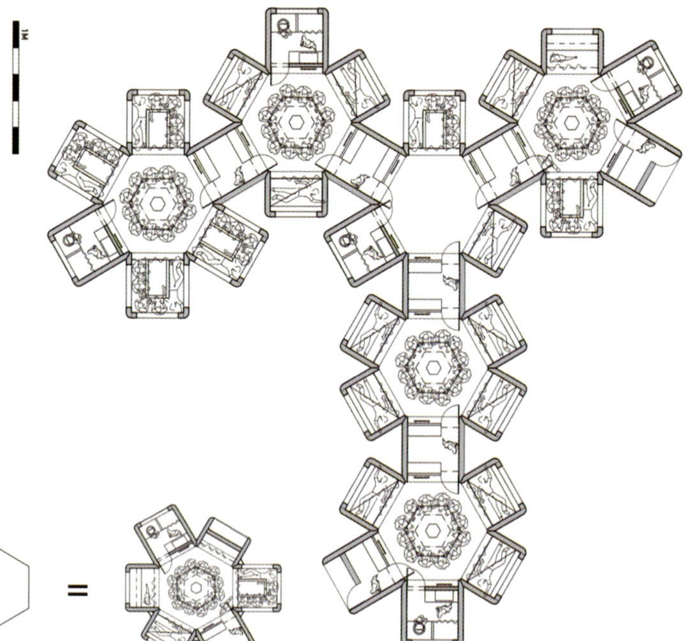

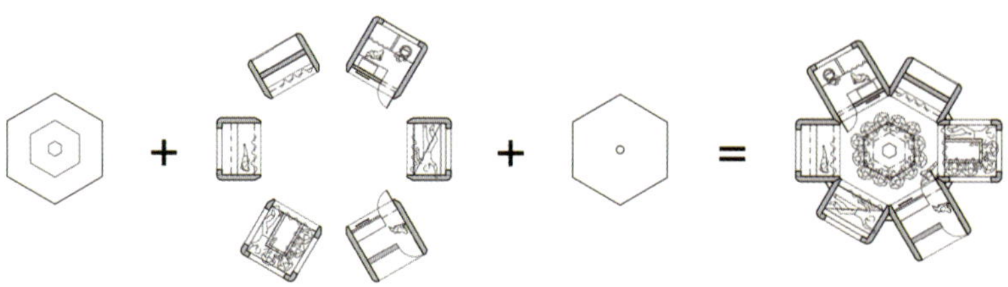

0053 ➤
The "add-ons" can be placed freely to maximize views and solar directions.

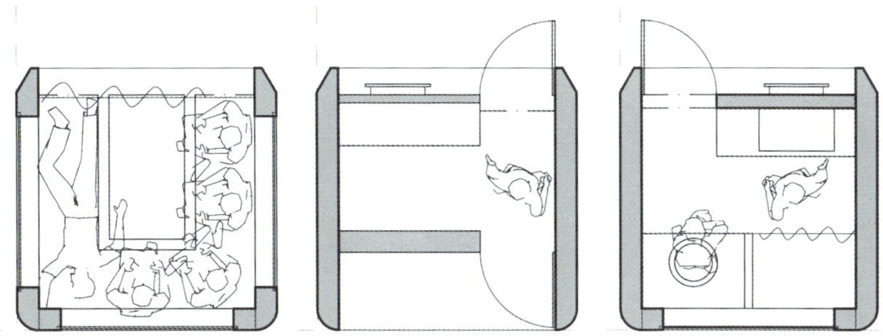

◄ 0059
An alternative use for the Bhouse is short term urban densification. Here as easily removable complement to the Olympic village of London in 2012.

0055 ▼
The resulting Bhouse addresses the need to reverse levels of over consumption in its energy-positive design and recyclability. Materials used in its production are sourced ethically and with respect for the environment, and are combined to create a luxurious space in which to relax and to be in.

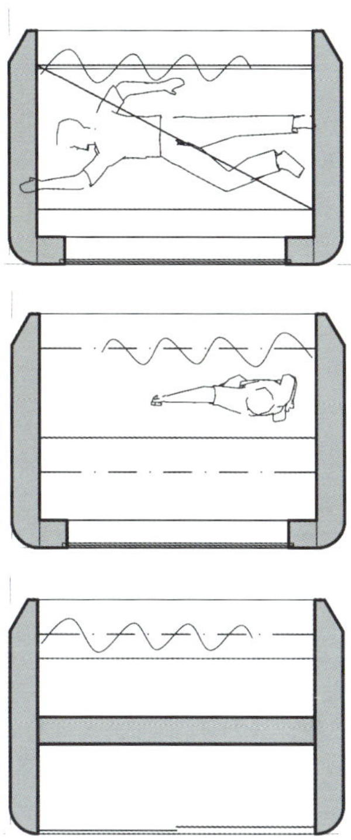

0056 ►
Individual units incorporate the highest standard of environmental design with sustainable solutions for the provision of energy, water and drainage, heating and cooling. All technical equipment is as simple as possible and is seamlessly integrated into the design. This extends to rainwater harvesting, purification and re-use, solar heating and energy, natural ventilation and refrigeration, and lighting.

◄ 0057
Designed by internationally-acclaimed Scandinavian architects, the BHouse is a response to environmental and social change, and provides a simple yet sophisticated solution to living and working spaces for a diversity of contexts where more ordinary and permanent buildings are not an option. The client's brief to the architects was to design a small, beautifully crafted, eco-building, which could be sited within sensitive rural environments where normal services and infrastructure are not necessarily available.

◄ 0058
A typical unit with six "add-ons" will have a footprint of 447 sq ft, with a bath with toilet, sink, and shower; a kitchen with stove and refrigerator; a storage unit with indoor as well as outdoor storage; an entrance unit with wardrobe function; a veranda room (insulated or open air); 11 beds (or 12 seats) and possible additional beds in the veranda room.

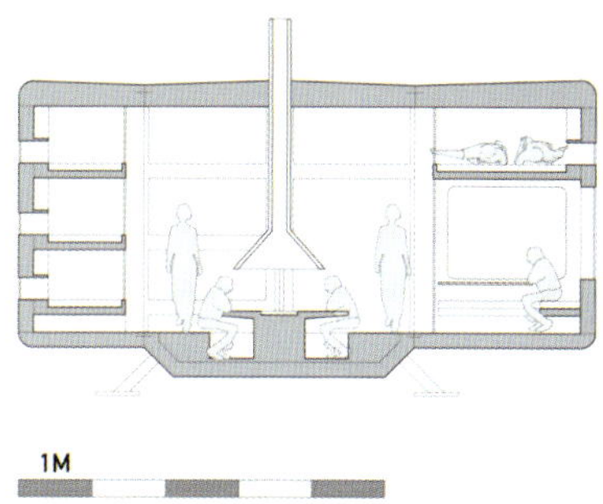

0060 ▲
The building should be designed to withstand hostile environmental conditions, and to be capable of providing "off-grid" living for short to medium term use. Its primary target market is made up of commercial buyers and operators in the leisure and hospitality industry, as it is capable of providing eco friendly "add-on" accommodation for guests looking for sustainable and beautiful places to stay.

Architekturbüro Reinberg ZT GmbH

Lindengasse 39/10
A-1070 Wien, Austria
Tel.: +43 1 524 82 80
www.reinberg.net

0061 ➤
This prototype home, designed for an Austrian solar technology manufacturer, complies with requirements similar those of the PassivHaus standard, such as good façade insulation and a bioclimatic design that favors solar heat gain.

0063
The home is self-sufficient in energy. It produces all of the energy it consumes to achieve a zero-net energy balance. The south frontage gains solar energy by means of vertical openings and the picture window found on the lower level.

0062
Another active strategy is formed by the solar thermal panels integrated into the roof and the photovoltaic panels used for electricity generation.

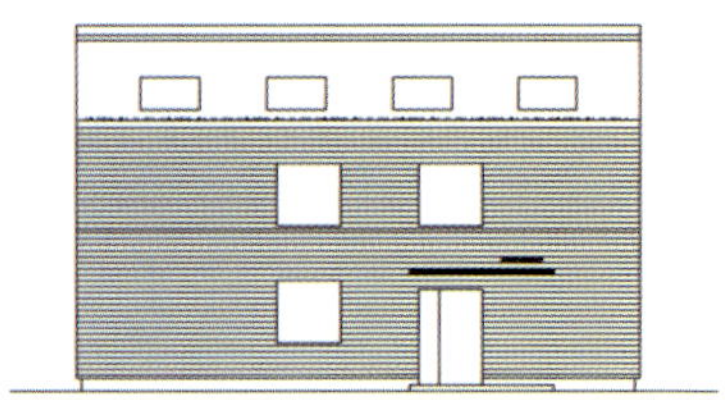

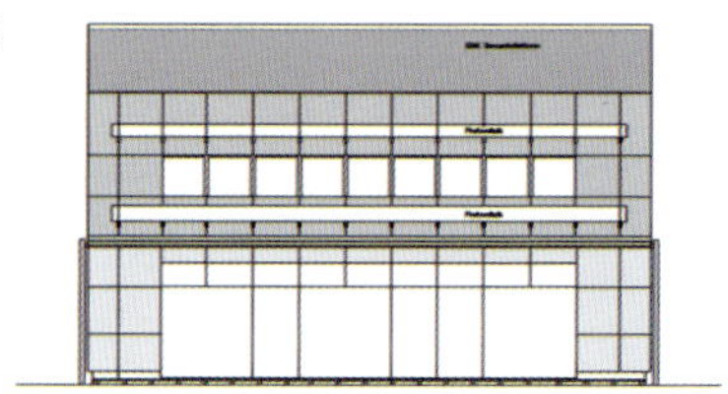

0064
In warm weather, the south-facing openings are protected from overheating by a fixed brise-soleil that forms 400 sq ft of photovoltaic panels. In winter, a heat pump provides comfort on extremely cold days.

0065 ➤
The energy for heating, hot water, ventilation, and to power home appliances and the heat pump are compensated with power from the photovoltaic panels and the heat-recovery systems, so that consumption is zero.

0070 ▼
The building is equipped with windows that open automatically only when oxygen levels are too low or there is too much moisture in the air.

◄ 0066
Radiant heating is designed under skirting boards and flooring to heat areas of the house. The high degree of insulation achieved with triple glazing and heat-recovery ventilation reduces heat loss drastically.

0069 ▼
The house features 269 sq ft of thermal solar panels, with storage for household hot water (in the plant room and on the lower level) and a heat pump run on solar power.

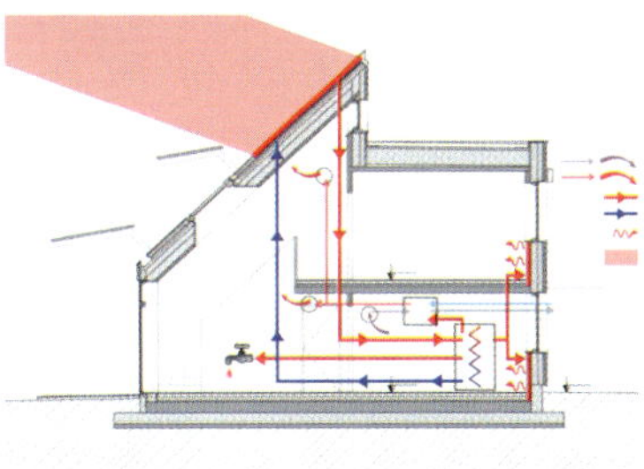

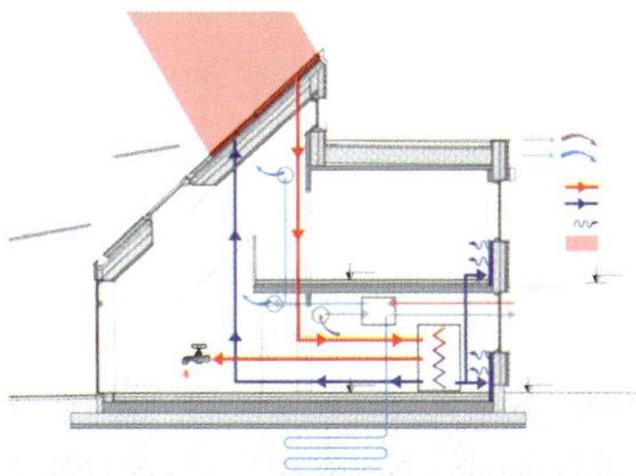

0067 ▲
The building features a larch wood and glass skin and a roof made from a material called Eternit.

0068 ▲
The interior walls are rendered in marl, a detritus sedimentary material with equal parts of sand, silt and clay particles.

Arconiko Architecten (Frido van Nieuwamerongen, Roswitha Abraham)

Postbus 399
3000 AJ Rotterdam, The Netherlands
Tel.: +31 10 4123181
www.arconiko.com

0071 ➤
1st Cradle-to-Cradle House
Use existing knowledge on materials and stimulate product suppliers to change their products into C2C (cradle to cradle). Innovative building projects are a great chance to motivate suppliers to invest in their materials to create C2C products. All parties can evetually profit from the investment if there is sufficient publicity to show the effects.

0072 ▼
Indes office
Use solar power for cooling.

a. Geothermal heat pump to heat in winter and cool in summer. The spaces are heated and cooled by a floor installation system.
b. The shape of the office reinforces natural ventilation throughout the building.
c. Blow-in of cold and warm air through textile ventilation pipes with low airspeed.
d. Photovoltaic cells on south façade to generate energy which can be used for the heat pump for cooling.

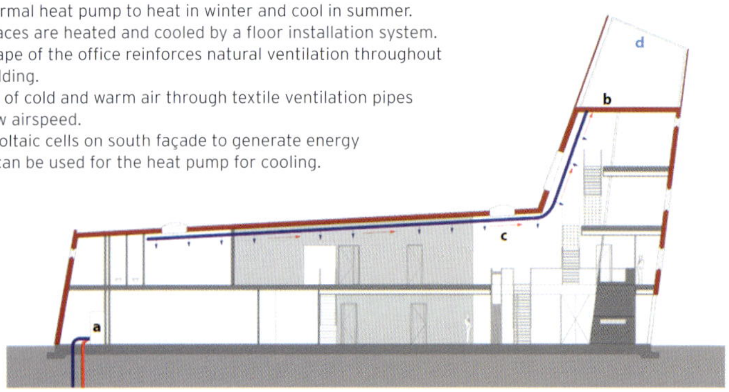

><

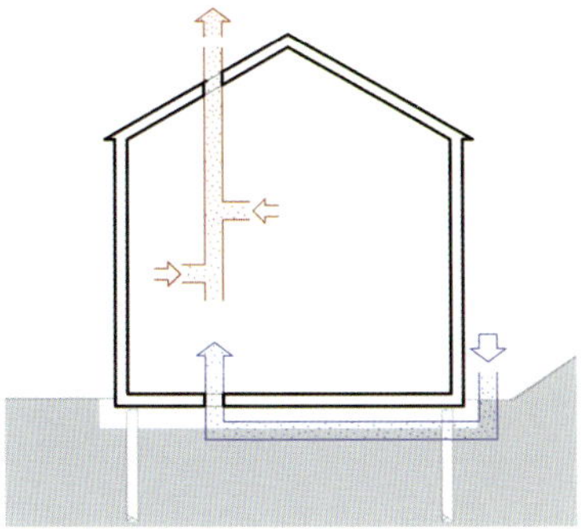

0073 ▲

1st Cradle-to-Cradle House

Prevail design before technique.
By integrating natural climatological principles within the design, high tech installations are of no need. In the 1st Cradle-to-Cradle House no mechanical ventilation is needed since the building itself creates a natural draft. Cold air is drained below the house through a shaft. Warm air is drafted by a chimney and rises up. The wind activates a propeller that leads the air outside - as simple as that.

0074 ►

1st Cradle-to-Cradle House

Better instead of less bad. The design mentality of the 1st Cradle-to-Cradle House is based on a positive theory instead of fearful criticism. Since the 1970s, environmentalists have emphasized on the reduction of our footprint in order to save the planet. We think that a positive mentality will be more effective and durable. Moreover, the technical possibilities have developed far enough to combine living comfort and sustainable building.

◄ 0075

Community school in Rotterdam

Daylight as a durable design principle. A former academy building was transformed to house two elementary schools, two gyms, a preschool and a child center. The inner courtyard was transformed by making an atrium to create extra space. The atrium brings daylight into the core of the building and serves as the central meeting place of the schools.

◄ 0076
Arconiko team
Think positive to create a better building environment. We think in terms of chances instead of threads.

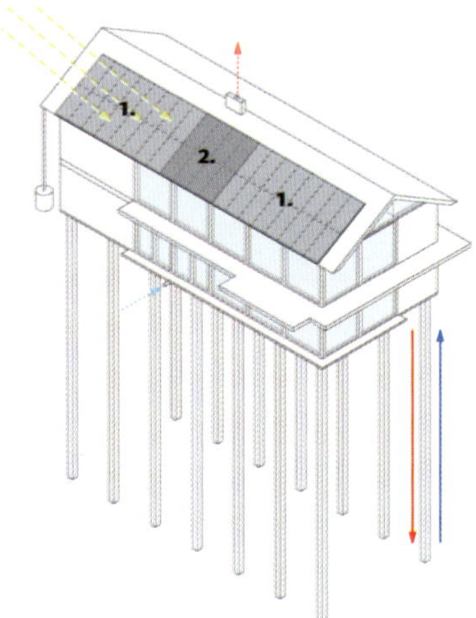

1. Photovoltaic cells for generating electricity.
2. Sun collectors for generating warm water.

0077 ►
House Harsta
Living comfort and sustainability should reinforce each other. Sky-related living and associations with a crow's nest were part of the requirements. The original house, which dates from around 1900 and was renovated in the 1960s and 1990s, can hardly be recognized now after the recent rebuilding. Only the wall on the east side is reused in the modern house. In the design, new identity voids connect the inner spaces and offer rich views that culminate in the crow's nest, a cantilevered panorama platform. Hereby the purposeful dealing with daylight is crucial. The interior is designed to respect the needs of the elderly with lazy stairs, respecting the environment and being flexible.

0078 ▲
1st Cradle-to-Cradle House
Use buildings as energy generators. Buildings can function beyond autarchy and even generate energy to supply the net. Photovoltaic cells on the southern inclined roofside collect sun radiation that is transformed from direct current into alternating current. This can directly be used in the house or delivered into the net for nearby buildings.

0079
Community school in Rotterdam
Make use of existing rooftops.

0080
Control center in Roosendaal
Improve existing buildings. The existing control center of the railway building in Roosendaal did not meet the high quality demands of security for both the staff and the railway system. The technical rooms were retained and a new space for the control staff was built on top of the exsiting building on a separate construction. During the transformation, the control center had to stay in function and was only paused for five hours.

Arkin Tilt Architects. Ecological Planning & Design

1101 8th St. #180
Berkeley, CA 94710, USA
Tel.: +1 510/528-9830
www.arkintilt.com

0081 ➤
The specifics of the site are the starting point
Working with the climate, landscape, views, and natural grade results in buildings that are harmonious and integrated into their surroundings. On sloping sites, buildings can be literally tied to the landscape via berms and living roofs.

0083 ▼
Build as little as possible
Create multi-use spaces that can change over time. Limit or add functionality to circulation space – for example, stairways can double as libraries, landings as study or reading nooks, etc. Smaller projects use less material resources and require less energy to operate.

◄ 0082
Employ the wisdom of previous generations
Look to local or climate appropriate vernacular buildings (buildings built before the 1940s or without HVAC systems) for passive climate response strategies. Agricultural and manufacturing uses often yield unique and interesting ideas for storing heat or moving air.

0084 ▲
Design windows to share daylight
High clerestory windows can bring light deep into a space. Salvaged interior windows can further share daylight and create spaciousness without the thermal penalty for single-pane glazing that older window sashes typically have. Films can be applied to glass in salvaged doors to achieve a required safety rating and obscure glass where desired.

0085 ▼
Buildings should primarily heat and cool themselves
Passive strategies can go a long way toward minimizing, if not eliminating, the need for mechanical heating and cooling. In hot climates a "ice house" roof adds a ventilated cavity above the thermal roof, providing shade for natural cooling, as well as tighter overall construction.

0086 ▲
Maximize resource efficiency
Salvaged materials can be from a multitude of sources and are often best used in unexpected ways: sunshades can be made from old airplane flaps, used billboard material makes a functional and playful wainscot in a school restroom, and bowling lane can be reused as a table or countertops.

0087 ➤

Integrate active systems to generate hot water and electricity

Photovoltaic panels and solar hot water collectors can do double duty. For example, adjustable photovoltaic awnings can produce energy, provide seasonal shade, and facilitate the shedding of snow in the winter, all the while generating electricity. Plus, there's an increase in energy production by optimizing the angle.

0088 ➤

Employ natural building systems

Straw-bale construction has multiple benefits: it is an annually renewed resource that is carbon-sequestering, it has high insulation values and high thermal mass, thus mediating temperature swings, it moderates humidity and absorbs sound, and it helps create a comfortable, nurturing building environment.

0089

Connectivity and delight

Introduce local materials and natural elements to reconnect to natural world. Local soils can tie the building to its place. A tree trunk can be an elegant focal point as well as a reminder of the origins of material resources.

0090

Blur the distinction between indoors and out

Create outdoor living spaces or ways to convert indoor spaces to be more connected to the outdoors. Healthier and more grounded, living outdoors can re-acclimate us to world around us. Covered porches can also provide solar control for interior spaces, west-facing ones in particular.

Atelier Riri
(Novriansyah Yakub)

Jl. Perkici 12 eb 3 #19
Bintaro Sektor V Tangerang, Indonesia
Tel.: +62 812 1032303
www.atelierriri.com
atelierriri.com/blog

◄ 0091

A simple window detail with the use of warm material such as wood can give a good solution to the natural ventilation of the house. As the wind breeze through the gap freely, the house can finally let go the use of mechanical tool like fan and ac.

◄ 0092

Nothing goes wrong when concrete meets vegetation. The need of safety and privacy sometimes can be solved with a steel-patterned bar. The existence of vegetation on this equation is not merely for the sake of a soft composition, but the setting can be a perfect plate for the tree to grow and give a sustainable quality to the house.

0093 ►

There are many ways to provide the small house with adequate ventilation for the wind to breeze through. The wall composition of cement block and grass block gives a natural and innovative solution to the cross-ventilation problem.

◄ 0094

Water element in a house has a double function when it has a proper location and execution. The tropical climate favors its existence as more than just an aesthetic part - also as a positive support to the microclimate. With the help of air movement, the surrounding semi-open spaces can benefit a cool breeze.

0095 ➤

Industrial material is still not a popular product to use in a small urban house. In order to use such kind of material, architect should care about the design and have a good calculation for the embodied energy and application skill of using this kind of material. This is a consequence of having a contemporary design to respond today's lifestyle, but the question of whether or not it is considered sustainable may have to be the highest consideration.

© Richard Salampessy

© Richard Salampessy, Novriansyah

© Richard Salampessy, Novriansyah

© Richard Salampessy, Novriansyah

0097 ▲

Selection of natural material is resourceful, therefore the use of such material lead to a sustainable criteria. This design attitude also narrowed down the overall look into a suitable sense of tropical.

0098 ▲

Houses in a tropical climate use sunlight to cut down the use of electricity energy during the day, so big glass walls are a common thing. However, it is best to avoid the direct sunlight, for it will raise the indoor temperature and spoil the comfort of the room. This is where window overhang and a terrace function as a buffer or transition.

0099 ➤

The use of bamboo has become more frequent in tropical-climate houses. This material is considered renewable and abundantly available in tropical countries. With a modern frame, the room looks uniquely romantic and natural.

© Richard Salampessy, Novriansyah

0096 ▲

An aesthetical part of the house design should function more than just visual look. While the sunlight nicely reflects into the room to brighten the space in a broad daylight, the choice of material gives the warm sensation. The parallel set of wood gives a play of light and shadow, but it also serves the purpose of lighting and ventilation at the same time.

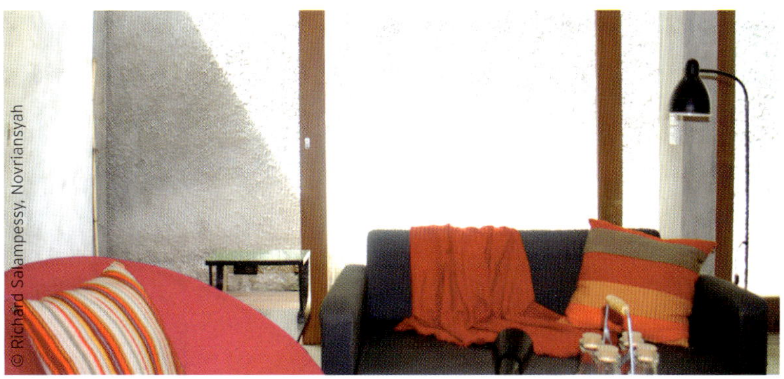

© Richard Salampessy, Novriansyah

◄ 0100

Tropical climate has an abundant source of sunlight during the day in dry season, and so much rain in rainy season. Therefore, house design need a different approach compared to counterparts in Europe or America. The interior will enjoy the brightness coming from the sunlight, but the building design should be able to regulate the intensity. This attitude will keep the indoor temperature in a comfort level.

Atelier RVL Architectes

43, rue d'Entraigues
37000 Tours, France
Tel.: +33 02 47 70 16 02
www.atelierrvl.com

0101 ➤
House in Saint Cyr-sur-Loire (2007)
MagicKub is a simple cube structure, which is an affordable, compact house, reduced to the basics, for young families. A steel-mesh sliding door keeps out excessive heat in the summer in front of the windows of the living room.

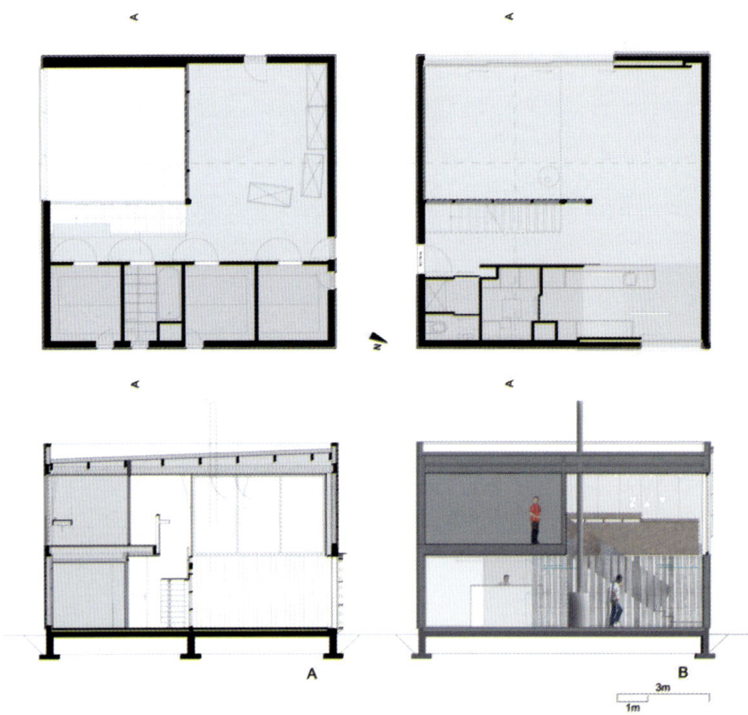

◄ 0102
House in Tours (2009)
This addition is characterized by an extension regrouping the kitchen and a small dining room. The extension acts as an umbilical cord connecting the garden to the house.

0103

Gym in Savigné-sur-Lathan (2003)

This extension represents the remodeling of a gymnasium and locker rooms brought up to standards for the disabled. Rather than enlarging and making an impact on the ground, we preferred playing with the incline of the wall of the building. Made from a prefabricated wooden frame, this project of building recycling presents a low impact on the environment.

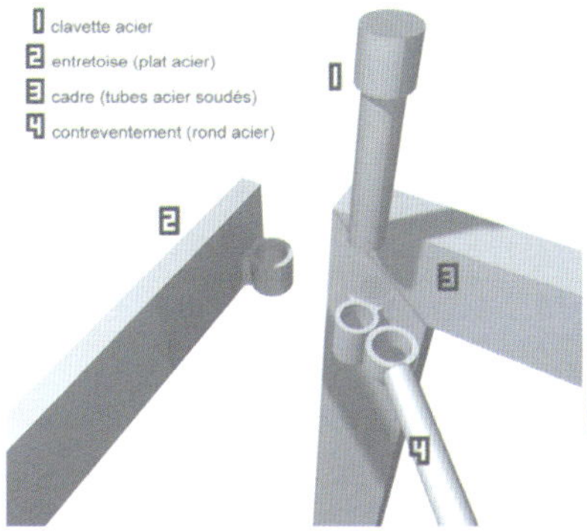

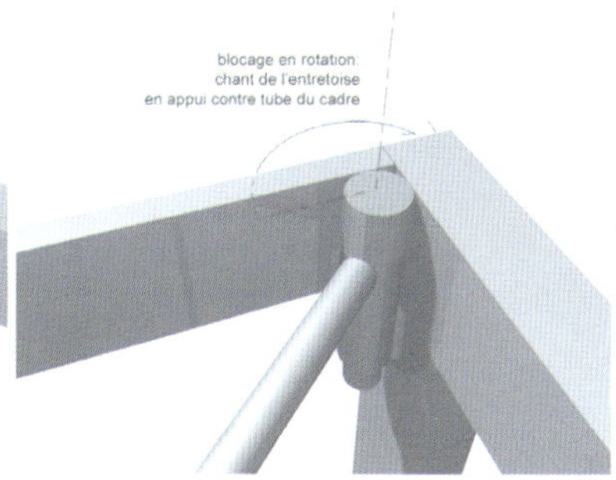

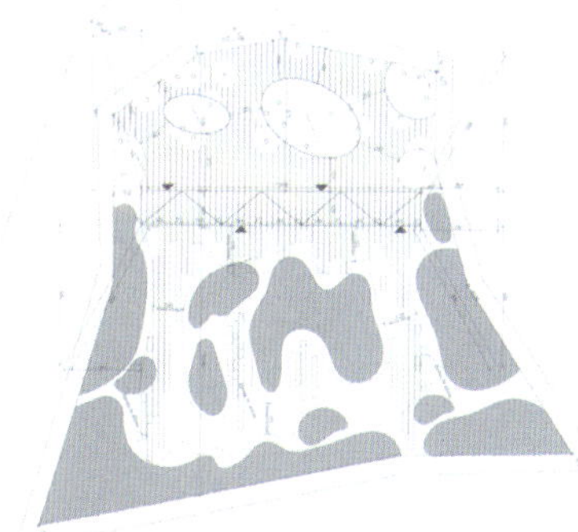

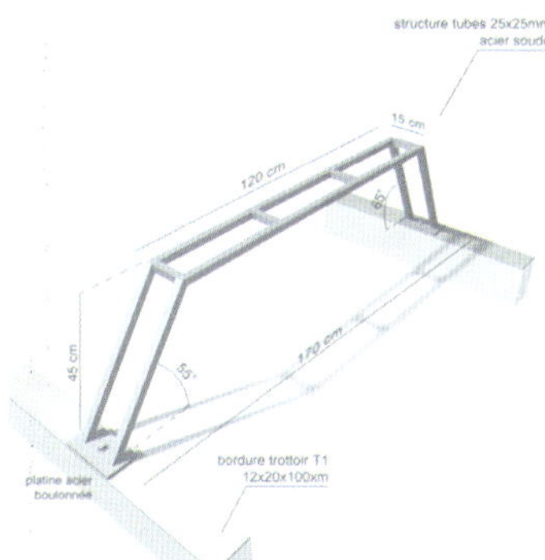

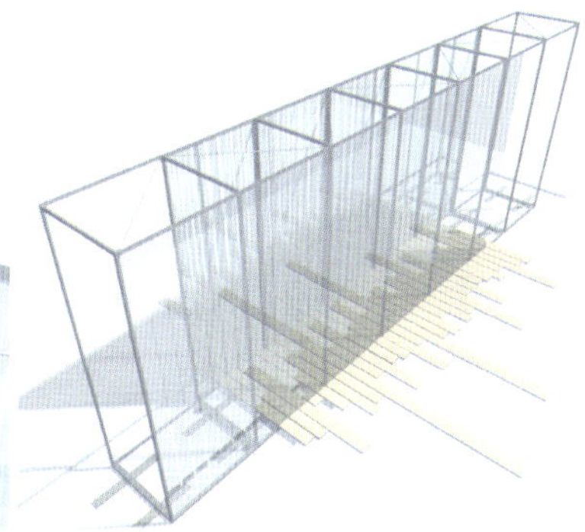

0104

Chaumont garden (2008)

We explore how the notion of sharing can create multiplicity and richness, the diversity of landscapes that make up the world being a case in point. In a deliberately caricatured way, the garden also portrays the North, temperate and navel-gazing, where artifice opulence and introversion reign, and the South, Mediterranean and still natural, with a fecund future.

0105

House meeting Passivhaus label in Angers (2011)

Thanks to its totally prefabricated timber frame, its double coated insulation (cellulose wadding and wood wool), its triple glazing and its high efficiency double-flow controlled mechanical ventilation and improved airtightness (0.09 m^3/hm), this house needs only 10 kW/m^2 year.

0106

Preschool in Ambillou (2011)

A wooden lattice-type trellis screens it from opposite buildings and provides protection from the sun. Evergreen creepers will complement the device. An element of shed roof type allows indirect lighting in classrooms while flooding the lobby with light. It is fully prefabricated timber frame and is covered with green roofing.

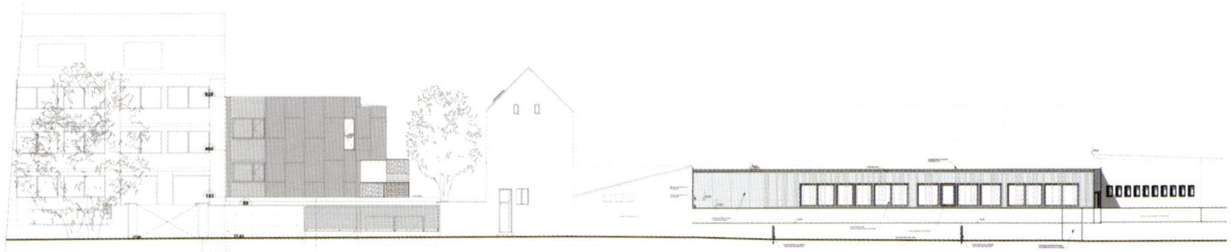

0107

OGEC school in Loches (2011)

Program: eight classrooms, a lecture hall, four youth clubs and thirty rooms for boarders. Over-insulation added to a wood concrete hybrid frame coupled with a double-flow ventilation has reduced the time of construction and the impact of the building on the environment.

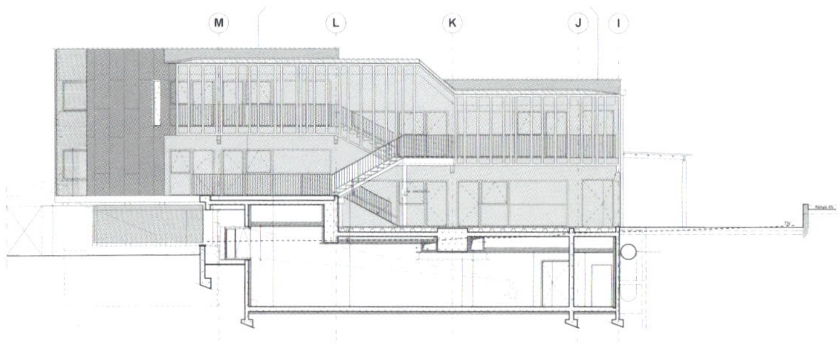

0108 ➤

Building in Charentilly (2011)

Contemporary, this house is a hybrid building fitting perfectly into the future suburban fabric. It takes advantage of the steep ground while looking over the magnificient views of the site. This house is based on the typology of our barns to adapt the program to a house in a rather unusual site. It is actually a series of four trellis-like gables.

◄ 0109

House in Tours (2009)

Functioning as a wooden covered green house, it allows the existing house to take in a maximum amount of sunshine. The wooden solar protection can be removed in the winter and put back in the summer.

◄ 0110

House in Fondettes (2011)

Surrounded by ancient trees, the construction, built against the hillside on the north side, has large windows on the south side, taking into consideration bioclimatic principles.

Baumraum
(Andreas Wenning)

Roonstraße 49
28203 Bremen, Germany
Tel.: +49 0 421 70 51 22
www.baumraum.de

0111

Tree houses are fragile structures supported by living beings, which means that its useful life depends to a large extent on the strength and life of the tree it is built in.

0112

From inside the cabin, thanks to wall-spanning windows and the skylight, the occupants can freely enjoy nature, which is literally within their grasp.

0113 ▲
The dream of living in and with nature comes true in this type of home, which puts most of its weight on the resilient oak trunk.

0114 ▼
Oak is the predominant building material. The railings that limit the habitable space are made of oak and steel.

0115 ➤
The side walls are covered in oak panels over rockwool, which serves both as insulation and wind foil.

◄ 0116
The name of the project - Between Alder and Oak - simply responds to the fact that the tree house is built between two different species of tree: an alder and an oak.

0119

The oak that partially supports the load was not strong enough, so the architect placed two posts over a concrete base for security.

0117

At the height of 13 ft, there is a platform-terrace with a table and a few chairs, and an upper cabin with a curved roof clad in wood and bitumen.

0018

Built for a family with grown-up children, this wooden cabin - 16 ft above the ground - provides its residents with space for rest and relaxation, and the possibility of adapting one of the compartments as a guest room.

0120

A few steps lead up from the terrace to the cabin.

Beals-Lyon Architects

119 Sinclair Road
W14 0NP London, UK
Tel.: +44 2076104638

Monseñor Félix Cabrera 23, of. 33
Santiago, Chile
Tel.: +56 2 2318824
www.beals-lyon.cl

0121

From objects to ecologies

In times when architectural production is governed and judged by issues of external appearance and originality of shape, we would like to think in sustainability as a way to move our understanding of architecture as the production of isolated and autonomous objects to one focused on relationships to context. A new ecology that emerges from more diffuse, vague, or ambiguous boundaries.

0122

Blend-in with surroundings

For a sustainable design it is important to understand and know the place, being responsive to local conditions. By borrowing shapes and textures from existing buildings in the area, a new construction can blend-in with its surroundings, creating a fragile image, as if it has always been there.

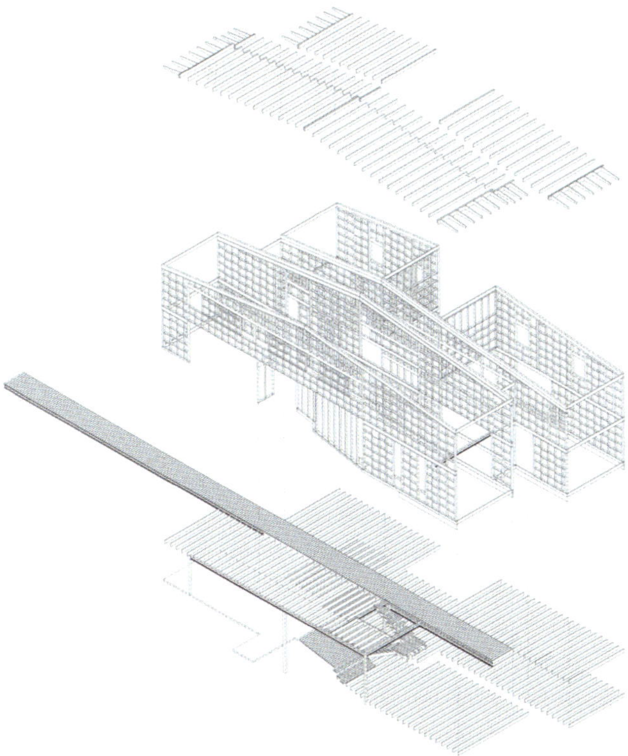

◄ 0123

Use local material and techniques

When working in remote and isolated site conditions, the use of available materials and constructive methods significantly reduces the environmental impact of new constructions. If using renewable sources, timber is the most sustainable alternative.

0124 ▲

Create an in-between space – not an interior, nor an exterior, but something in-between

An in-between space blurs the limit between interior and exterior, creating a more ambiguous relationship between buildings and landscape, natural and manmade.

◄ 0125

Do not design objects, but environmental conditions

A roof that extends beyond the interior provides a surrounding shadow, a more temperate environment.

0126 ➤

Build as light as possible

The less material is employed, the more sustainable is the building. Thus, structure is the result of the search for efficiency in performance, which is frequently found in older and traditional constructions.

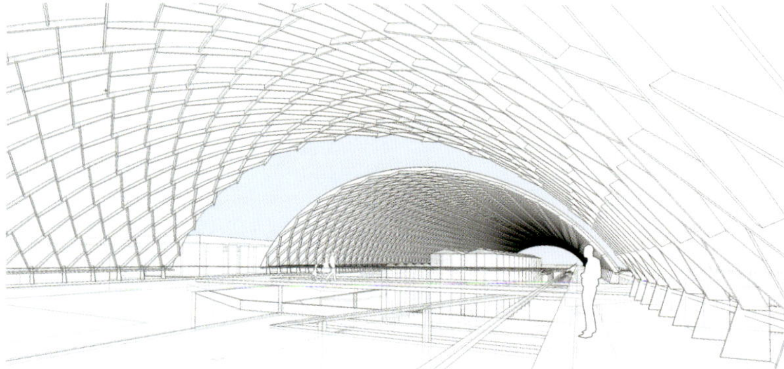

0127 ➤

Touch the ground lightly

Projects must emphasize nature by respecting the landscape, creating a new approach to it, not against it.

0128 ➤

Erase architecture by reflection

By means of reflection, it is possible to disappear in the landscape. The "puddle fountain" resembles a puddle in a park, mirroring the sky and creating a looking glass on the damp ground.

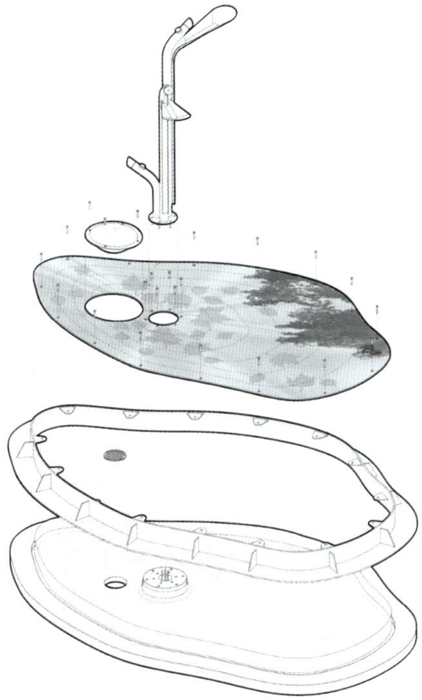

0129 ▲

Use porous boundaries

More permeable walls allow the migration of the exterior into the interior, and vice versa.

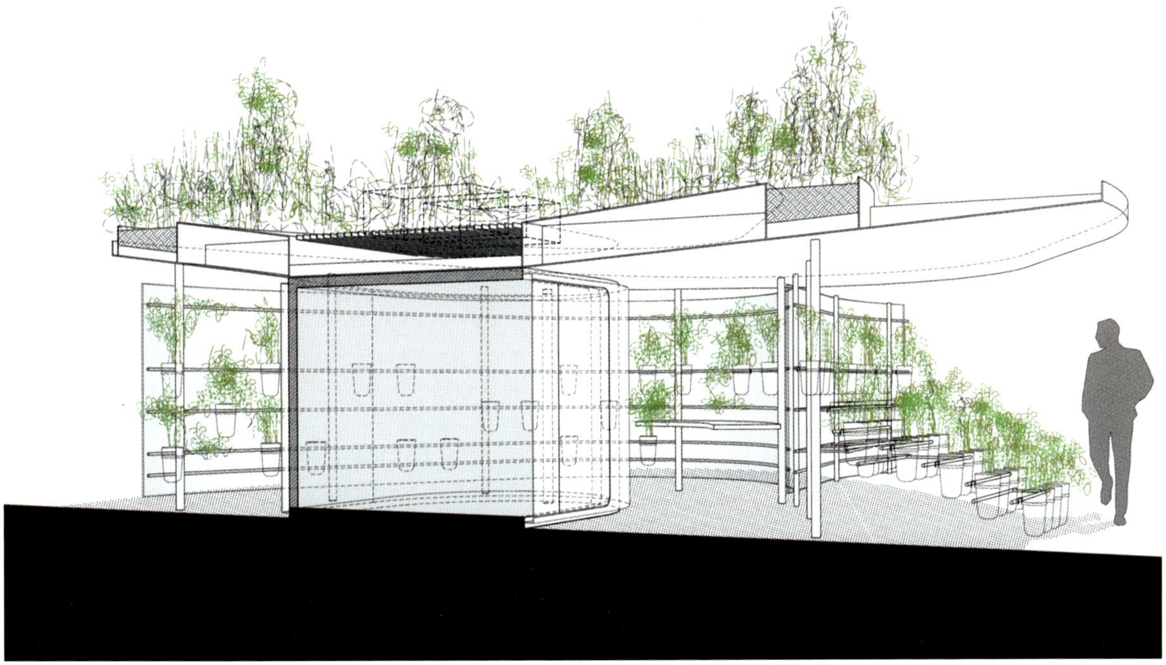

◄ 0130

Repeat the envelope

Limits created by successive layers create a thick border. Not just a dividing line between interior and exterior, but a space that can be inhabited.

Bipolaire Arquitectos (Miguel Arraiz García)

Mauro Guillén, 3, pt. 3
46009 Valencia, Spain
Tel.: +34 963 476 566
www.bipolaire.net

0131 ➤
In situ design
We decided, on a trial basis, to make partially open-ended decisions, so as not to have to define everything in the project phase.

0134 ➤
Accessibility
Accessing the home, located on a level below the entrance level of the lot, should always be possible, even in the long-term, anticipating the possible decreased mobility of the users.

0132 ➤
Materials
The choice of suitable materials is made depending on their location, how they will be used and their manufacturing process.

➤ 0133
Energy
Use of geothermal energy for heating, solar energy and for hot water and gas for cooking. The combination of good insulation in the façade and the roof, properly thought-out air circulation and the use of renewable energy are obligatory for a contemporary home.

0135 ▼

Water

Rainwater is collected and stored. Grey and sewage water is purified and stored. Rainwater and purified water are mixed and reused for watering. Water becomes an important element of the garden producing a touch of freshness, sounds, reflections etc.

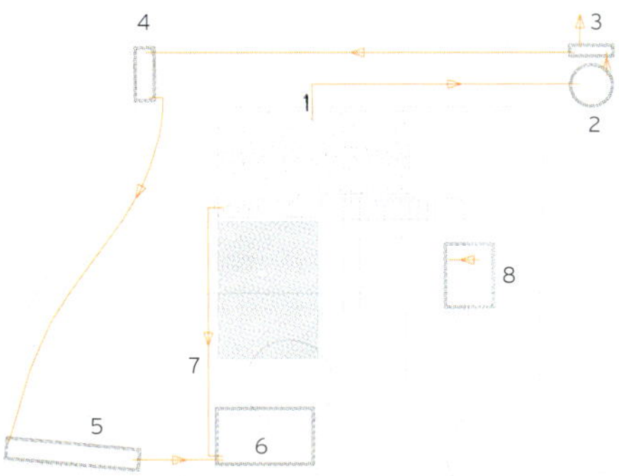

1. Sewage and graywater outlet.
2. Biological purification plant.
3. Overflow into the sewer.
4. Overhead recycled water tank.
5. Second phase of water treatment: sand and reed filters.
6. Rain and recycled water tank.
7. Rainwater outlet.
8. Rainwater tank.

0137 ►

Tree-building relationship

Trees are a starting point for a project. Each opening in the façade is linked to an existing or new tree that frames views, protects from excessive sun and provides end perspective and interpretation of the environment.

© Bipolaire Arquitectos

© Bipolaire Arquitectos

0140 ▲

Roof garden

It acts as the threshold of the landscape, banishing the nearby views of roofs and embracing distant views. It reinstates the green surface occupied by the plan of the home and provides excellent insulation.

© Bipolaire Arquitectos

0136 ▲

"Time is money" is not compatible with sustainable development.

0138 ►

Reusing waste

The slow pace of the work can reduce waste generation to an unimaginable minimum. The few remains of the materials produced are carefully stored and reused in subsequent stages of the construction. The 4,090-sq-ft project has generated a volume of 388 cu ft of waste.

0139 ►

Natural resources

Cross ventilation, exposure to prevailing summer winds and protection from prevailing winter winds provide a comfortable indoor climate with a very stable temperature.

© Bipolaire Arquitectos

© Bipolaire Arquitectos

BNIM

106 West 14th Street Suite 200
Kansas City, MO 64105, USA
Tel.: +1 816 783 1582
www.bnim.com

0141 ➤
Add vitality
Every act of building must add vitality and resilience to the surrounding community and ecosystem. Sustainability does not have to be exclusive of design excellence. Each must coexist for either to be achieved. In Greensburg, KS, after the entire town was destroyed by a tornado, they vowed to build back better and stronger.

0142 ▲
Promote obsolescence
We can design buildings, landscapes and communities that are compelling enough to make our current ideas of community obsolete. These new designs improve the health and quality of life of each inhabitant, while increasing the vitality of our environment.

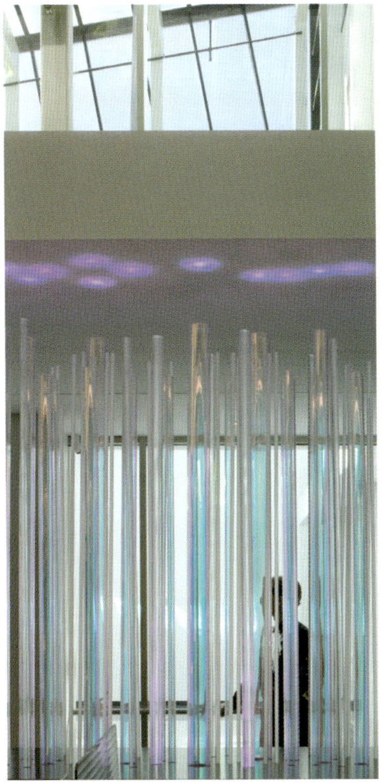

0143

Celebrate human and nature

Buildings are for people. Sustainable architecture should celebrate beauty and connect us to our innate knowledge of the living world.

0144

Reuse existing building stock

The most sustainable act of building reclaims from the vast inventory of existing stock to create new life and purpose.

0145

Generate more than you consume

A building can give back more resources than it consumes through carefully orchestrated strategies designed to achieve a net zero impact. In a cycle of restorative design a building can renewably generate energy to operate (and often with a surplus). It can also capture, treat and use its own water (and that of surrounding buildings) and function by using only what the site can provide.

0146

Use intuition and science

Though we begin with intuitive design ideas, it is through scientific energy and daylight modeling that we predict how that intuitive approach will perform in a given climate, often retooling the design to achieve the greatest opportunities and the appropriate technologies.

0147

Building as pedagogy

Look at buildings and sites as teaching tools. Each element of a project has the potential for pedagogy, filled with the promise of imparting knowledge to those who interact with it.

0148

No one knows as much as everyone

Collaborative intelligence creates ownership, facilitates the sharing of resources and allows the best ideas to emerge. Whether it's collaboration within an integrated design team or a community vision that emerges from social media tools, using a "collaborative dialogue of discovery" can and does produce the best ideas.

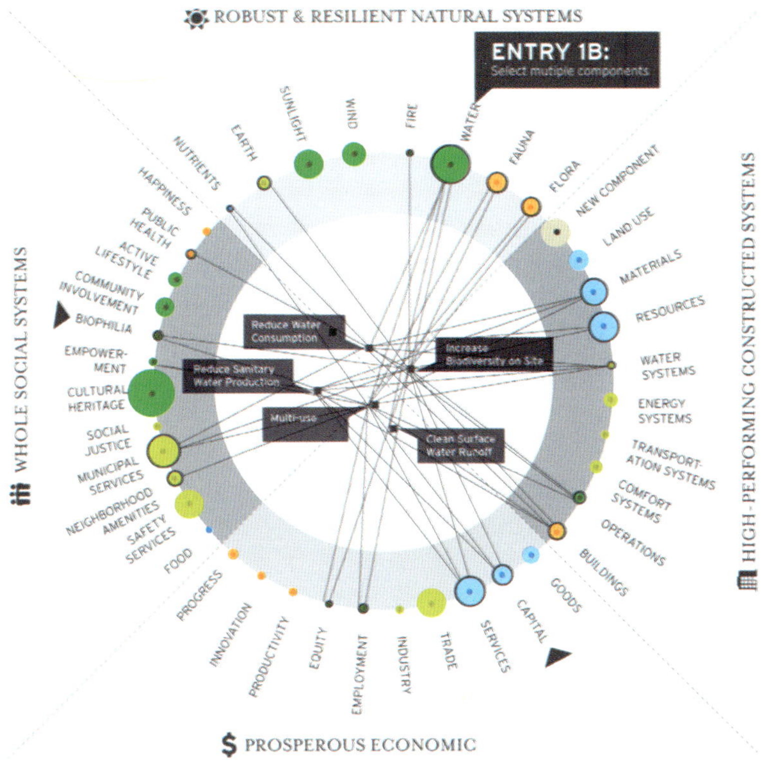

0149

Analyze and measure

High-performance design for new buildings – and sustainable improvements to existing buildings – realize quick paybacks from reduced utility costs, increased productivity and improved social and corporate equity.

150

Plus Ultra

Latin for "more beyond," this mantra causes us to challenge what we know, go deeper to ask questions and find answers, ultimately to seek ways of building that are restorative and symbiotic with nature. The Packard Foundation Sustainability Matrix and Report and the REGEN Tool for the U.S. Green Building Council are two tools we have created to help designers make more informed decisions.

Bourne Blue Architecture

PO Box 295
Newcastle, NSW 2300, Australia
Tel.: +61 02 4929 1450
www.bourneblue.com.au

0153
Design buildings well, so that they are well used and do not become obsolete as the client's needs change. Good design will be timeless, delightful spaces will always be utilized fully.

0151
Recycle buildings if possible rather than knock down and rebuild. Look for the positive elements within the existing buildings and reinforce them. This building was a small seaside cottage, which was pulled apart and converted to living space, with new sleeping spaces added as pavilions in the garden. Where walls were removed, contrasting floorboards were added in the floor so the previous entity could always be understood.

0152
Design a building to use minimal energy in its use. Incorporate solar panels. Use low energy light fittings, hot water heating and appliances. If possible in a temperate climate, orient the building East-West to maximize the ability to catch summer sun.

0154
Position openings which will allow the occupants to maximise cross ventilation in summer. By placing large louvre panels close to the ceiling at both ends of this hall, convective currents will always force air out on hot days.

0155 ▲
In temperate climates, insulate the building well to reduce heat loss in winter and heat gain in summer. This project has insulation (both bulk and reflective) in all wall and ceiling cavities.

0159 ▼
Collect all rainwater and use onsite for toilet flushing and garden use.

© Simon Whitbread

0160 ▲
In temperate climates, incorporate floor slabs that are shaded in summer and flooded with sun in winter. This way the floor stays cool in summer, but, as more sun hits the surface later in the year as seasons change, it radiates more heat into the room.

0157 ▼
Use materials that have minimal environmental impact in their manufacture: reconstituted or plantation timbers, recycled polyester insulation, plywood, low VOC paints.

© Simon Whitbread

0156 ▼
Encourage outdoor living, in a partially covered "in between" zone. Spaces not fully inside, nor outside but protected, require little energy to sustain and provide a delightful location to dwell.

© Simon Whitbread

© Simon Whitbread

© Simon Whitbread

0158 ►
Install screens or shutters, and large opening doors and windows so that the building can be "trimmed" like a sail on a yacht. These shutters can fully close, fully open or sit somewhere in between, allowing the inhabitants to adjust the building to suit the weather.

Casagrande Laboratory

Tamkang University Department of Architecture
151 Ying-chuan Rd.
Taipei, Taiwan
Tel.: +886 2 2621 5656
www.clab.fi

0161
Can't push a river
Chen House is raised above the ground in order to let the frequent heavy storm waters run free under the house. The house is not an obstacle in the natural flows of energy (Chen House, Casagrande Laboratory, Taiwan, 2008).

0162
Break the box
Modern man in an air-conditioned box is a degraded animal. Bio-climatic architecture aims in breaking the modern box in order to let nature to step in. Chen House gaped walls are essential to the bio-climatic architecture (Chen House, Casagrande Laboratory, Taiwan, 2008).

◄ 0165

Local knowledge

Local knowledge builds a connection between modern man and nature. Industrial city is alien to the local knowledge, which pushes the built human environment towards the organic (Bug Dome, WEAK! - Marco Casagrande, Hsieh Ying-Chun, Roan Ching-Yueh -, Shenzhen, 2009).

0164 ►

Insect architecture

To design is not enough. Design should not replace reality. The building must grow from the site. It must react for its surroundings, it must reflect life and it must let to be itself, like any other living creature. Architectural control is against nature and it is against architecture (Bug Dome, WEAK! - Marco Casagrande, Hsieh Ying-Chun, Roan Ching-Yueh -, Shenzhen, 2009).

0163 ▲

Dominate the no-man's land

Same space shared by man and nature, human nature as part of nature. In the organic settlement of Treasure Hill, the balance between man and jungle is constantly changing. This is a living ruin (Treasure Hill, Casagrande Laboratory, Taiwan, 2003).

0166 ➤
Maximum existence
The only rule of nature is to produce maximal life. House and city should be part of the life providing system, not an enclave in it. Industrial city has many rules (Ruin Academy, Casagrande Laboratory, Taiwan, 2010).

0167 ▼
Ultra-ruin
Ruin is when man-made has become part of nature. Modern architecture and industrial city must be ruined. You can drill holes through the building in order to let rain inside (Ruin Academy, Casagrande Laboratory, Taiwan, 2010).

0168 ➤
Cave-man style
Modern man has to take the liberty to travel 1,000 years back in order to realize that the things are the same (Ruin Academy, Casagrande Laboratory, Taiwan, 2010).

0169 ➤
Flesh is more
Architecture is a meditative space between modern man and nature. Site-specific knowledge is gained through physical labor (floating sauna, Casagrande & Rintala, Norway, 2002).

0170 ▼
Land(e)scape
You can build legs for abandoned farm-houses so that they can follow the farmers to the cities of the South (Land(e)scape, Casagrande & Rintala, Finland, 1999).

Center for Design Research, University of Kansas

School of Architecture, Design & Planning
University of Kansas
Lawrence, KS 6645, USA
Tel.: +1 785 864 2700
www.saud.ku.edu

0171 ➤
This program run by the University of Kansas for graduating students in its Architecture and Urban Planning Program focuses on prefabricated building systems and responds to the general problems of adapting building prototypes to suit local contexts.

0172 ➤
Located in the Rosedale neighborhood, this home is ideal for those who want to live "off the grid" without missing out on the amenities offered by living near the city's urban core.

0173
The program aimed for a LEED Platinum certification for the house, and to be the first home in Wyandotte county to use renewable energies.

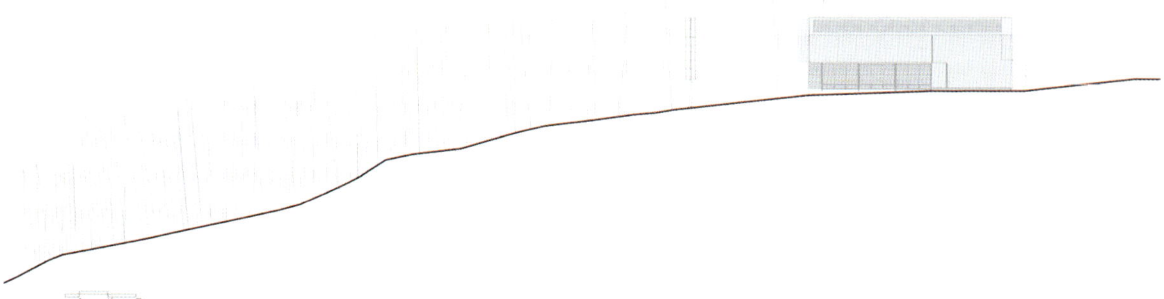

0174
The house is designed to produce surplus energy and sell it back to the grid. The roof features 600 sq ft of photovoltaic panels. These are complemented by a wind turbine and a geothermal energy source. The cellulose insulation in the walls and roof has a value of R-20.

0175
The solid hardwood timber used on exterior walls was sourced from South America and is FSC certified. Interiors and the frame make use of 70-year-old recycled Douglas fir.

0176
This sustainable prototype was built and delivered a year after a tornado devastated the Greensburg area. The design responded to the specific brief of the 5.4.7 Arts Center, the principal client, and was intended to act as community center for the area.

0180
It features wind turbines that supply an estimated 430 kWh per month of energy for a mean wind speed of 11 mph. Photovoltaic solar panels contribute 1.4 kWh.

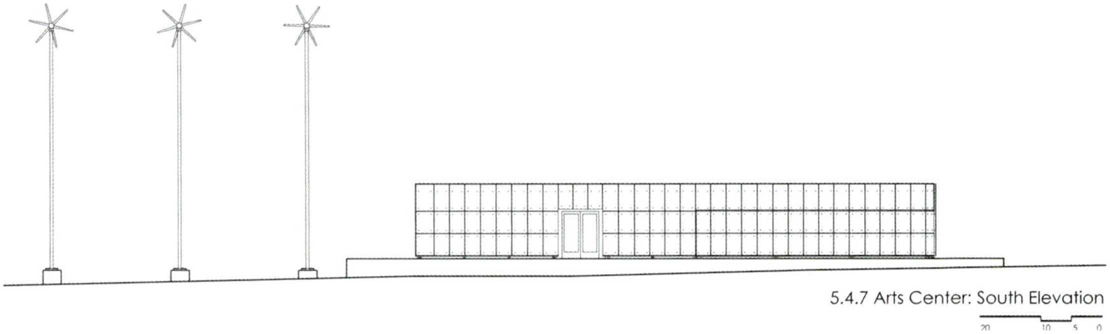

5.4.7 Arts Center: South Elevation

0179
Greensburg is located in Kiowa county, in southwestern Kansas, with a large farming sector. In May 2007, the town was devastated by a tornado that destroyed 95% of its buildings and left 11 people dead.

0177
According to the student team that designed it, the chief environmental positives of the prototype were its seamless blending with the landscape, strategic use of active and passive strategies to meet energy requirements (80-120%, depending on the season and wind speed), use of recycled materials, and flexibility for use as an exhibition space, community center or offices.

0178
Although the Arts Center did not require public funding, they chose to follow the guidelines of this rating system as an act of responsibility, and actually became the first building in Kansas to receive LEED Platinum level certification.

Christina Zerva Architects

Ossis, 3
Lárissa, Greece
Tel.: +30 2410 258003
www.christinazerva.com

© Milan Li Sakis

0182

An operable roof system allows the cool air to enter and the warm air to escape through the opening, thus perfectly ventilating the space. You can watch the stars at night or sit snug in a rain shower. It adds value and enhances the living space or, in this case, the dining area of the restaurant. When open, the natural light illuminates the dining area, creating a special atmosphere, while also providing energy savings.

0181

The façade is equipped with smart glass and a movable shading system in order to comply with thermal comfort requirements. Creating a "moving air chamber" between the wood panels and the smart glass prevents condensation behind the panels and provides thermal and acoustic insulation. The airflow through the glazing cavity is driven by natural buoyancy aided by wind pressure differences.

0183 ➤

Green roofs are biological sponges and filters that regulate building temperatures by acting as insulators. They increase urban wildlife habitat and reduce the urban heat island effect in our cities by dramatically absorbing and slowing the rate of storm water runoff from buildings.

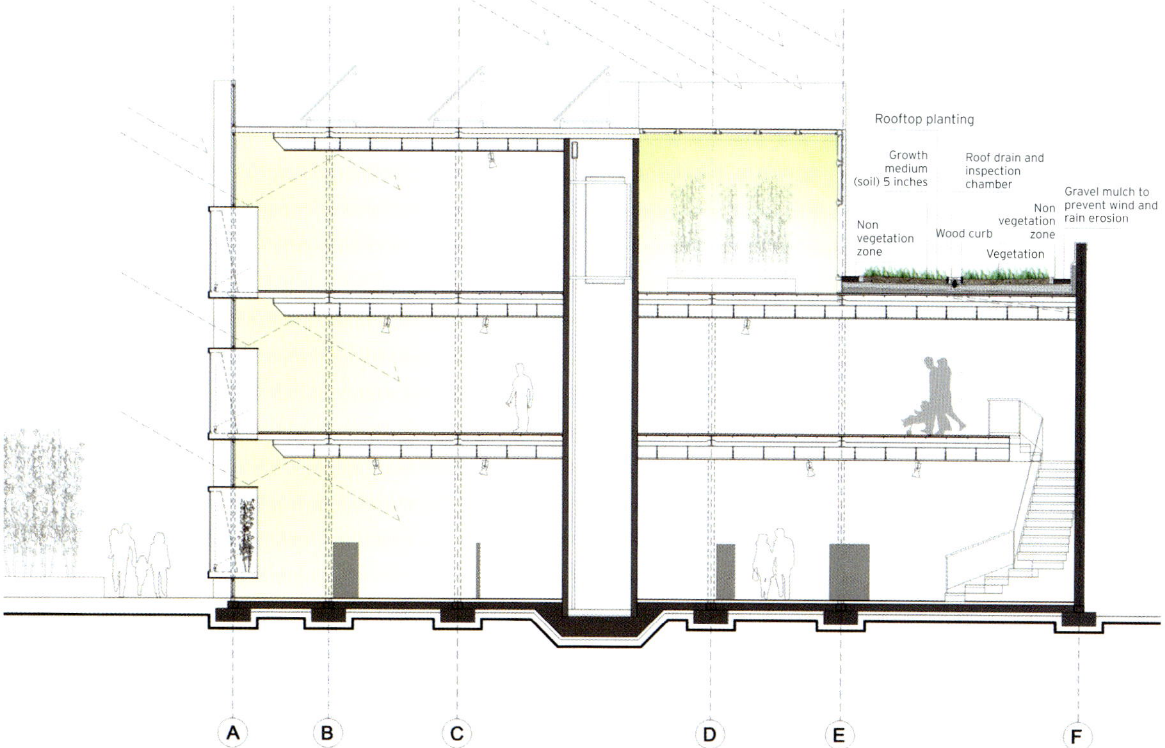

0184 ➤

Environmental design considerations shape the architecture of advanced naturally ventilated buildings. By splitting the building in two separate cubic forms and lifting it up from the ground level, the force of the wind splits too. This contributes to the cooling of the floors and roofs of the building.

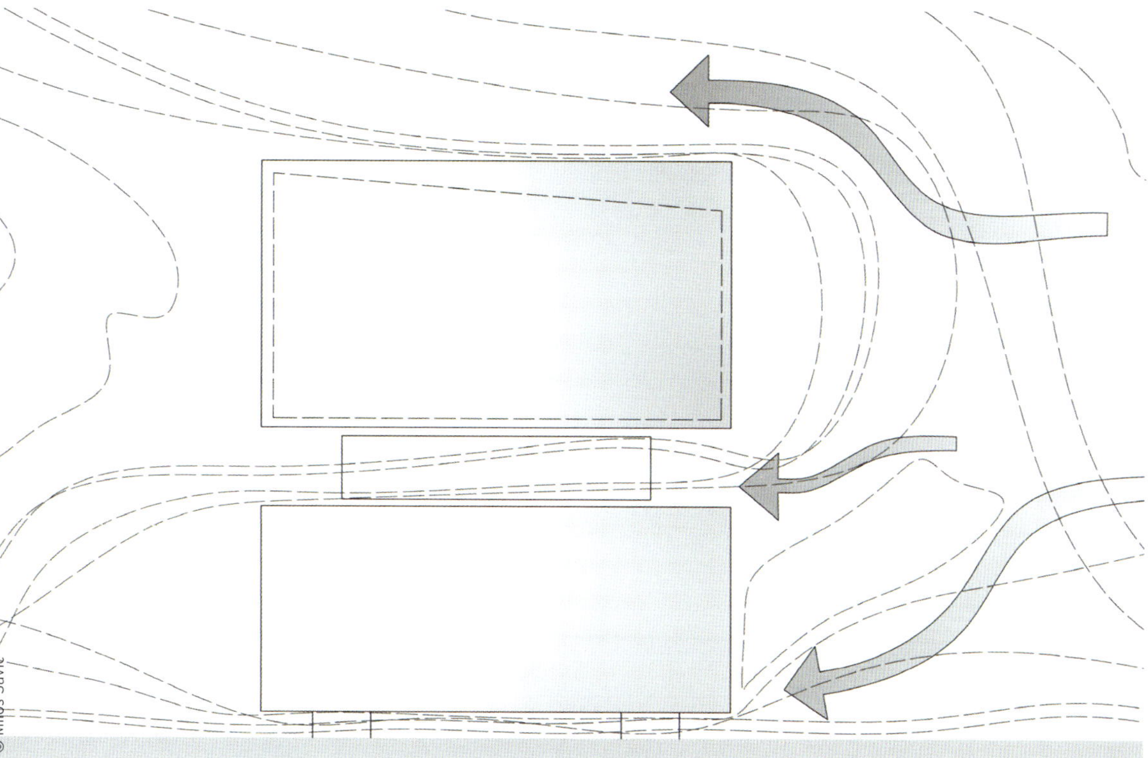

0185 ▼

Eco-friendly building materials provide environmental and health benefits that traditional materials typically don't. The production and application of these materials mean less energy consumption, less natural resource depletion and pollution, and are generally less toxic for the planet and its occupants. Green materials are: reusable, renewable, recycled, durable, locally available and low or non-toxic.

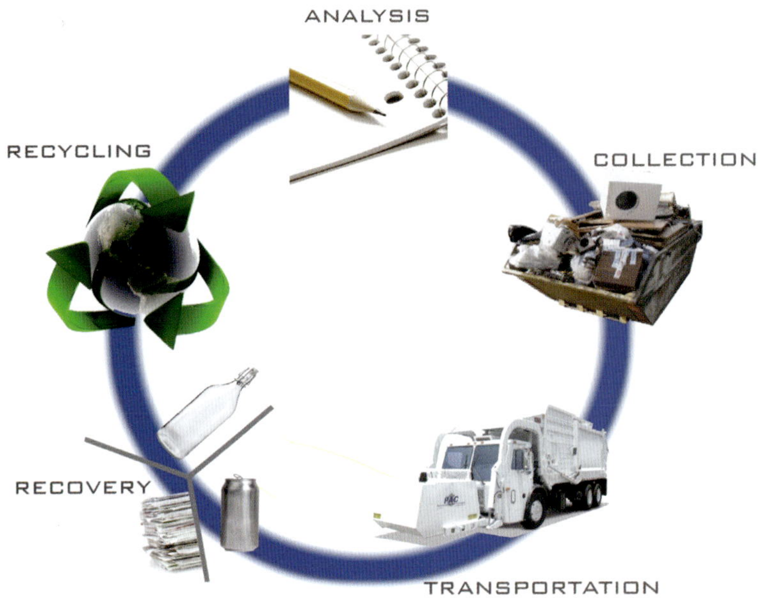

◄ 0187

Design decisions can make a significant contribution to preventing and reducing waste in the first place. The purchase of the materials with less or returnable packaging and the pre-order of the materials to specification reduce the waste. It is very important to reuse any excavated soil to landscape other areas. Bringing this philosophy early on can dramatically change and ease the process of waste management.

0186 ►

The role of shades is very important and is one of key passive design elements in eco-friendly architecture. The wooden shades can be spaced to maximize winter sun penetration, allowing passive solar heating, yet still offering protection in summer to minimize heat gains. Adjustable shading is recommended for elevations that receive a combination of high and low angle sun throughout the day and year.

0188 ➤

Vegetation should play a significant role in architectural design, due to the many advantages it offers to the internal environment, occupant's satisfaction and overall aesthetics. Vegetation systems become an active cooling agent to buildings, reducing the need for air-conditioning. Indoor plants purify, humidify and oxygenate air, improving indoor air quality and also adding a psychological value.

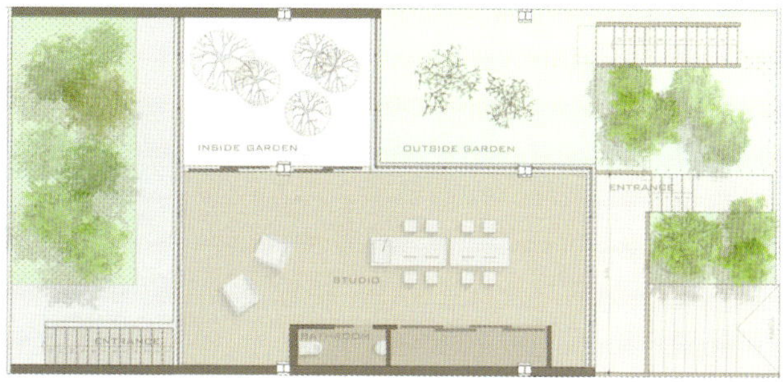

0190 ▼

Solar performance glass can help prevent heat gain and insulate against heat loss, improve thermal comfort and reduce glare and UV radiation. In the winter, much of the warmth given off by the heaters inside the building is bounced back into the room. In the summer, the sunrays bounce off the glass and the heat stays outside. Eco-glass creates a healthy and comfortable environment.

0189 ▼

Windows performance and orientation is crucial for determining the amount of solar radiation a house receives. The main south-facing façade, with the large angled opening, receives more solar radiation than a vertical one, thus capturing as much solar energy, "free heat," as possible, for best energy-saving winter performance.

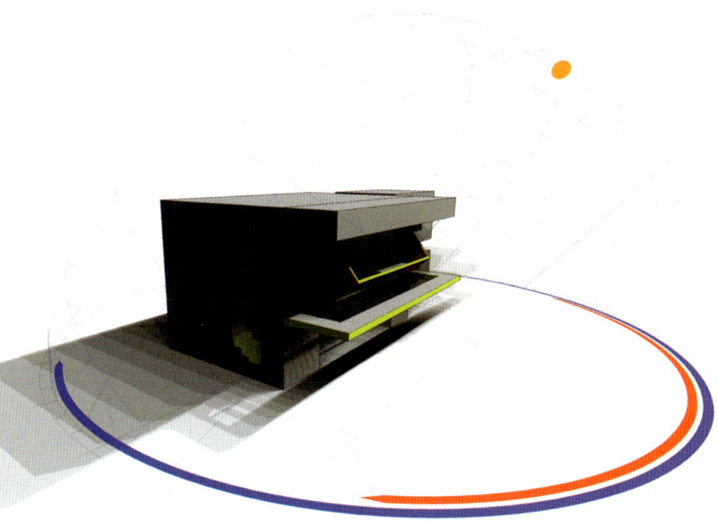

© Milena Stojkovic

Correia/Ragazzi Arquitectos

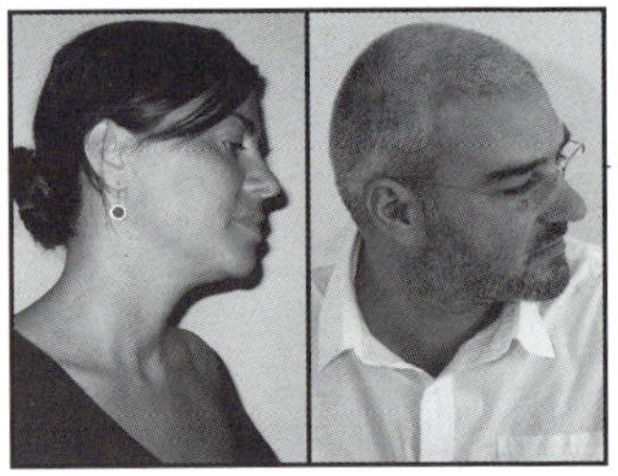

Rua Azevedo Coutinho, 39, 4º Sala 44
4100-100 Porto, Portugal
Tel.: +351 226 067 047
www.correiaragazzi.com

0191 ➤
The house opens itself in all directions in order to maximize the views towards the beautiful vineyards as well as sun exposure (with adequate shading on the sunny side), preventing the need to use cooling systems.

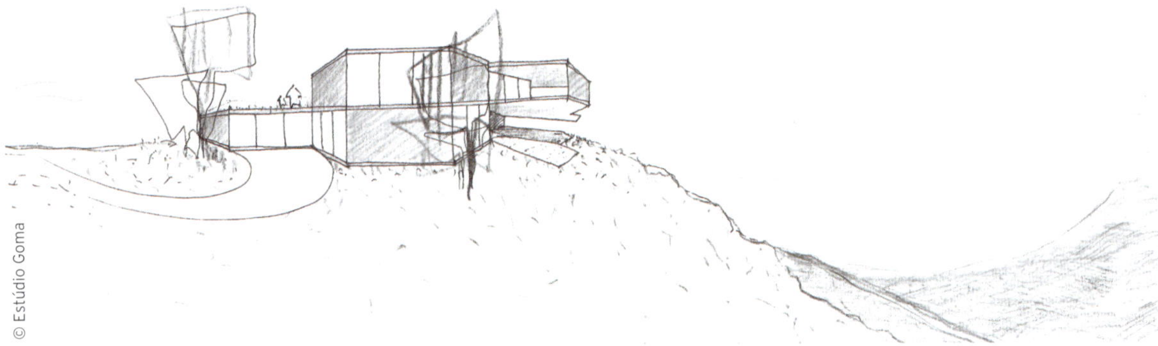

© Estúdio Goma

© Luis Ferreira Alves

◄ 0192
The project placement on the plot was essential, given its surroundings. The house could only act as a significant element on the landscape and, at the same time, the exceptional outlook should be an element of the house that frames the landscape as if it was a painting.

© Luís Ferreira Alves

◄ 0193

No trees where cut down to build this house on the National Park. The house overhangs the riverbank cliff and reduces land occupancy. From the river it appears as a clear glass frame dissimulated on the vegetation, almost non-existent.

◄ 0194

Two tiles that reinvent the Portuguese tile tradition. Produced from recycled materials and leftovers of tile production. In high and low relief.

0195 ►

From both tiles, together or separately, several different surfaces of high plasticity can be created. Countless patterns and textures result from different combinations.

© Alberto Plácido

0196 ➤

The courtyard establishes urban relations and allows the transition between outside and inside private housing spaces, creating a new layer of privacy and occupancy.
The platforms dissimulate the natural plot undulation. Artificial and natural complement each other and compose a new landscape idea. Vegetation and water are introduced also as means of controlling the heat island effect, promoting shading, cooling and diminishing pollution.

◄ 0197

A system of cell growth, each individual cell being an apartment in a honeycomb criteria that can be increased according to housing needs. Flexible layouts allow the needed adjustments in terms of topography, sun exposure, ventilation, areas, etc.

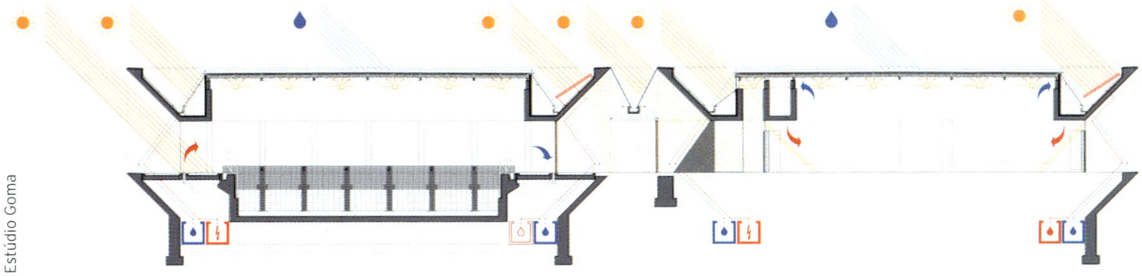

◄ 0198
As a big public structure is of vital importance to be as sustainable as possible in term of energy efficiency and use of natural resources. Also, the use of prefabricated elements improves cost-efficiency construction in terms of budget and time spent.

0199 ▼
SYN comes from the Greek and means "with" or "together" .SYN is both light and ventilation, a one piece that combines both functions, ideal to use on rehabilitation of old buildings and houses of smaller are compartments, as in bathrooms. SYN is made from 90% recycled material.

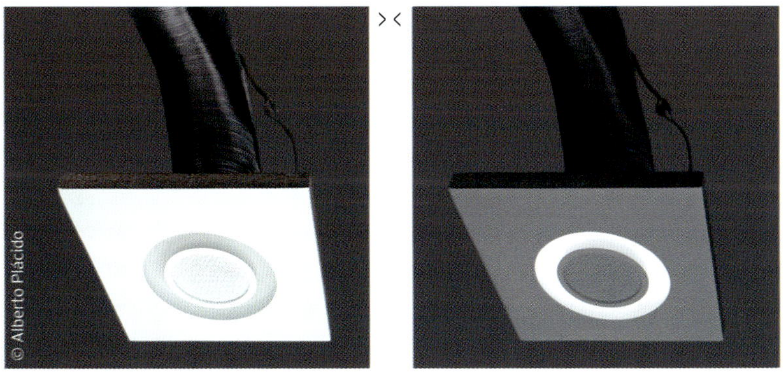

0200 ►
The existent ruin was rebuilt and is now a guest bedroom; this solution allowed the existence of another bedroom in order to accommodate the entire family without increasing the waterproof area in the plot, on an area of heavy rain.

Coste Architectures

11, rue de la Prévoté - BP 19
78550 Houdan, France
Tel.: +33 1 30 59 54 95
www.coste.fr

0201 ▲
From the outside, the residence appears to be made up of fairly classic cube forms: a rectangular shape and gable roof. The outer cladding on the walls is wood.

◄ 0202
This latest model for a prefabricated home was designed by Coste Architectures, but the actual construction is the responsibility of the Geoxia consortium (Maisons Phenix).

0203 ▼
The property incorporates thermal solar panels, located on the roof, which provide over 50% of the energy required to heat the water used in the home.

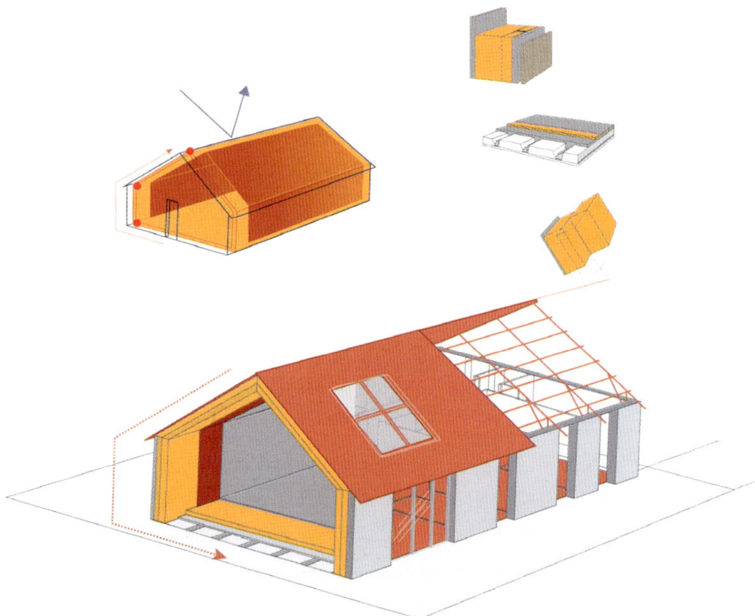

◄ 0204
Thanks to this disposition and to all the other bioclimatic features, the property does not need to be heated by electricity. To achieve optimum insulation and prevent heat loss, the project integrated triple-glazed windows and the total elimination of thermal bridges.

◄ 0205
In addition, the walls were erected with a double R-value in terms of thermal resistance, in accordance with French technical regulations.

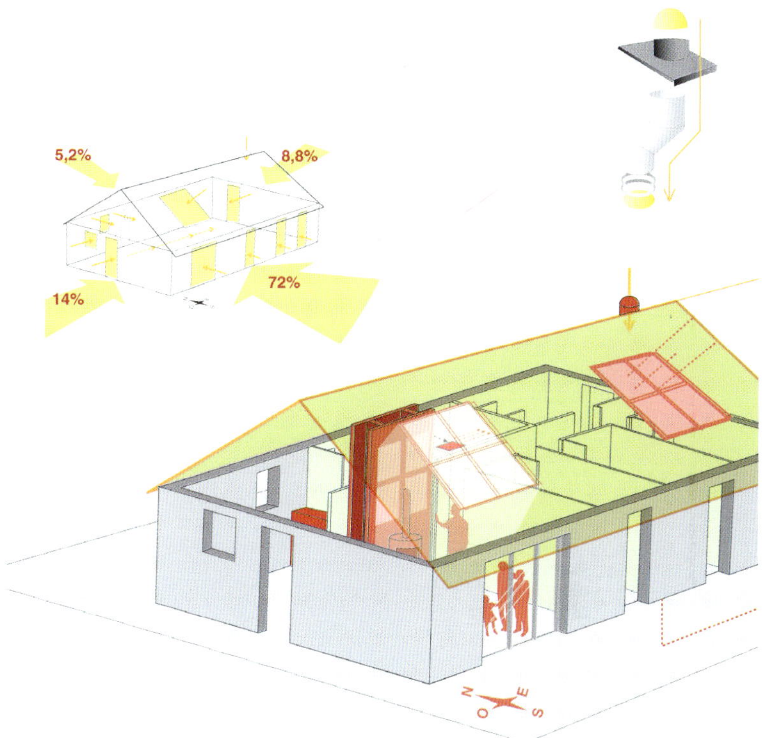

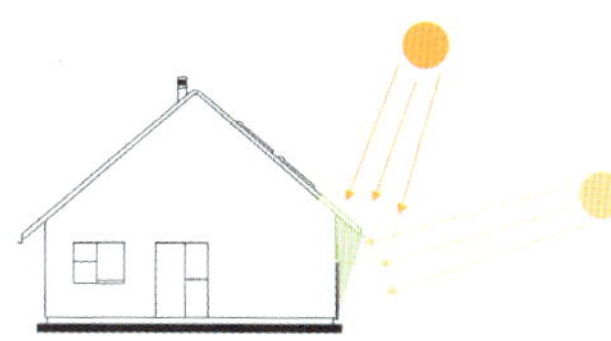

0206 ►
From the perspective of sustainable architecture, the house offers a multitude of solutions for greener living. The first is its optimum orientation to the sun, since 72% of the natural light penetrates the building on its southern side.

0207 ➤

The energy consumption for the entire house is 12kW/m² per year, whereas in normal conditions, without taking any measures to increase energy efficiency, it would amount to roughly 70kW/m² per year.

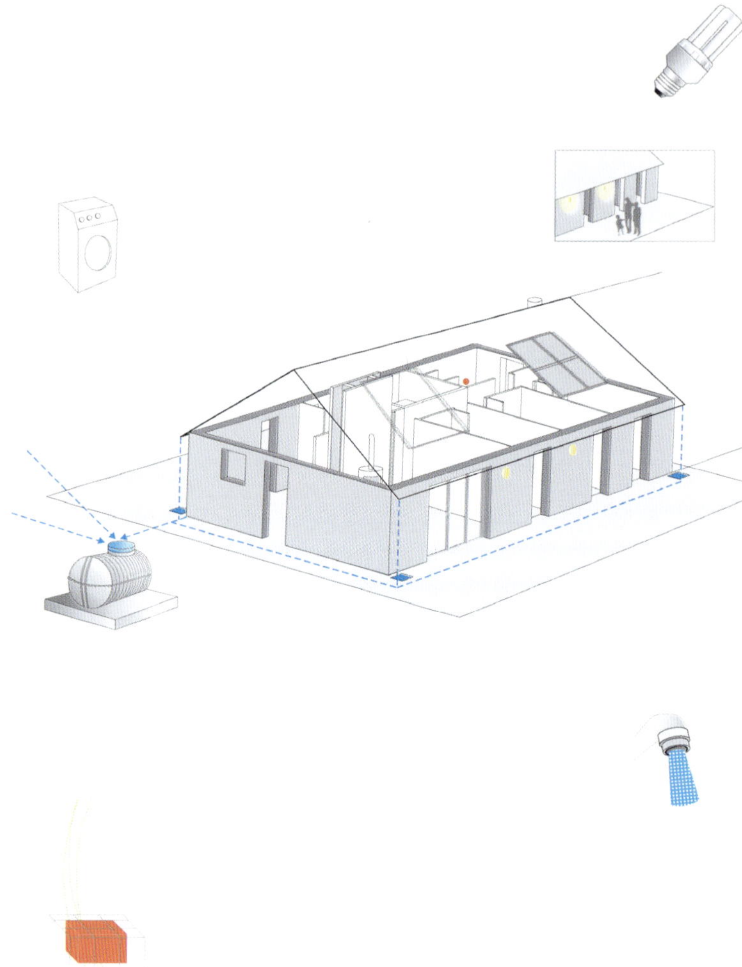

◄ 0208

The air passes through a double-flow thermodynamic system and is distributed by two diffusers that help to renew the atmosphere inside the house throughout most of the year. A wood-burning stove has also been installed to enhance the heating system.

0209
An earth tube (earth-air heat exchanger) buried in a trench at a depth of 8 ft feeds a ventilation system with air at constant temperature of 57 ºF (with variation of +/-4 ºF).

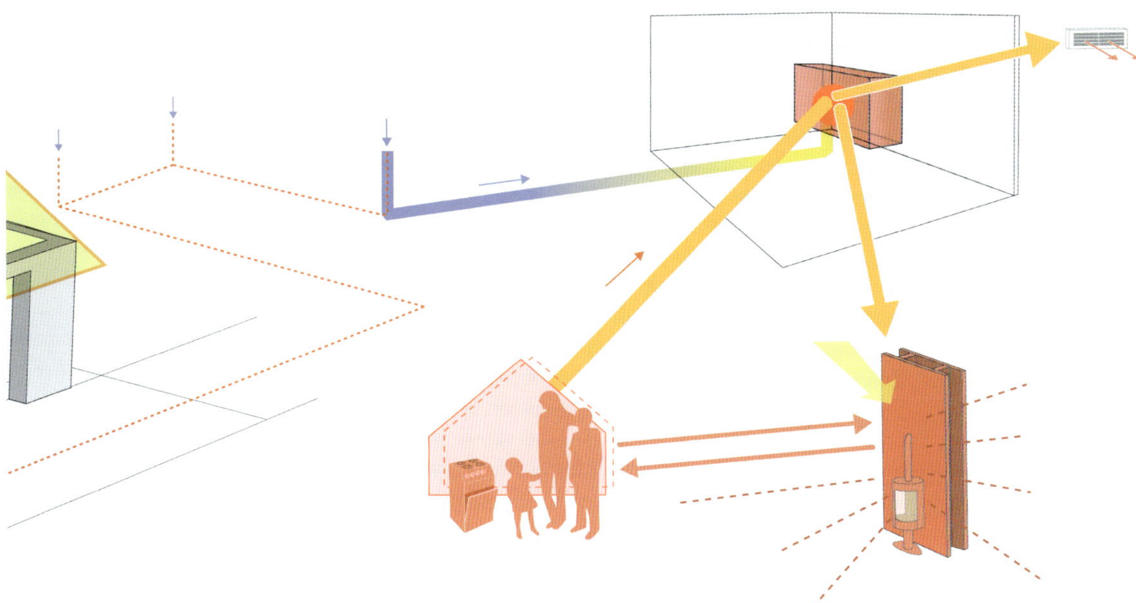

0210
This savings in energy, which are calculated to be around 80%, and in water, estimated at about 38%, translate to a reduction in CO_2 emissions into the atmosphere of some 2,755 lb a year- figures that are by no means negligible, showing that reducing emissions is a viable position.

Designs Northwest Architects

10031 SR 532 Suite B
Stanwood, WA 98292, USA
Tel.: +1 360 629 3441
www.designsnw.com

0211 ➤

Limit the footprint

Building small reduces the amount of impact on the existing ecosystem by allowing a larger amount of natural vegetation to remain intact. A smaller house also uses less energy and leaves a smaller carbon footprint. It also uses less material, saving resources, which is beneficial to the environment as a whole.

0212

Use passive cooling

You can reduce the need for mechanical cooling by using passive strategies. Windows can be located to provide cross ventilation. Sun shading devices can be used to reduce solar gain. Operable walls can be used to create semi-outdoor rooms.

0213

Use concrete floor systems

Concrete floors can be used as a thermal mass to store energy gain during the day and release it during the night. This moderates drastic temperature swings and reduces the need for mechanical heating and cooling. Concrete floors can also be used for hydronic heating, which can be as much as much as 30% more efficient than a forced air system.

0214

Borrow light for dark spaces

Take advantage of natural light whenever possible. This saves energy and is also beneficial for psychological health. By using skylights large windows and delicate structure you can bring light into interior spaces. Bright colors or reflective materials can also be used to reflect natural light into farther into darkened spaces.

0215

Use native landscaping

Preserve as much of the native vegetation as possible and look for opportunities to restore areas to their natural state. Using climate appropriate plants will reduce the need for irrigation and be easier to maintain. It will also be beneficial for the surrounding ecosystem.

0216

Prioritize your use of glazing

Orient major glass openings to views or to a desired sun exposure and limit the amount of glazing in other areas. Prioritizing in this manner will allow you to reduce the overall amount of glazing, making the building envelope more efficient.

0217 ➤

Use a rain screen system

A rain screen cladding system creates a breathable air space between the siding material and the air barrier/drainage plane. This prevents moisture from being trapped behind the siding, which increases the longevity of the materials and helps prevent the development of toxic mold and mildew.

0218 ➤

Choose materials carefully

Sustainable materials, such as engineered wood products, composite materials and steel, often use less raw material and are more durable than traditional building materials. Also look for opportunities to salvage and reuse previously used materials. Try to think beyond just the aesthetic when choosing your materials.

0219

Adaptive reuse

Existing buildings can often be salvaged and repurposed for new uses. Even if the entire floor plan, aesthetic character, and use of the building are being changed, saving elements, such as the foundation or exterior walls, can eliminate a lot of disruptive site work and keep materials from reaching landfills.

0220

Green roofs

Green roofs have many sustainable properties. They provide superior insulation without using synthetic material, they retain and filter storm water runoff, and they provide a microhabitat for various native species of flora and fauna.

Despang Architekten

1040 N. Olive Road
PO Box 210075
Tucson, AZ 85721, USA
Tel.: +1 520 626 9350
www.despangarchitekten.com

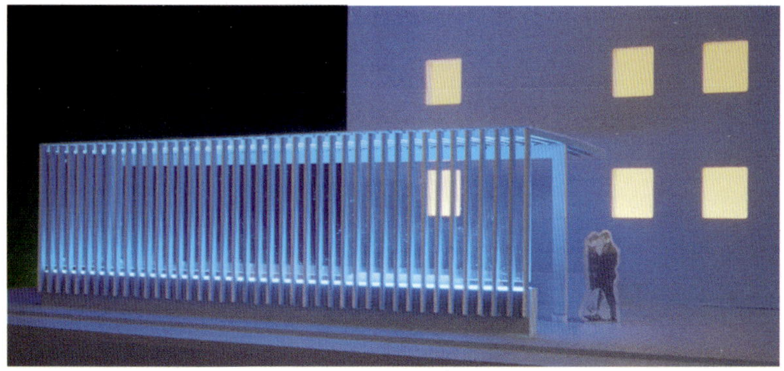

0221 ➤
Ecology as a universal system requires a comprehensive methodology of architecture as a facilitator of human events. The individual ecological human activities create typological prototypes which together form a holistic bioclimatic way of living.
A fundamental type is movement between public transportation spaces, riding in style with an architectural aesthetics engaging the senses.

◄ 0224
A grocery supply decentralized and walkable encourages a healthy customer attitude. The Hannover Jibi grocer is a composition of a green vegetative façade food volume supplying the majority of energy by way of its PV roof, and a beverage pavilion with a shading textile cloud hovering over it, creating a biodynamic mercantile spectacle.

0222 ▲
To get people off the anti-environmental personal transportation, public infrastructure must be made sexy. The subway canopies for the city of Bochum adjust the eye from the dark to the bright and provide a lowest maintenance texture. The Karlsruhe signposts deliver the information to the traveller gestural with a minimalist approach of anti-cluttering.

0223 ➤
The next three tips represent dwelling types resulting from the concept that the most ecological building is the one not newly built, but the one kept in the life cycle through rejuvenation. Here climate change serves as inspiration for innovating vernacular traditions of rooftop sleeping in the cool summer breezes. The Hannover case study interprets Schindler's theme as an assemblage of thermally modified timber.

0225 ▲
Regarding the fact that 90% of the buildings in 2030 are expected to already be in existence, the ecological mission of rejuvenation for the Hannover project uses the thermal improvement of the building envelope as the initiation for responsible conversion. An unfinished attic is morphed into a loft and composes outdoor spaces around a typical 1960s multi-dwelling house.

0226 ➤
The most effective way of infusing ecology deeply into society is education. This allows emerging inhabitants to grow up in environments of optimized eco-friendliness and simultaneously have them disseminate the environmental message. The Ilsede project adapts an existing school for societally required all day use by offering universal space with a bio-regulative exoskeleton.

0229 ▼
The Göttingen University passive-house kindergarten is a monolithic concrete thermal massing hybrid of landscape and architecture bermed into the campus park, gesturally radiating out towards the south with textile shades in frames for unobstructed views.

◄ 0228
The first passive-house kindergarten for the city of Hannover innovates the US frame system in deepening it with TJI wall trusses and cellulose insulation. The curvilinear glazed south façade optimizes group intimacy, seamlessly transitions into the outdoor classrooms and solar gain. The other three fronts soften their hermetic thermal enclosure with slices of light.

0227 ▲
Reviving the ecological relationship of working close to dwelling both in the urban and rural, the Krogmann Headquarters exemplifies the transitioning of a traditional small town wood contractor into the 21st century. In plan and section, the cone-shaped structure demonstratively embraces the sun and the center of the small town, signalizing a "passive house / active working" environment.

◄ 0230
A 300-year-old farmhouse gets its embodied energy further amortized through a critical restoration of replacing strategic parts of the half-timbered loam brick infill with a new spatial and thermal threshold of triple pane glass. Recessed from the exoskeleton, the glazing creates transitional outdoor spaces and internally features a hybridism of Miesian free plan and Loosian Raumplan.

Dick van Gameren Architecten

Willem Fenengastraat 4B
1096 BN Amsterdam, The Netherlands
Tel.: +31 (0)20 4627800
www.dickvangameren.com

0231

The design steps off from the existing house, so that, along with comprehensively improving the quality of both space and building performance, it makes the most of the materials already on site. Components of the existing house that had to be removed have been reused elsewhere in the design where possible.

0233

A floor heating system has been laid into the new concrete deck floor that can heat or cool the rooms using low temperature heating (water <95 °F). A second system has been installed in the bedroom ceilings to facilitate additional cooling in the summer.

0232

Roofs and façades have been insulated or reinsulated (R = 3.5). The floor too has been insulated (R = 3) and finished with a smooth continuous concrete deck floor on compression-resistant insulation. The old wood frames have been replaced with new aluminium-framed facade units of insulated glass (U = 1.1)

0234

Ventilation is premised on the natural circulation of air throughout the house. Ventilation units in the outer walls make it possible to regulate the exact quantity of air entering the building. In the summer, ventilation can be stepped up using a mechanical discharge system in the roof lights of the central hall.

0238

All living spaces receive daylight from more than one direction. Storage units, bathrooms and other ancillary spaces also receive daylight, some of it indirect. All artificial lighting is LED-based.

0235

The entire system is fed by a thermal storage unit. Self-generated energy is not being treated as an option for the time being. The surrounding trees mean that there is much shade for a large part of the year and little wind. The part of the roof that does catch the sun all year long is provided with a solar boiler for hot water facilities (head pipe system).

0237

Rainwater on the roofs is run off directly into the brook. All waste water (greywater) is run off into a tank where it is purified organically and then discharged into the brook. Only biodegradable cleansing agents are used in the house.

0236

The living room heats up quickly in winter by being oriented to the south and having all-glass façades, and thus serves as a heat source for the house as a whole.

0239

The garden is sprinkled exclusively with water from the brook. An electric lawn mower robot keeps the grass at the correct height, and the planting in the garden can be tended without the need for herbicides and artificial fertilizers.

0240

Much of the furniture is built-in and, where possible, made of sustainable materials: bamboo for wood floors and wardrobes, and for the floor covering in the sunken sitting area; Ecoplex (poplar) laminate for the kitchen cupboards, and wool filt for settees in the living room and kitchen, and curtains in the nurseries.

Djuric Tardio Architectes

17, rue Ramponeau
75020 Paris, France
Tel.: +33 1 40330641
www.djuric-tardio.com

0241 ➤
Home that adapts to an urban context owing to its volume and varies through the roof/pergola creating a sunny and intimate suspended garden or terrace. Eco-sustainable building system with Finnish wood panels positioned on a base.

0242

Dense and pleasant urban typology, consisting of houses and small collective houses of 5-7 diversified and BBC (low consumption buildings) apartments with terraces and gardens. Preservation of existing vegetation and pre-planting of removed trees, as well as double orientation of the homes (northeast and southeast) for better sun exposure and protection against the wind, are some of the techniques used in this sustainable district.

0243

Construction of new low-cost rent housing. We wanted to give a new image to the existing neighborhood, make the residents feel safe and create a sustainable neighborhood. The wooden constructions are between apartment buildings and houses.
A wide variety of solutions for homes, interior/exterior relationship and the building forms was used.

0244

In Langoiran, an eco-district project that provides environmental solutions, we used wooden construction, solar panels, English gardens and various advanced technologies in energy savings. The urban concept is developed from different types of houses and materials. The houses are built around the principle of a common yard, a hub for social life.

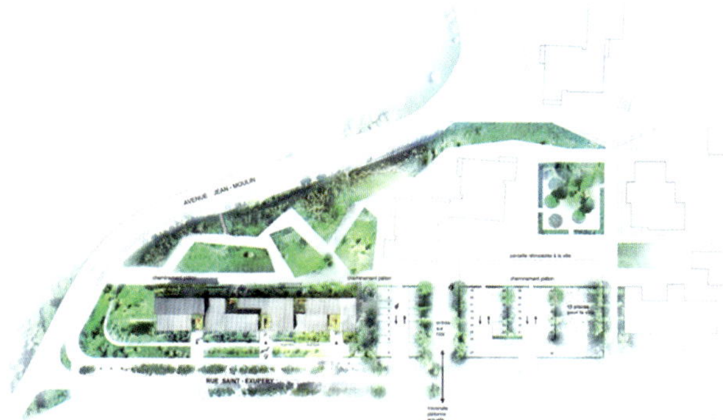

◄ 0245
Lights and shades. This hotel in Nador, Morocco respects the historic urban fabric and it is built around a marina allowing direct access to the sea. The very hot weather requires a double skin façade that generates ventilation and prevents the overheating of the walls.

0246 ►
Moroccan national television headquarters in Rabat. Vegetation of the forest around the site invades the site. This ensures the building''s climate control providing shade and cool air, creating a natural barrier and dominating the entrance to the building with a garden.

◄ 0247
Reconversion of military barracks. The project respects the existing plaza and improves the quality of life of the surroundings, enriched by the social density of an urban barrier.

0248 ▲
"A train called desire". Sustainable urban, suspended movements. This entirely, wooden suspended path can be covered on foot or on bike. It is a strong and dynamic link. The plaza is an urban magnet, a place of exchange.

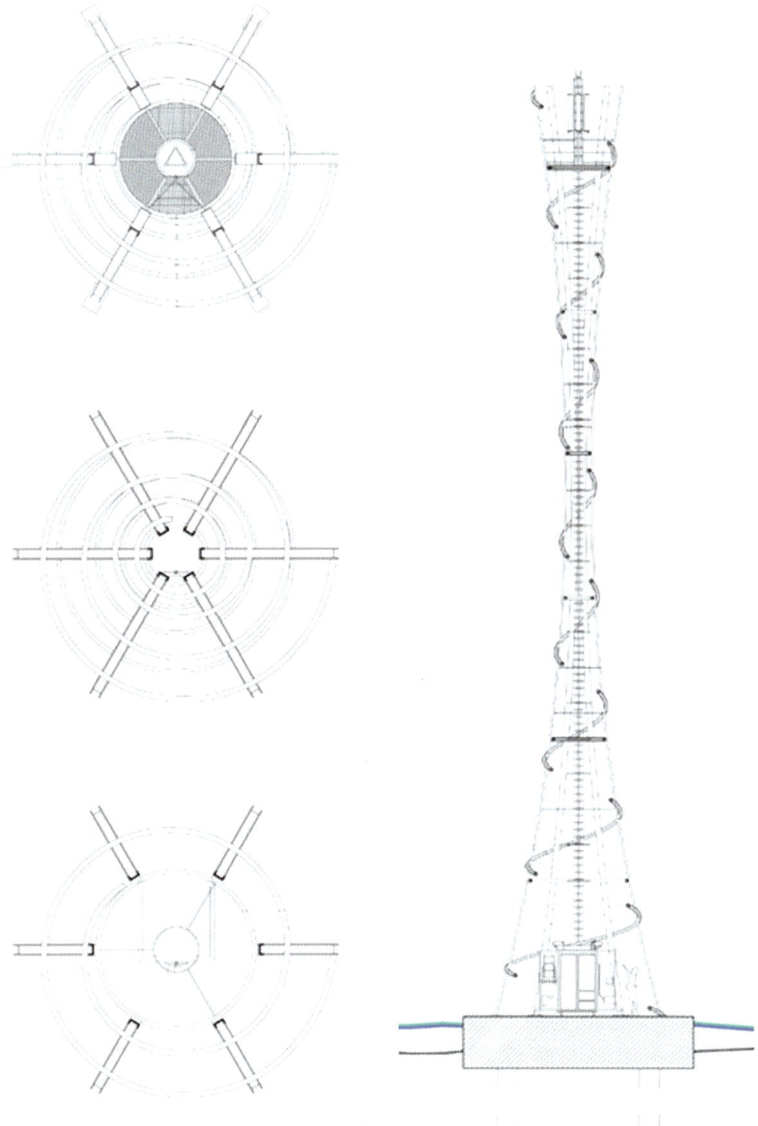

0249 ►
With its slim and atypical form, the mobile phone antenna in the Lagoon of Venice becomes a metal sculpture and light of life. The objective is to highlight its technological aspect and give it an additional role. Technology is at the service of the environment.

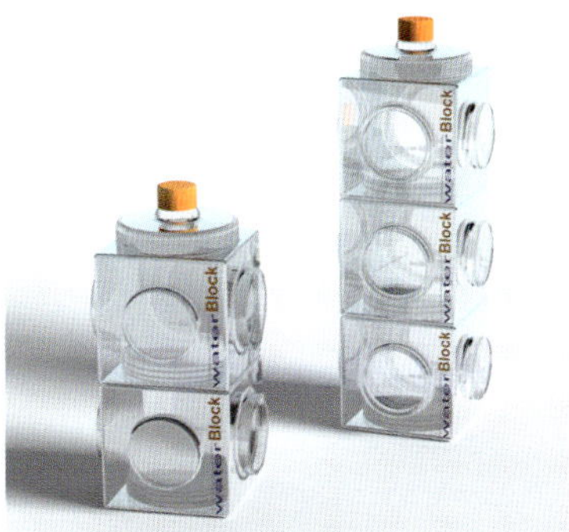

◄ 0250
It's a bottle but not only a bottle. Reusing plastic bottles is environment-friendly. It produces less waste. After being used, it becomes a multipurpose object. It can be recycled as an object and not only as PET plastic. Blocks are embeddable with each other. It's a recyclable object before becoming a recyclable material.

Dorte Mandrup Arkitekter ApS

Nørrebrogade 66 D 1.sal
2200 Copenhagen, Denmark
Tel.: +45 33937350
www.dortemandrup.dk

0251
Think passive
The heating and lighting power of the sun can be used in various ways, but the most efficient is the simple one. Letting the light penetrate the building in an efficient and manageable way to facilitate the functions of the building, and keeping the heat of the sun store in the heavy parts ensure efficient use of the sun-energy throughout the entire life-span of the building.

0252
Think active
From a holistic way of thinking sustainability, the amount of time a building is actively in use directly reflects the actual need for a building. In short, a building that is not used very often can be measurably sustainable, but if it is only used very rarely, the energy used to erect and maintain the building easily surpasses the energy saved, when the building is in use.

0254
Why build?
Every time a building-process begins, the main objective needs to be clear and well-based. If the program of a building is not clear, change it. The Herstedlund Community Center is an evolution of a well-known building typology in Denmark, but this building typology is closed 90% of the time. In order to clarify and enhance the need for the building, the program was changed and expanded to facilitate more functions and groups of people at the same time.

0253
Explore all options
This community center had the agenda of sustainability added at a very late stage in the process, and the sustainable measures built in were, therefore, based on the exploration of options at hand: soil and sun-based heating, semi-passive ventilation and active lighting systems.

0255
Economical accessibility
Sustainable building only matters if it is accessible for the masses. Platform is a single-family standard-house project that combines the economic benefits of mass-production with a low-emission, low energy-consumption building.

© Torben Eskerod

0257

Fit in

Consider the hierarchy of the city-structure before deciding, which part needs to be added to the context. Add only buildings and expressions that will find their place in the context to prevent the city-structure from having to change repeatedly, resulting in an overall increased energy-consumption.

© Torben Eskerod

0256

Think social

The success of a building like a community center lies entirely on its ability to attract and mix as many different people as possible, as often as possible. Make sure that the building serves as an invitation, especially to users that wouldn't normally consider the possibilities of the building. This goal is only achieved by thinking all-in, thinking and building social.

© Adam Mørk

0259

Densify

Non-built areas are a main consumer of CO_2 otherwise emitted to the atmosphere. By densifying the cities, as much as possible without losing the special qualities of the cite spaces, our total emission to the atmosphere is deducted.

0260

Early incorporation

An early mindset of a sustainable and holistic approach should be the precondition of any new building. The Platform house was done with the precondition of lowering energy-consumption and emission to 30% of the building code.

© Torben Eskerod

0258

Reuse

Reusing materials, especially if they are already on the site, will minimize overall energy-consumption, as well as adding a historic layer to a new architecture. The bricks of an existing but un-saveable school-house were reused in the completion of the new school-house.

© Torben Eskerod

© Torben Eskerod

© Jens Markus Lindhe

Ecospace® Ltd.

3 Iliffe Yard
SE17 3QA London, UK
Tel.: +44 020 7703 4004
www.ecospacestudios.com

0261 ➤
Find your natural space in life
Made from sustainable cedar wood with an optional plant covered roof, low-energy heating, lighting and insulation, Ecospace homes are right with the environment as well as your garden.

◄ 0262
A pitched roof is a different storey
A sloping roof with skylight creates a bright and airy interior. The extra space above becomes a mezzanine chill-out pad fora two-storey loft style living.

0263 ➤
Built to modern housing standards
This means it is made to last a lifetime using the latest in modern methods of construction. We use the highest specification of structurally insulated panel systems (SIPS) to achieve exceptional structural and insulation performance, as used on many new eco homes.

◄ 0264
An office, a studio, a gym, or an extension of your home
An Ecospace building is whatever you want it to be.

0265

It's cost-effective

An Ecospace studio costs less than a home extension or a loft conversion and has a fixed price, so there are no "unforeseen costs" from the builders.

0267

Ecospace is eco-friendly

Sustainable cedar wood, planted-covered roof, low-energy lighting and under-floor heating, plus high-performance insulation and double glazing.

0269

Tailored to you

Everyone's perfect Ecospace studio is different. As an architectural practice, we can design any space you want, with a shower room, mini kitchen or something totally unique. We have even grown Ecospace studios into homes, holiday retreats, commercial and educational buildings. Just give us a call.

0268

A decade and still evolving, naturally

We were the first to develop the contemporary modular garden studios, nearly 10 years ago. Contemporary architecture, sleek lines and natural beauty, all at home, at the bottom of your garden.

0266

Just five days to install

That's right, just five days. A lot less disruption than any extension or conversion. We'll usually get your Ecospace studio to you within 12 weeks of your order too.

0270

No planning permission

That's right. In many cases, your Ecospace studio can be erected without any hassle at all. And where planning permission is required, such as conservation areas, as an architectural practice we can carry it all out for you, as part of the package.

Ecosistema Urbano

Estanislao Figueras, 6
28008 Madrid, Spain
Tel.: +34 915 591 601
www.ecosistemaurbano.com

0271

Develop constructive criticism as an optimistic approach to existing reality

In order to bring up creative solutions the EcoBoulevard in Madrid periphery has been conceived as an operation of urban recycling to achieve the reconfiguration of the executed urban development. Three pavilions or artificial trees function like open structures to multiply resident-selected activities.

0272

Believe the concept of the city is completely linked to the creation of public space

From a row of projects to improve public spaces in central Madrid, selected points were chosen as catalysts to initiate a broader reconfiguration of the city's public spaces.

0273

Rely on low-cost to make big projects with less resources

Create a shadow space of 26,910 sq ft to held summer activities. The starting point is a low budget to cover the whole space with standard means. Citizen participation and the reuse of a standardized object are the tools selected to make it possible.

0274

Bring instant change through urban actions

We believe everything is architecture. Small actions provoke huge reactions and everything is connected. Through these actions in the public space we have built a park in five days that a mayor had been promising for the last 15 years. We created a new "fake municipal government" to denounce the real one, which was planning crazy new "Guggenheims" for a small city.

0275

Build networks to share knowledge and experiences

1. Our blog ecosistemaurbano.org is an internet platform to show worldwide experiences on creative urban sustainability.
2. EUABIERTO.com is an open network of professionals to share experiences and knowledge on creative urban sustainability.
3. ecosistemaurbano.tv is an interactive television channel for exchanging multimedia concepts related with urban sustainability.

0276

Integrate the citizens into the processes of changing their environment

The ecological reconfiguration of Philadelphia is a strategy, based on the localization of a series of low cost-interventions on the street network, for creating mechanisms that promote citizen participation: a launch pad for the auto-regeneration of the urban fabric.

0277

Create open systems in order to allow the development of a changing reality

In an area occupied by the Maribor municipal landfill in Slovenia, presently in a phase of ecological rehabilitation, we took this temporary circumstance as a leitmotif of the project, understanding that temporary processes should be highly related to architecture.

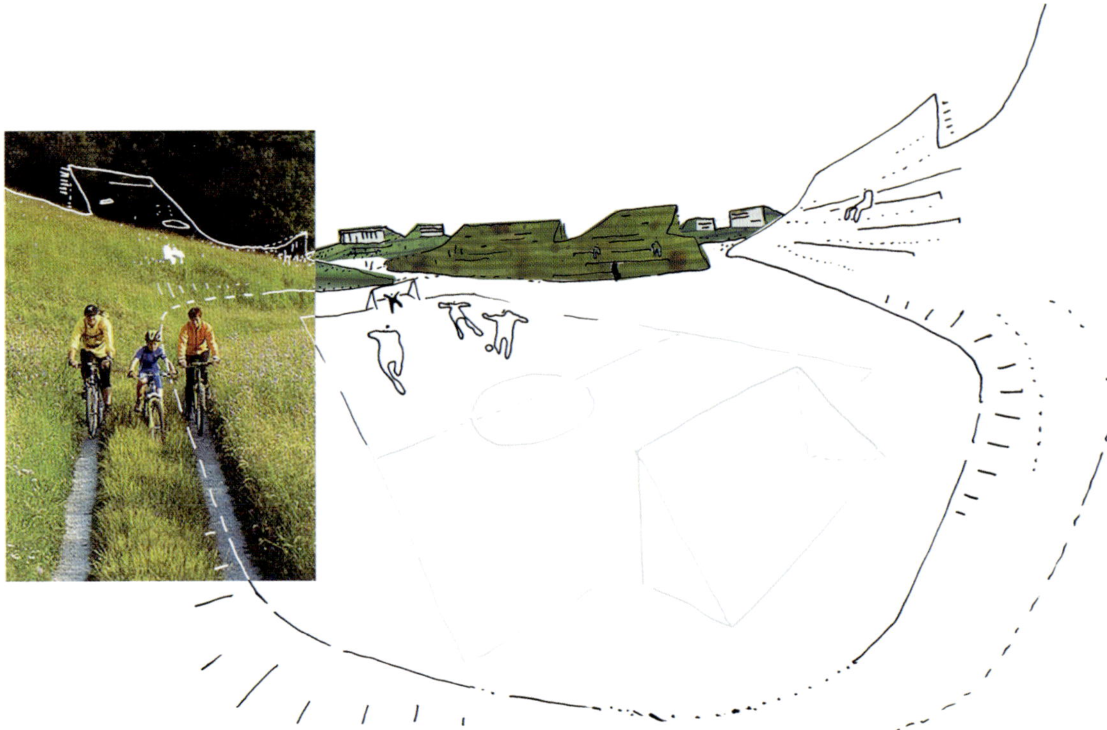

0278

Reactivate the existing as an alternative to uncontrolled expansion

How to improve the public space of a neighbourhood in Madrid's outskirts? Demolishing the limits that separate different urban facilities from each other and from public space, reconnecting this activity points to reconfigure the whole network, and considering the city as a playground.

0279

Take account of the intangible using new technologies as a mechanism to create complexity

Architecture as a management of energy resources (water, wind and sun) becomes the driving force for activity, forming the mutations of the landscape. A network of technological elements characterizes the image of the waterpark to demonstrate that nature can turn any urban waste into a new resource for the city.

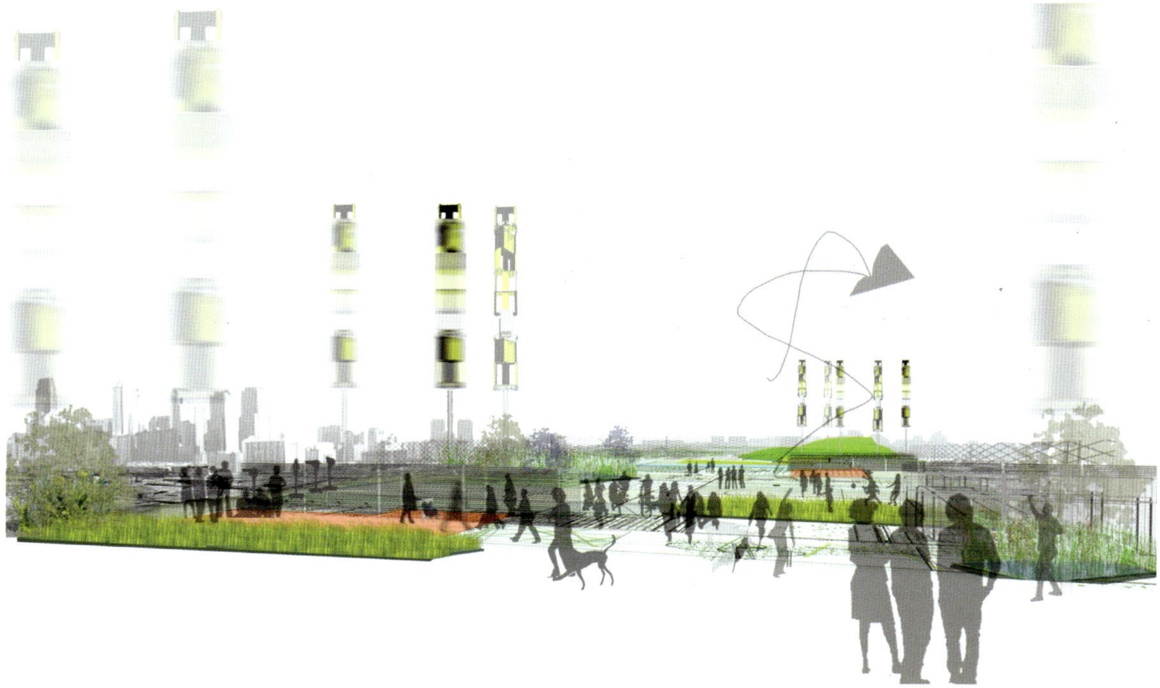

0280

Keep positive to be able to change reality

In contrast to traditional problem-solving methods for reactivating degraded public spaces in historical centers, we believe another form of intervention is possible where the citizen plays an active role in the creation of public space.

FLOAT architectural research and design (Erin Moore)

erin@floatwork.com
Tel.: +1 541 868 6074

0281
Consider the lifespan of each building material and plan for its replacement, removal or reuse.

0282
Consider the habitat that a building can offer around its exterior and make comfortable, ecologically unique places.

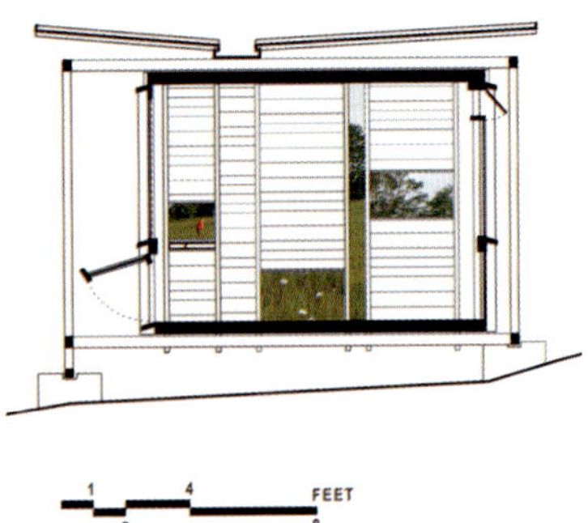

0283
Place window openings to reveal different aspects of the environmental context and use near, middle and far views to include multiple levels of detail in those views.

0284 ▲
Consider the physical experience of moving inside and outside and how each moment of that transition relates to a detailed sense of being in that place.

◄ **0285**
Find beautiful ways that the building can record the life around it.

0286 ►
Maximize direct solar gain during the cold season and eliminate it during the hotter months.

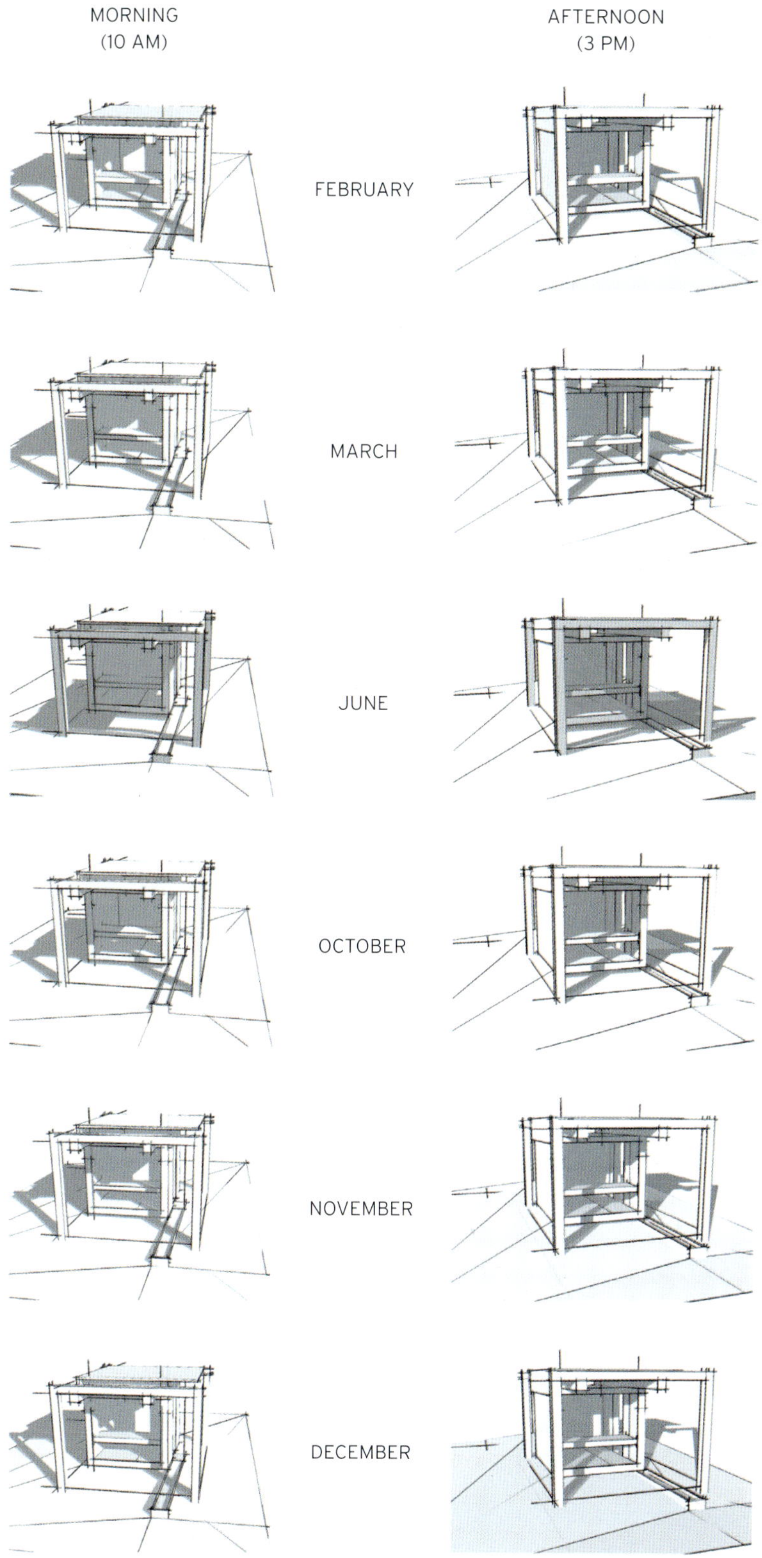

0287 ▲
Make the most of every drop of rain that falls on the site. Even a small basin will draw many animals.

0288 ➤
Start with the idea of putting people in a place rather than with the idea of putting a building there. Grow the building up around the people in a way that makes the most of the place.

0289
Let the structure be the building.

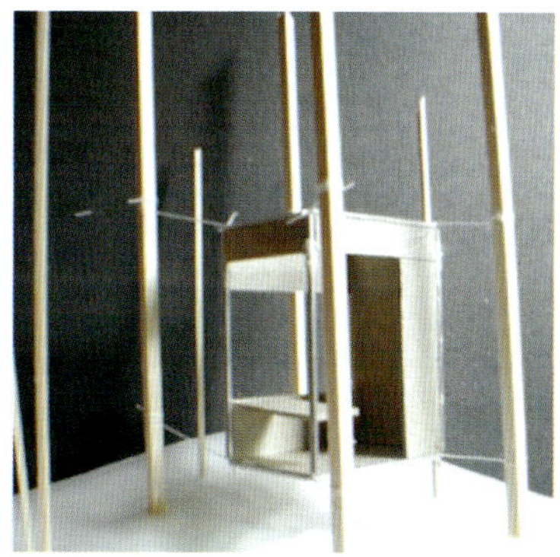

0290
Attend carefully to how the building meets the ground. This connection embodies the project's relationship with its ecological context.

Francisco Portugal e Gomes, Arquitecto

Rua de Vale Formoso, 602, 2º Esq.
4200 - 510 Porto, Portugal
Tel.: +351 228 303 803
arquitecto@franciscoportugal.com

0291
Cork inside and outside the building is provided for thermal protection and reduced energy consumption. In the exterior surface of the expansion areas of the house, the cork will be apparent with panels of high performance thermal insulation measuring 5 x 1.6 x 0.31 ft.

© Jorge Garcia Pereira

0292
The insulating characteristics of the cork allow keeping a constant temperature inside, avoiding the high costs of energy consumption resulting from the use of mechanical cooling systems. Unlike other insulating synthetic materials, cork is an environmentally friendly material that does not contribute to CO_2 production.

0293

The issue of external glazing in this work is one of the challenges the client made us before the project started. He wanted the interior space with a large area of glazing in order to observe the landscape and simultaneously guaranteeing privacy for the residents.

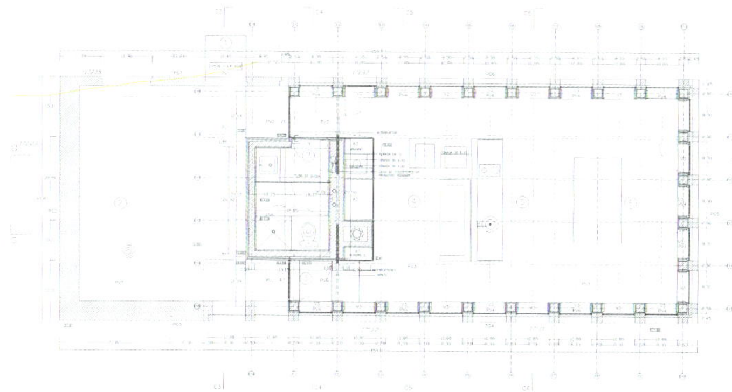

© Jorge Garcia Pereira

0294

Regarding solar impact, the opaque areas are formed by pillars that represent 25% of the areas of the façades, while the glass surfaces account for 75%. In the winter, direct solar gains are achieved through the glazing and the application of slate on the floor to retain the heat absorbed by thermal inertia.

© Jorge Garcia Pereira

© Jorge Garcia Pereira

© Jorge Garcia Pereira

0295

The solution that emerged at early stages of the project was targeting the gateways traversed by slate cards brise-soleil. This solution, combined with the composition of the façades and the use of local materials, allowed immediately think of a solution with the implementation of energy efficiency concepts, such as control the solar impact and heat loss, as well as a natural ventilation system.

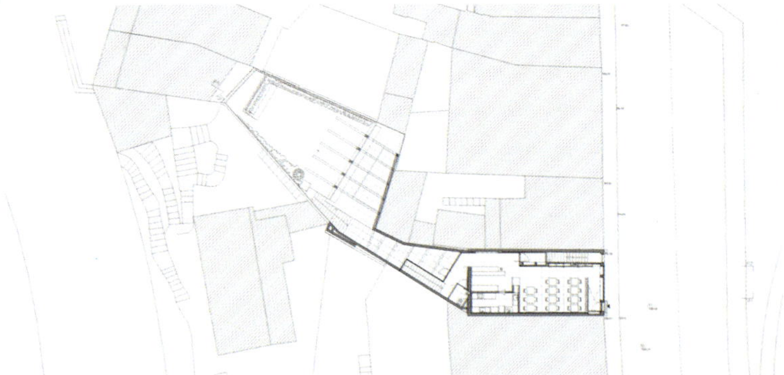

0296 ➤
The work consists in the full redevelopment of a small urban lot that has the peculiarity of having an exterior space not aligned with the building implanted side to the street.

0297 ▼
The situation makes the non-built space invade the back of the surrounding buildings.

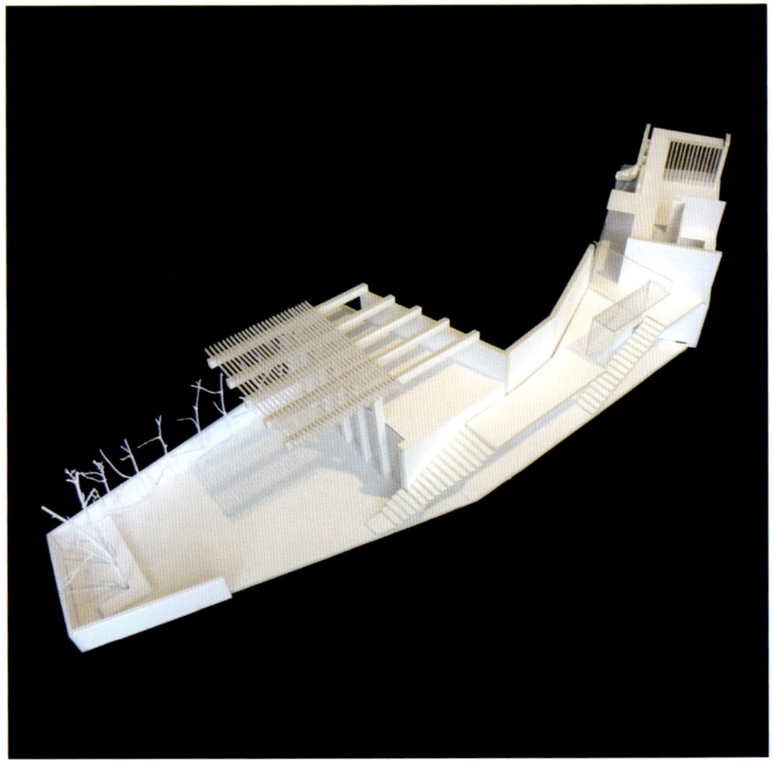

◄ 0298
The exterior space was converted in a bamboo garden that has a significant percentage of permeable urban land. This garden, an extension of the visual field of the tea house, plays a contemplative function and simultaneously generates a qualified green space inside the block.

0299 ➤

In Porto, the temperatures in July, August and September are frequently around 86 °F. The extension building has been designed with an architectural shading device that prevents the direct impact of sunlight on glass surfaces to reduce energy consumption with artificial cooling.

© Fernando Gabriel

© Fernando Gabriel

◄ 0300

Another contribution to the reduction of electricity consumption was designing the interior lighting with LED technology. Some lighting fixtures were specifically designed for this work.

François Perrin

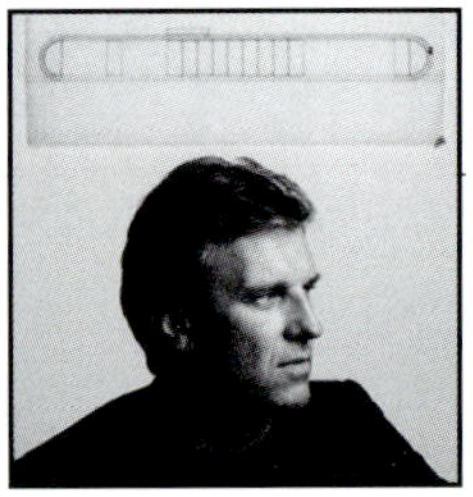

1511 Portia Street
Los Angeles, CA 90026, USA
Tel.: +1 213 590 7096
www.francoisperrin.com

0301 ➤
Build with the air
A layer of air is created in between the interior wood structure and the exterior plastic skin. It acts as a natural insulation and keeps the building at the same temperature all year long. It is free, non-toxic and creates zero carbon footprint. It is highly efficient as well (no air conditioning).

© Michael Wells

© Michael Wells

0302 ▲
Build with the sun
A sunroom is added to a California bungalow to create a transition space in between a cold and dark interior and a hot and sunny backyard. Made of a translucent skin on top of a wood structure with several windows, skylight and sliding doors, it brings natural light and the sea breeze into the house (no air conditioning).

© Michael Wells

0304 ▲
Build with local materials
Wood is one of the main construction materials in California. It is produced in the State and used for structures, underlayers, decks, floors and exteriors sidings. California cedar or redwood are perfectly fit for the local weather. No need to deforest another part of the world.

© Michael Wells

◄ 0303
Build with the earth
The site is carved to place half of the house underground in order to protect it from the heat during the day and from the cold at night. Each floor extends outside to catch the sea breeze. Like the first habitations of human beings, it acts as a grotto (no air conditioning).

0305

Build with new geometries

The volume that is designed for the house extension responds to the orientation of the site. The solar envelope is the geometrical shape that takes advantage of the sun's path for a natural energy gain through the use of passive solar heating.

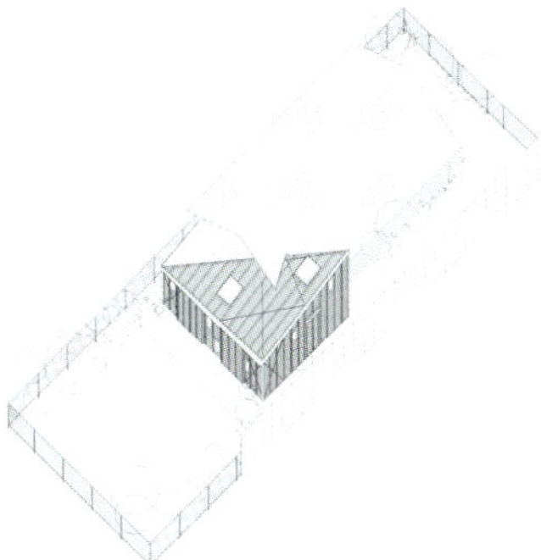

0307

Build with local technique

The wood frame is the typical construction system in the USA, and especially in California. It is the easiest, the cheapest, the fastest and the most flexible system. In this project, the structure is kept visible, only wrapped by a translucent plastic skin.

© Michael Wells

0306

Build with the wind

A light structure made of a silver aluminum mesh acts as a temporary structure to host the students of the Mountain School of Art during Art Basel Miami Beach. The shape of the structure, as well as the specifics of the material, allows the strong winds in that time of the year to go through it without impacting its stability while cooling down the temperature.

0308

Build with local people

Dante Cacace is a carpenter based in Venice Beach, California. He usually likes to work very locally, only a few blocks from the Ocean (West of Lincoln). His knowledge of the local building code, materials, techniques, as well as his deep commitment to the local environment, are the key to many successful projects.

© Michael Wells

0309

Build with new products

Some high-tech products built and tested for the agricultural industry, such as this highly reflective silver aluminum mesh to protect plants from extreme sunlight or these translucent polycarbonate panels to cover greenhouses, can be adapted to any project.

© Michael Wells

0310

Build efficiently

This is the only remaining waste of a 1,000 sq-ft house prototype built entirely out of wood. The design was created according to the panel and studs dimensions in the market to avoid any extra cuts and unnecessary waste.

© Michael Wells

Garrison Architects

45 Main Street, #1026
Brooklyn, NY 11226, USA
Tel.: +1 718 596 8300
www.garrisonarchitects.com

0311 ➤
Staten Island Animal Care Center, New York, NY
Prioritize passive approaches and supplement with active systems only when required. At the Staten Island Animal Care Center, translucent multiwall polycarbonate panels permit natural, diffuse daylight to permeate the space making electrical lights unnecessary during daylight hours.

0312
Syracuse University School of Architecture, Syracuse, NY
Seek opportunities to introduce passive ventilation. A central atrium with an operable skylight provides a place for buoyant warm air to move upwards and out, promoting fresh air ventilation without mechanical equipment.

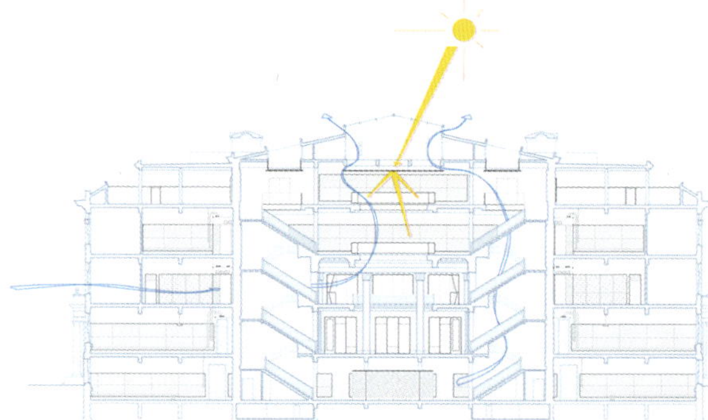

0313
Ambassador's residence, Apia, Samoa
Incorporate an understanding of climate into the earliest stages of design, and learn from the strategies of vernacular building types. Solar orientation, shading and wind breaks are effective, inexpensive strategies for reducing cooling and heating loads. Deep roof overhangs and louvered shades keep the tropical sun off the façades while promoting natural cross-ventilation.

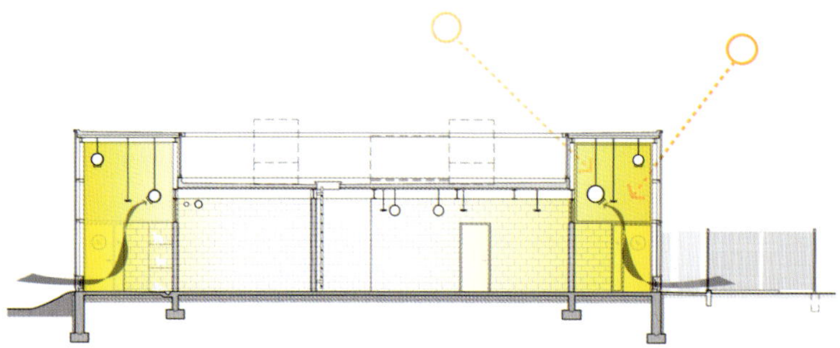

0314
Staten Island Animal Care Center, New York, NY
Recycle heat energy. Using a heat recovery wheel in the ventilation system exhausts indoor pollutants from the air without losing heat. In the cooling season, the system reverses, transferring excess heat in the ventilation air to the cooler exhaust air, reducing the need for mechanical cooling.

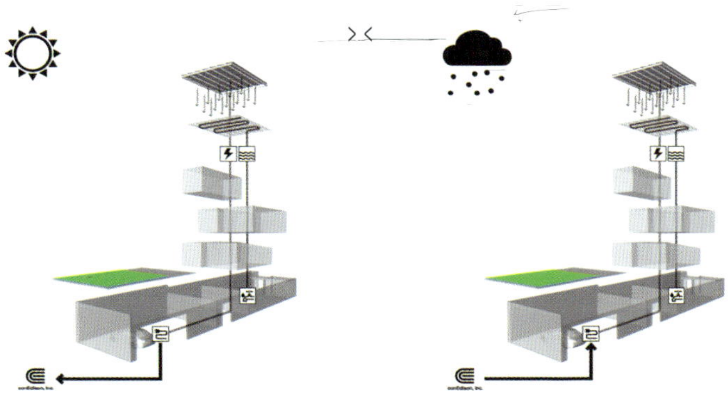

0319

Red Hook Green, Brooklyn, NY

Realize net-zero energy by connecting rooftop photovoltaic arrays to the municipal power supply grid. Red Hook Green sells back excess solar energy from sunny days to the grid, maintaining reliable backup power for rainy days. At the end of the year the overall energy production meets or exceeds the building's consumption.

0315

Koby Cottage, Albion, MI

Consider the factory. Buildings constructed offsite can recognize huge efficiencies by consolidating time and resources. Modular designs are driven by the efficient use of space and materials, resulting in buildings that can be incredibly functional without sprawling. Spending less on construction allows flexibility in the budget to provide for high performance fixtures, low-energy systems and environmentally-sound finishes.

0320

Lehman College Child Care Center, Bronx, NY

Integrate plantings into vertical surfaces. Plants can be grown in layered façades with shading devices or rainscreen cladding. For low maintenance installations, thermostatic control of operable façades and hydroponic watering systems maintain optimal conditions for plant health.

0318

Red Hook Green, Brooklyn, NY

Think beyond the photovoltaic panel. Highly efficient technologies to harness the sun's thermal energy have been developed for applications ranging from heating to electricity production, cooking and distilling drinking water. The Red Hook Green project uses high efficiency solar collectors to provide its domestic hot water.

0316

Border Patrol Station, Murietta, CA

Take advantage of natural daylight to reduce electrical lighting costs. Use light shelves to bounce daylight off of building surfaces, preventing glare and creating even, diffuse ambient lighting. Similar techniques, such as cove lighting, can also be implemented to increase the effectiveness of artificial lights.

0317

Border Patrol Station, Murietta, CA

Hybridize. Use natural ventilation in circulation and common spaces while providing active cooling dedicated to enclosed spaces. The spill air from the enclosed spaces can be used to temper areas that accept higher temperatures.

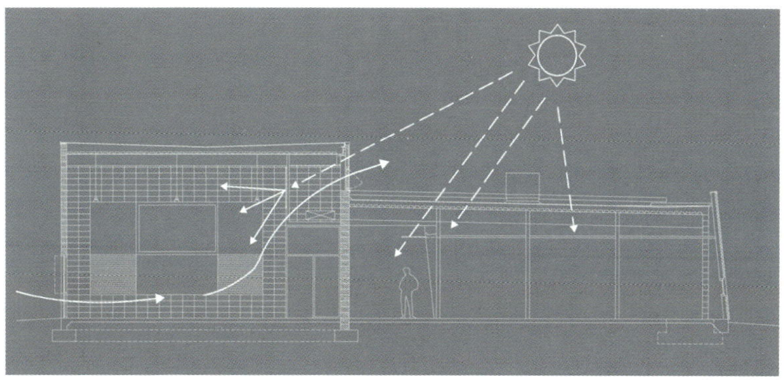

Green Dwellings/Leger Wanaselja Architecture

2320 McGee Avenue
Berkeley, CA 94703, USA
Tel.: +1 510 848 8901
www.greendwellings.com

0321 ➤
Old aluminum highway signs, attached outside in, make a durable siding on this bay window. Reusing materials before they are recycled can save significant energy and reduce environmental impacts of processing. For this project, old highway signs were also bent for light shades and stair railings.

© Leger Wanaselja Architecture

© Leger Wanaselja Architecture

© Scott McGlashan

◄ 0322
Junked streets signs are incorporated into this pedestrian fence and gate. A Volkswagen headlight lights the entry at night.

0323 ▼
Using locally sourced junk and recycled materials can significantly cut back on environmental impacts. This green renovation and new construction project that features small, energy and resource efficient units also relies on extensive salvage and reuse, including 3.5 tons of discarded street signs.

© Cesar Rubio

0324 ➤
The upper level of this house is clad in over 100 grey car roofs. The roofs were carefully selected for color and sawn out in the junk yard. This new, two-bedroom, 1,140 sq ft, virtually passive solar house is an infill in one of Berkeley's oldest neighborhoods.

© Leger Wanaselja Architecture

0325

Tempered car windows are versatile as building components because of their size, three- dimensional shape and mounting hardware. Here, Mazda hatchback glass is repurposed for as a railing. Tip one shows a Porsche rear window used as an awning.

© Leger Wanaselja Architecture

© Leger Wanaselja Architecture

© Leger Wanaselja Architecture

0326

Wood and wood products remain among the most environmentally friendly and versatile materials we use in construction. The lower walls are clad in poplar bark, a waste product from the furniture industry of North Carolina. FSC-certified wood was also used for framing. And, the walls and ceilings are insulated with shredded old phonebooks, newspapers and cardboard.

0328

Built to exacting specifications (to withstand tremendous loads) and with refrigerated units (to maintain low internal temperatures efficiently), shipping containers make excellent building blocks for architecture. Even after many trips around the globe, they still easily meet or exceed the building codes for construction. As a net importer, the US ports are filled with them. Here, three insulated containers are used to create this airy yet compact 1,330 sq ft, three-bedroom house.

© Leger Wanaselja Architecture

© Leger Wanaselja Architecture

0329

The awnings are fabricated from junked Dodge Caravan side windows. Once advertised as "America's best selling minivan," now a common item in junk yards.

© Linda Svendsen

0327

Other car parts also perform well in construction. Here hatchbacks were used to make a railing. In tip one, eight Volvo rear doors are fashioned into a fence and remotely operated electric parking lot gate.

© Ethan Kaplan

0330

Two 200-year-old oak trees fell on the property during the design phase. Not letting their demise go to waste, the trees were incorporated extensively into the design of this remodeled house. In fact, almost all of the finish wood in the project, including fencing, siding, cabinetry, and flooring is salvaged, totaling over 6,000 board feet of wood.

GROUP A Architects

Pelgrimsstraat, 3
3029 BH Rotterdam, The Netherlands
Tel.: +31 (0)10 244 01 93
www.groupa.nl
www.groupalive.com

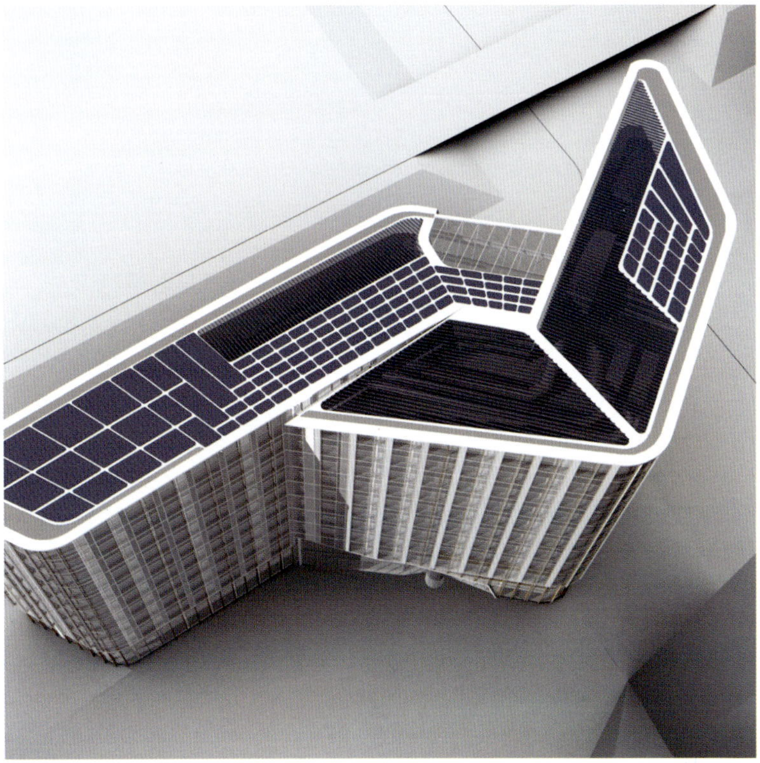

0331

Do think ahead

Essential to the early stages of planning and designing a green build is to think ahead to environmental impact, orientation, existing surrounding qualities, technical practicalities, social and cultural cohesion, selected materials and finishes, the design and construction process, the long term sustainable value, maintenance, education of end-users, and future change in expectations and demands.

0332

Do the Rs

The classic Rs can't of course be missed in any Top-10: reduce, reuse, recycle. When reducing, savings are both economic and sustainable. Explore reduction before deploying reuse and recycling. Reuse (adaptive reuse) can happen on a big scale and often results in significant savings and environmental benefits, but it takes planning. All selected building materials, components and parts should be recyclable.

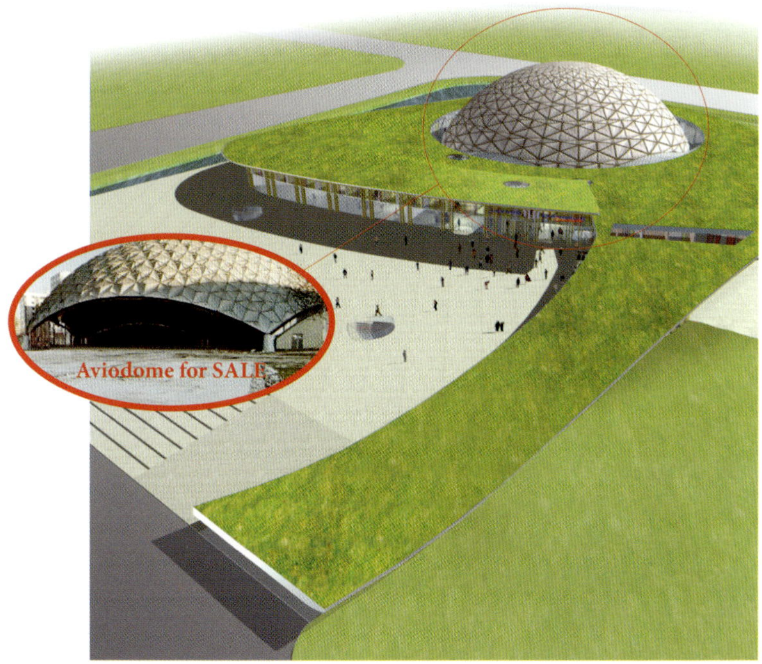

◄ 0333

Go "new world of work"

Consider in the early stages of design also the actual space end users believe they require. Discuss for example office's real occupancy rates, the potential of multi-functional spaces, the value of team tables, and open plan activities. Develop together with users a more compact office environment with less fixed workspaces, anticipating realistic occupancy rates. Prepare for "new world of work."

0334 ►

Go compact

If finally decided proceeding with building activities, and all stages of reflection and appropriate sustainable considerations have been completed, it is certainly an additional "green" asset to build as compact as possible. Smart urban growth, clever higher densities, expanding vertically rather than horizontally, minimising circulation distances, atrium embracing floors, and "new world of work" concepts, all contribute to this ambition.

0335 ➤

Do reconsider

Even before considering any physical preparation and building activities on site, parties involved in the planning should make sure that actual building is really well-considered at all. It should be absolutely clear to everyone that the envisaged build has social, cultural, environmental, and economical relevance, for now and in the future. Reconsidering should always be part of any planning process.

◄ 0336

Be inspired

Acting "eco" can only be considered succesful when the final product fits the user, fullfills their expectations, and creates an atmosphere that motivates and inspires them. Reference to this objective in GROUP A designs is their own studio. Although the 1930 monument still shows shortcomings, the building has contributed highly to the creative process and solid social cohesion amongst staff.

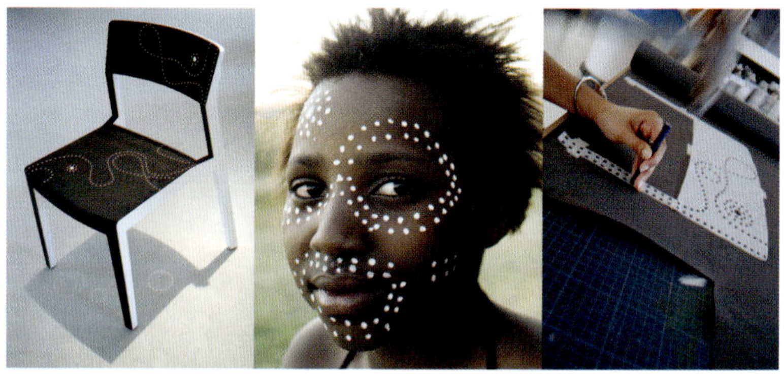

0337 ▲

Do love

Unconditional love for our profession (designer, creative architect, educator, communicator, value adder, social and cultural worker, urban planner, motivator, initiator, or team member) is the ultimate motivation in the way we live up to our principles. Only with this mentality and passion we can start inspiring other people and processes to be eco-ware, and ready to implement 1,000 eco-tips.

0338

Be natural

Vital to any build environment is the resulting impact it has on people's physical and mental well-being. The natural quality and performance of building materials, internal climate, daylight, and interaction with the outside are key to prove a healthy, sustainable environment. Choices should, therefore, be inspired by the ultimate balance and principles, as they apply in nature.

0339

Be receptive

Planning, designing and building is teamwork, its success often depending on the willingness of parties being receptive to each other's opinions. Open up and get inspired by cooperating disciplines. Start listening more with your heart and your intuition, instead of your mind. Get rid off the habit of "being heard" to be able to really contribute to innovation and sustainability.

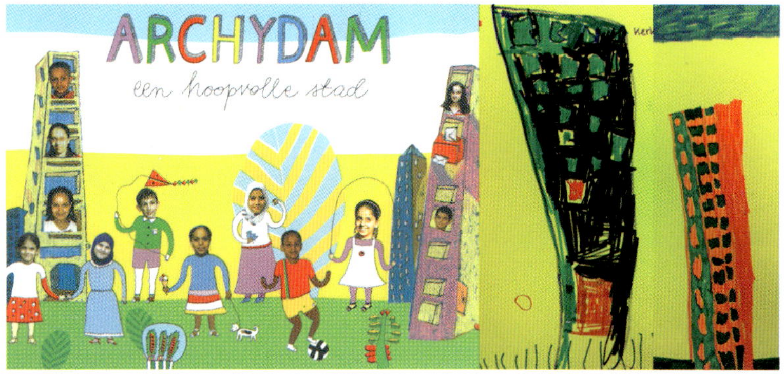

0340

Go underground

By deploying relatively "low tech" means, building performance can improve substantially. Exposed internal concrete structures, for example, allow its mass to inhibit temperature fluctuations. The natural steady temperature reduces energy consumption and requires smaller plant facilities. But wouldn't it be even more effective minimizing the external impact of extremes in temperature, all together by going underground, and introducing "green" roofs?

Gudmundur Jonsson Arkitektkontor

Hegdehaugsveien 24
0352 Oslo, Norway
Tel.: +47 23 20 23 50
www.gudmundurjonsson.no

0341

The layout of the plan is related precisely according to the most important views at the sight, giving glazed fronts towards the view and closing the rest of the building as much as possible otherwise to emphasize the idea.

0343

Thus the choice of materials becomes important in order to match the landscape and acting as energy consuming as well as materials with sustainability.

0342

The materials being concrete (with pattern from nature), Zebra wood (very strong and durable) Icelandic Blágrýti (bluestone).

0344

Make the use of glazed openings a priority in order to emphasize the most important view where it is really needed and closing the rest of the building in order to make expectations for the view to be experienced.

0345 ➤
Use of the roofs in order
to recreate the landscape and
to isolate the buildings below.

0349 ▲
The materials are virtually
free of maintenance.

0346 ➤
The slate is a material obtained from
the production of larger stones.

0348 ➤
Using natural materials, such as slate
and durable slow-growing wood (e.g.
Siberian wood), gives anlow energy-
consuming and age-resistant building.

0347 ➤
Materials are to be related to the
climate of the site in order to be
climate-resistant and simultaneously
needing minimum of maintenance.

◄ 0350
Make architecture by interpretating
the culture of the place and
using the elements consciously
in order to enhance energy-
consuming building parts.

Guz Architects

3, Jalan Kelabu Asap
278199 Singapore, Singapore
Tel.: +65 6476 6110
www.guzarchitects.com

0351 ➤
Keep built form to a minimum to maximize space for nature and greenery.

0352
The smaller and the more efficient the house, the lower the carbon footprint.

© Timothy Shankar

0353
Lay out the building to make the most of the surrounding environment. Don't destroy it, but keep the "magic" as much as possible.

© Timothy Shankar

© Timothy Shankar

© Timothy Shankar

0354
Design for massive cooling/heating as much as possible.

0357 ➤
Use locally available materials where possible. Cut down on materials from far away.

0358 ▼
Use sustainably formed timber if possible, since as a carbon store in itself, it has a much smaller footprint.

0355 ▲
Recycle water and use sunshine for photovoltaics panels where possible.

0356 ▼
Green roofs create more greenery, which is easy on the eye and in the tropics keeps a house cool.

◄ 0359
Keep to a human scale - overly large buildings don't look good and don't relate nature.

0360 ▼
Bring light to basement.

Harquitectes

Montserrat, 22, 2n 2a
08201 Sabadell, Spain
Tel.: +34 93 725 00 48
www.harquitectes.com

0361 ➤
Our design approach is based on common sense, closer to a radical normality than "strident exhibitionism."

0362 ▼
We are interested in popular architecture. Anonymous. And, most of all, the circumstances that technically condition its construction and make it a formal and technical reference.

0363
We believe in sustainability, not as a new paradigm or as a single or sufficient objective, just as a more professional circumstance.

0364
We want to become experts in all materials - those available, making best use of them and understanding their characteristics, focusing on the constructive logic peculiar to them, or finding new ones. Getting the most out of them in terms of both material and space.

0365
Architecture requires a total turnaround. It needs to be redefined. We must listen to the social demand (real) and try to anticipate needs. As architects, we should try to lead this social redirection, especially regarding the territories that are more typical in our profession and that, in theory, we master better than anyone.

0366 ►

We have an obsession with a concept we call "space-structure," and we are always committed to make the most of the materials we use. Casa 205 perfectly exemplifies both concepts (space and material).

0367 ▲

We review vernacular architecture and we name it "available architecture": available materials, available techniques, available typologies. If we understand vernacular in this way, nothing prevents us from imagining the existence of a modern vernacular construction. The availability today is not based on geographic terms, but economic terms. Construction should be catalog, prefabricated, lightweight, systematic: using market systems that are assembled rather than built. Screwing instead of sticking.

0368

We opt for those strategies that achieve the highest architectural and environmental quality as well as simplifying, reducing or reinvesting costs in order to give you greater living comfort and greater management of the building.

0369

Using incorporated low-energy biospheric materials, designing passive strategies to reduce demand and enforcing both reversible and reusable building systems seem consistent with both available and sustainable construction.

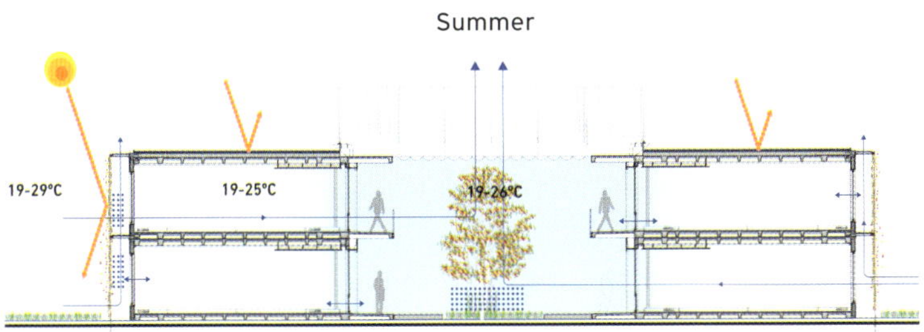

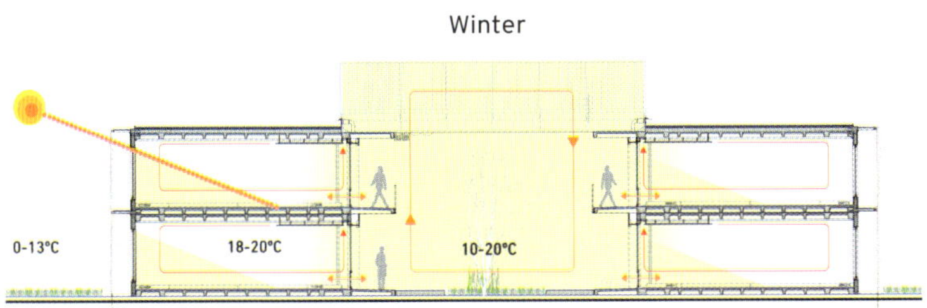

0370

We take sustainable architecture seriously, starting from the understanding of the life cycle of the building: materials, construction, and energy demand.

H2o Architects

29 Northumberland Street
Collingwood, VIC 3066, Australia
Tel.: +61 3 9417 0900
www.h2oarchitects.com.au

0371 ➤
Brise soleil
The 10-ft-wide balconies to the north elevation of the same building double as a sunscreen device whilst providing access to internalacademic spaces as a substitute for an internal corridor. The use of open "pores" in the precast façade provides borrowed light to internal rooms (Swinburne University of Technology, Advanced Technologies Building, Hawthorn, Victoria).

0372 ▼
Recycled materials
Face bricks from a former building demolished by the University prior to construction were stored off site and reused extensively to balcony faces of internal areas to maintain thermal performance and provide a weather proof, "urban" low-maintenance finish (Swinburne University of Technology, Advanced Technologies Building, Hawthorn, Victoria).

◄ 0373
Thermal mass
Universal application of precast concrete panelized façades adapts flexibly to a variety of user conditions. Combined with minimum acceptable glazing to satisfy briefed requirements and limited glazing to the East and West, this ensures high thermal mass (Swinburne University of Technology, Advanced Technologies Building, Hawthorn, Victoria).

0374 ▲
Off site construction
Off site factory manufacturing under controlled factory conditions were utilized for all envelope components, including structural framing, walling, roof trusses and roofing, seating platforms and seats (North stand, Lakeside Stadium, Albert Park, Victoria).

0375

Adaptable reuse

An existing 19th-century rope factory in inner Melbourne was simply converted to a state-of-the-art 24x7 IT "barn" by utilizing inserted acoustically and environmentally contained pods with a grid 'ceiling' acting as a carrier for introduced services (RMIT University, Building 512 Computer Barn, Brunswick, Victoria).

0376

Screening device with multiple uses

Folded and undulating timber screen in Celery Top pine (unique to Tasmania) acts as a trellis for a heritage grape vine and provides sun protection, visual privacy from an adjacent public footpath and, by extending 4 ft above an upper roof terrace, also acts as a handrail (Hobart Tennis Club, Hobart, Tasmania).

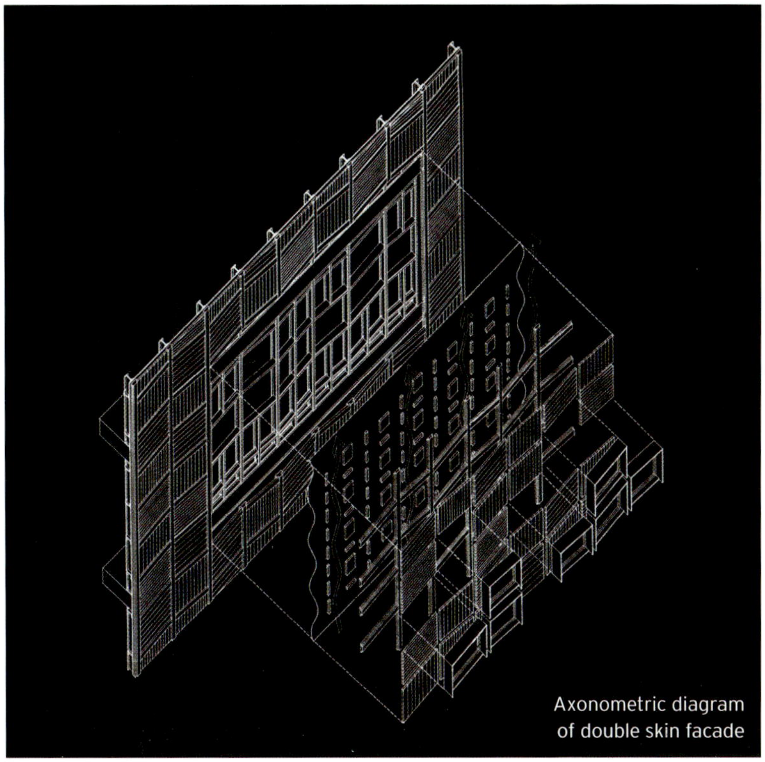

Axonometric diagram of double skin facade

0377

Rain screen

Textured Western Red Cedar panelized façade recalls textile analogies and acts as a rain screen in front of Tyvek sealed building envelope behind. A 3-in air gap separates the two skins and aids the partial cooling of the north façade through induced thermal chimney effect (RMIT University, Building 513, Brunswick, Victoria).

0378 ➤

Glare and sun minimization

Use of classical roof profile and "saw tooth" south light as sun control device to a library briefed to have minimum glazing (Avondale Heights Library & Learning Centre, Moonee Ponds, Victoria).

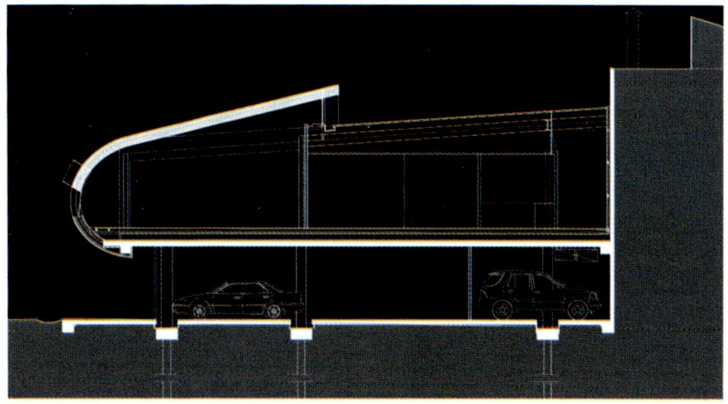

0379

Cross ventilation

Establishment of sectional profile to linear, extrapolated plan form to maximize cross ventilation. Use of mechanically operated – via BAS system, low level labyrinth style vents (to maximize clean air intake) to south side and high level louvre vents to north side (State Emergency Services Headquarters, Southbank, Victoria).

0380

Thermal chimney

Internal multi-level antrums along the main spine of a large educational center act as thermal chimneys to extract hot air at nights via mechanically-operated high level glass louvres controlled by a BAS system (Deakin University, International Centre & Business Building, Burwood Campus, Victoria).

Heliotrope Architects

5140 Ballard Ave NW, B
Seattle, WA 98107, USA
Tel.: +1 206 297-0442
www.heliotropearchitects.com

0381

Energy: envelope

A high-performance thermal envelope is the critical first step in the development of a low-carbon building. The Passive House performance standard is perhaps the most rigorous in use today. In our first Passive House compliant project, we are utilizing a super-insulated, nearly air-tight envelope with high-performance glazing in order to drastically reduce energy requirements for heating.

0382

Energy: inputs

Leveraging free energy provided by nature is another critical component in a low-carbon building. Thoughtfully placed glazing can drastically reduce necessary supplemental heat, and thoughtfully designed openings can eliminate the need for air-conditioning in mild climates. In our Passive House project, solar heat gain is provided through an expansive skylight with unobstructed southern exposure.

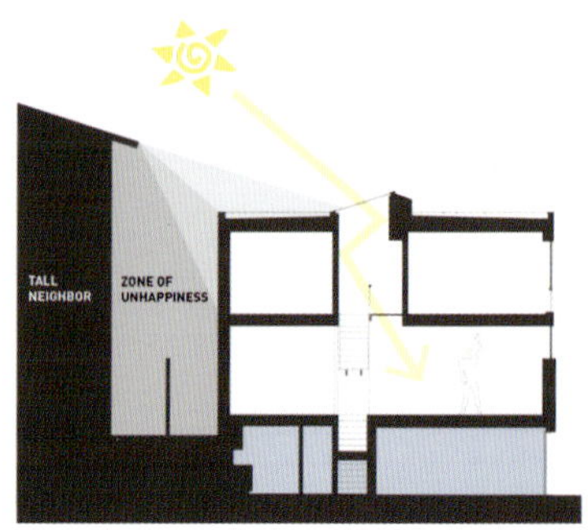

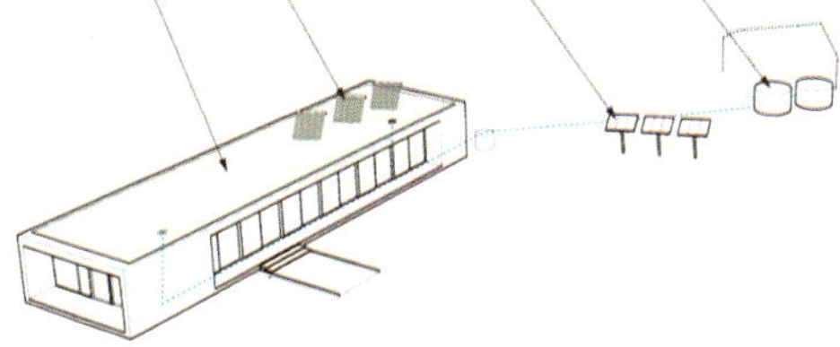

0383

Energy : systems

Use of appropriate technology is an important tool in reducing carbon-footprint. In our North Beach project, a solar hot water system provides inputs to both potable hot water and radiant space heating systems, a rain-water catchment system cuts down on potable water use and a PV system provides supplemental electricity. These systems have varying pay-back dependent upon climate and local incentives.

0384 ▲

Ecology: water

Much of our work is on or near the shoreline of the Salish Sea, which is imperiled by the cumulative effects of thoughtless development. It is important to understand and respect natural surface and sub-surface water flows in order to prevent further damage to our environment. Our Suncrest residence utilizes garden roofs, dispersion trenches and pond replenishment to filter all rainwater captured by building roofs.

0385 ▲

Ecology: resource use

Over a 50-year period, carbon utilization in building renovation and repair roughly equals that of initial construction. Proper control of moisture, use of durable materials and thoughtful detailing are important components to reducing this statistic. Equally important is creating esthetically timeless works.

0386 ➤

Ecology: flora and fauna

In the Salish Sea our endangered orca feed exclusively on salmon, which feed upon forage fish, which feed upon insects, which in turn depend upon a healthy near-shore habitat. The interconnections are vast, and it is critical to understand them in order to minimize harmful impacts.

◄ 0387

Experience: light

In our region we experience over 200 days of cloudy weather per year. Daylighting in this climate is a critical component to mental health and wellbeing of both individuals and community. We desire a luminous quality in our work and utilize carefully placed fenestration to bathe wall surfaces in light - and always from more than one side of a room.

0388 ▼

Experience: place

Imagine someone blindfolded and brought to a project from far away. When looking around, do they have a sense of being in a unique region and place? How is that uniqueness conveyed? Beyond views and landscape, the interrelationship of building and landscape, as well as materiality, color, quality of light, etc., all work together in creating a unique sense of place.

0389 ►

Experience: connection to environment

Establishing a strong connection between building inhabitants and the surrounding environment is central to our work. We seek to celebrate the best features of the site while also highlighting the overlooked smaller moments - a tree stump or an interesting rock can become a focal point of a more intimate space. Identify opportunities to provide connections and exploit them to the extent possible.

0390 ►

Experience: environmental health

Fresh dust and bug-free air, generous daylight, clean water - these are critical elements to a healthy environment. The search for healthier and more sustainable systems, materials and coatings is a never-ending process. We have spent years accumulating a lengthy list of manufacturers and suppliers to draw from, and the search is a part of our regular daily routine.

Hiroshi Nakamura & NAP Architects

2-15-7-1F Sakurashinmachi Setagaya-ku
154-0015 Tokyo, Japan
Tel: +81 (0)3 5426 0105
www.nakam.info

0391
"Building form snuggles up against trees."

0392
Wood columns and beams were used, since they can be easily worked to match the complicated shapes of the walls and the ceiling, and structural plywood was applied to create a monocoque structure. FG board (strengthened with inorganic fibers) was used on the inside to follow the many curves, and it was finished with an elastic coating material.

0393
Specially ordered asphalt shingles that likewise follow the curves and still have a good appearance when there are leaves on them were applied to the outside. The trees were planted according to the plan formulated when the building was designed after all other work was completed.

0394
"Bringing nature, buildings and people closer together." There is a small private art museum in the city of Oyama, in Tochigi prefecture. The owner wanted to build a room to showcase paintings that were collected by his late father, Roku Tsukada, and a cafe that had the ambiance of a salon where people could drop in anytime .

0395
For protective layer and finish of the roof slab, we used soil of the site, and to prevent an outflow of it, we planted the wild grass seeds.

0396
This grass-soil roof has an effect on insulation and reduces the cost of the exterior sheeting. And using the soil of the site reduced the cost of transportation. The exterior walls also need to be coated by something to prevent from the salt damage. We mixed the soil, cement, and resin and spread them thick on the roof 2-in maximum.

0397
The roofline and colors were decided by the plants the soil brings up. After the completion of the construction, they will continue to be changed by the seeds which birds or winds carry, the pruning by the resident, weathering, and seasons.

0398
At first, I devised a large room getting the view and the wind from the sea to the mountains and insulating the eyes from the next-door houses on both sides.

0399
Working with the soil in a garden is an action of the owner conversing with the soil permanently depending on seasonal changes. So, at the gardening-architecture, the owner and nature have decisive power.

0400
Clients also joined to work. They scratched off the soil freely with various tools, such as a metal skewer, a metal broom, and a spatula.

HOK

211 N. Broadway, Suite 700
St. Louis, MO 63102, USA
Tel.: +1 314 754 4215
www.hok.com

0401 ▼

Use what's free

A fundamental sustainable strategy is to use resources that are available and in abundance. Just as nature doesn't import energy and materials from distances, we need to embrace our conditions and seek innovative solutions to use it. The Project Haiti replacement orphanage plan is strategically designed to maximize natural ventilation by harnessing eastern trade winds.

◄ 0402

Look to nature for solutions

Nature's survival strategies can be directly adapted to design at all scales. Using biomimicry, we need to identify a design's functional challenges and then look to nature for solutions. With Project Haiti, the variegated bamboo screens surrounding the walls function like bark on a tree, protecting the building by reducing heat, providing shade and maximizing airflow.

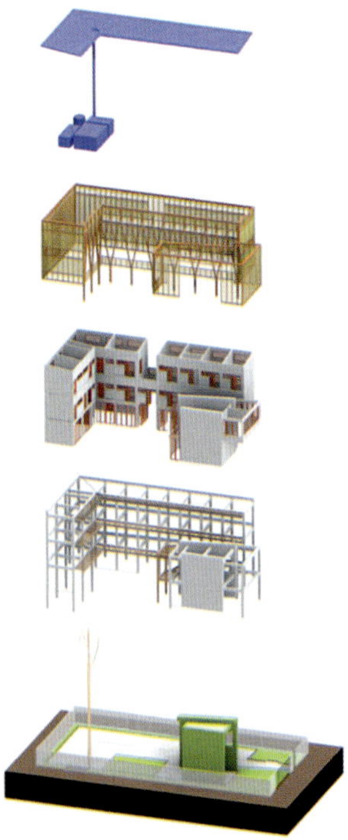

0403 ►

Build resilience through diversity

"Diverse structures form in response to abiotic disturbances, resulting in an overall structure that creates a more resilient system." To ensure continuity in all conditions, the design of the Project Haiti replacement orphanage incorporates multiple sources for energy generation, including wind generation, natural ventilation, photovoltaics and a biofuel generator for load balancing.

◄ 0404

Architecture without architects

"Vernacular architecture does not go through fashion cycles. It is nearly immutable, indeed, unimprovable, since it serves its purpose to perfection." Bernard Rudofsky got it right; there's so much to learn from understanding vernacular solutions – and nature's principles – in seeking high-performance, inspirational, lasting design solutions.

◄ 0405

Passive solutions first

Use every means at your disposal to drive down energy and water loads before integrating systems solutions. This starts with early design analysis to optimize orientation, massing, openings, building envelope and renewable energy generation.

0406 ▲

Failure is multiplicative

Performance-driven design requires all strategies to work together in harmony. If the natural lighting strategy doesn't work, the lights will stay on longer, the increased heat gain will cause the MEP systems to not perform as designed and the total loads will increase.

0407 ▲

Daylight rules

Optimization of natural light is a major design driver. This single goal brings a number of benefits, including reduced electricity usage, decreased greenhouse gas emissions, reduced heat gain from lighting, and improved indoor environment for occupants. For Process Zero, a zero-footprint retrofit of an existing office building, the design team "carved" the city-block-long building to bring natural light.

0408 ▼

There is no "silver bullet" solution

There is no simple solution in sustainability. Ideas must be integrated into all aspects of the design. Every opportunity to elegantly optimize performance and environmental, social and economic benefits should be employed.

0409 ▲

Embrace your limits

Don't see limits as roadblocks to get around, but rather as ways to force an entirely new approach to developing creative solutions. After all, "Necessity is the mother of invention" - it's how we leapfrog to entirely new solutions. Process Zero's breakthrough design idea uses energy-producing microalgae to help power the building by capturing carbon monoxide emissions from the nearby Santa Ana Highway.

0410 ►

Be of place

A sustainable project should tell us about its place. Like in nature, it should be locally attuned and responsive. The building orientation and massing, fundamental energy and water strategies, types of materials and design aesthetic should all tell a story about the specific climate, habitat, culture and people of a place.

House + House Architects

1499 Washington Street
San Francisco, CA 94109, USA
Tel.: +1 415 474 2112
www.houseandhouse.com

0411

Small footprint

Careful analysis of rooms and their relationships to each other can create efficient circulation without the need for hallways. By rethinking spaces that are often separate (family and living, for example), it is possible to design beautiful combined environments that don't waste materials or systems.

0412

Accessibility

Making accessibility an integral part of design, rather than a special added component that must be legislated and prescribed, is a more holistic approach to creating space. This 165-ft long ramp provides universal access and is experienced as a sculptural, three-dimensional movement through the garden, with the views unfolding as a surprise.

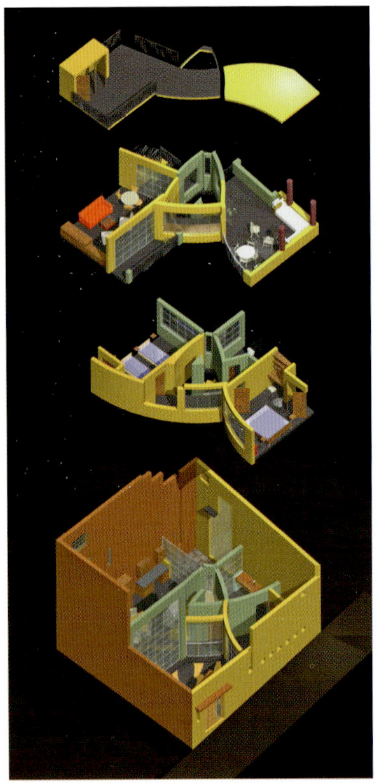

0413

Solar shading

Trellis shading offers the opportunity to create beautiful moving shadow patterns that surprise and delight the eye while offering relief from unwanted sun intrusion. A careful analysis of sun angles can provide the criteria required to allow the sun in during winter while blocking it in summer.

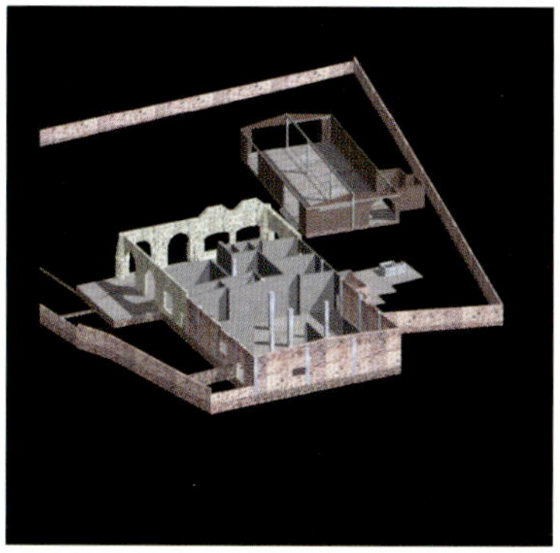

0414

Adaptive reuse

Adaptive reuse is a good way to keep from depositing into landfills the massive debris created when a building is torn down. This abandoned factory was transformed into a gracious home and art studio. Debris from demolished walls was used in the foundations.

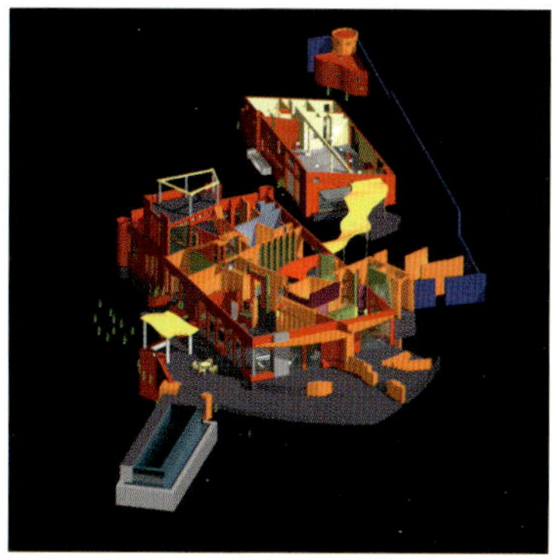

0415

Recycling

Using recycled materials can add warmth, texture and a bit of history to new, modern buildings. An old barn was transformed into beautiful wood flooring in this home in northern California.

0416

Furniture

Use old materials in unexpected new ways. In this example, an old, deteriorated carpenter's work table is reframed and converted to a new dining room table that is a conversational centerpiece and invites the users to touch the markings of work done generations before.

0417 ➤

Courtyard

The central courtyard is a vernacular concept that developed in almost every country, allowing light and fresh air into each room and inviting the inhabitants to partake of protected outdoor space. It offers the opportunity for large windows without the need for privacy screening and frames views from one part of the house to another.

◄ 0418

Natural light

Make the sun work for you. Creative positioning of skylights and windows can provide natural day-lighting to give a soft glow, make a deliberate streak or add a dappled texture. Capture its heat in the winter months in a concrete floor to re-radiate its warmth on chilly evenings.

0419

Sun control

Know where the sun is and how to really access it to your advantage. This home in California closes down at its outer perimeter to deflect the summer heat, but opens huge window walls to a small central courtyard where the sun has carefully controlled entry.

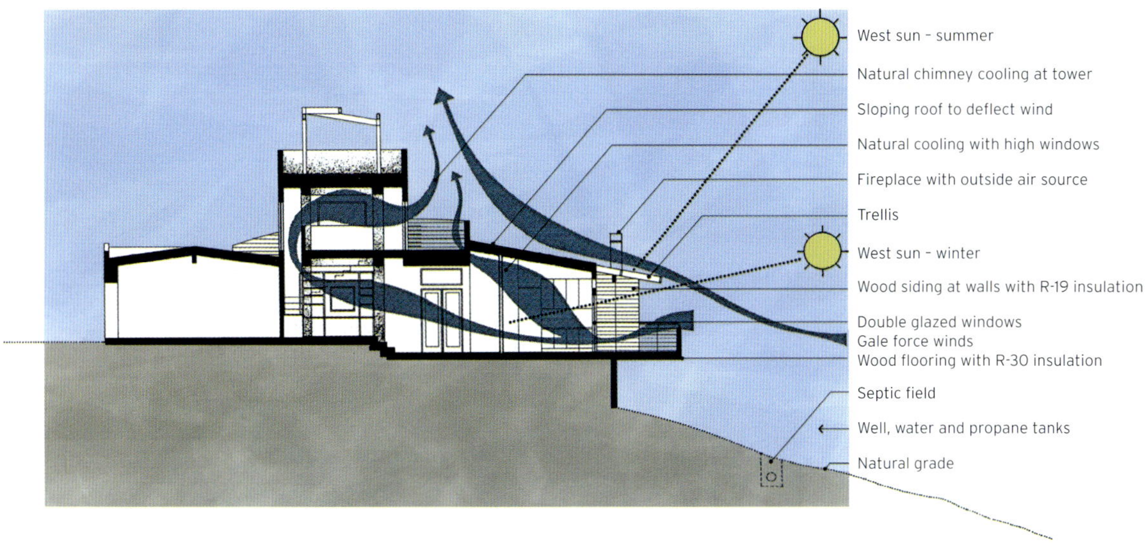

0420

Convection

Use convection. Hot air rises no matter where you are or what the budget is so make it work to ventilate your home naturally. Incorporate high operable windows to let the warm air out and low windows in shady, protected areas to let cool air in to ventilate the house naturally.

Huttunen-Lipasti-Pakkanen Oy/Ltd

Iso Roobertinkatu 41 LH8
00120 Helsinki, Finland
Tel.: +358 9 694 7724
www.h-l-p.fi

0421 ➤
Everything starts with the site
The biggest decisions in the energy consumption/gain of the building are made when placing the building and giving it its form. Every design should be a result of a thorough site analysis.

0422 ▼
Places can be built with gestures
The work of an architect has a lot to do with articulating spaces for functions. It is not always needed to build a heated and insulated room to create a defined space.

0423 ▲
Architecture grows from the chosen materials
All the decisions from large scale to the smallest details should follow the choice of materials and the way they need to be treated. The materials should turn old in a beautiful way to prevent a constant need for renovations.

◄ 0424
Buildings should be designed considering that the users and functions will change
The more flexible a plan is, the better chances there are for a long survival of the building. In the case of this ice skating cafeteria, the building is designed to be divided in two pieces and moved between a beach and a ice skating arena, and vice versa, twice a year.

0425

Buildings take an enormous amount of natural resources

For this reason, they should be built to last for generations. All the aspects of working with architecture are involved in this. The following points are there to illustrate this.

0426

Architecture must grow from the site and the local culture

If a building does not manage to gain the acceptance and pride of local people, it will not be taken care of and it will not last for a long time. In the best case, the building is a fresh interpretation of its surroundings and a continuation of the whole built culture.

0427

Things that have quality in them are to be preserved

Wether it's a city or a door handle well made things survive the challenges of both new ideologies and being used over decades. The quality is defined in taking the detailing all the way to the very end.

0428

If a building is built to be temporary, it should be considered very carefully how it is going to be recycled after its use

In this day care center, the concept consists of movable warm core modules and cold façade structures that can also be undetached and transported inside the modules.

0429

Architecture grows from the structure

The chosen structure defines the architectural language. To minimize the use of building materials, it is worth considering if the structure can be shown as it is. Clear, simple, beautiful and understandable buildings don't go out of fashion.

0430

Every building should be unique

It is not needed to spend vast amounts of money, energy and material to reach this. Simple ideas are sometimes enough. The aim is to get a big effect from a little change.

I-Beam Design

138 Spring Street, 2nd Floor
New York, NY 10012, USA
Tel.: +1 212 244 7596
www.i-beamdesign.com

0431

Reuse

The ascending grassy knolls accommodate urban residents with public gardens and private lawns at their doorstep, even for people living in a 4th floor duplex. The grass roofs provide water storage during periods of high rainfall, reducing runoff to the local drainage system, and the rain water that percolates through the roof can be filtered and used on site.

0432

Regenerate

Green Springs help to absorb carbon dioxide, release oxygen and mitigate the presence of greenhouse gases in the atmosphere. They reduce energy consumption by keeping the building cooler in the summer and minimizing "heat island" effect.

0434

Integrate

Boating is the most energy efficient means of transportation. This is capitalized by allowing apartments along the canal come with a barge summer home that plugs into the apartment, extending the living space into a floating sunroom with extra bedroom, kitchen and bath.

0433

Enjoy nature

Water is synonymous with health and life. Swimming, ice skating, and floating performances are just some of the activities that could take place in the water plaza at the center this housing development.

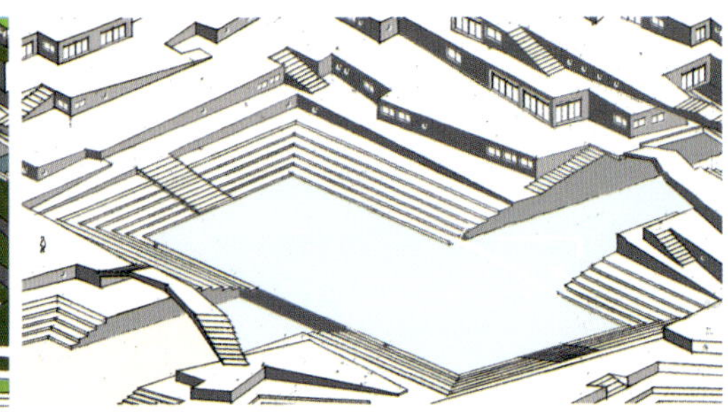

◄ 0435

Reappropriate

The principal building module for the refugee housing project is the wooden shipping pallet, which is widely available in most countries, versatile, recyclable, sustainable, easily assembled and inexpensive.

◄ 0436

Adapt and change

The pallet matrix permits families to build according to their own needs with local resources, thereby fostering empowerment, employment, and economic growth within the community. A simple pallet structure evolves naturally from emergency shelter to permanent house with the addition of indigenous insulating or cladding materials, such as rubble, stone, earth, mud, plaster and concrete.

0437 ▼

Recycle

40 million bed springs are dumped into American landfills each year. By combining two rapidly growing industries, green wall systems and mattress recycling, Green Springs intends to reduce landfill waste and encourage the beautification of urban landscapes by using discarded bed springs to create green walls and roofs.

0439 ▼

Remove and relocate

By combining pallets with local construction methods, such as thatch roofing or wattle and daub, The Pallet House provides a hybrid solution that is prefabricated, environmentally sustainable and culturally appropriate.

0438 ▲

Connect

This is a living park, transformed each season by the imagination of its users. Residents participate directly from their windows in selecting, growing and planting the flowering vines and ivy which constitute the hanging garden. Seating, playing and entertainment are integrated into a playful landscape of paving, planting and water that inspires joy and interaction between people and the parkscape.

◄ 0440

Enliven

By using the sky plane as a garden, the design reduces noise and air pollution to the surrounding residences, animates the park, and provide shade.

Iredale Pedersen Hook Architects

Suites 5 & 6, Murray Mews
329-331 Murray Street
Perth, WA 6000, Australia

PO Box 442
Leederville, WA 6903, Australia
Tel.: +61 08 9322 9750
www.iredalepedersenhook.com

0441 ➤
Walmajarri Community Centre
Culturally responsive architecture that seeks to bind ancient culture to place while helping to preserve a rapidly disappearing language.

0442
Tjuntjuntjarra Community Housing
Community architecture designed with flexible individual use patterns while encouraging a connection to the community.

© Peter Bennetts

0443
Sheep House
A heavily grounded architecture with a minimum carbon footprint producing power and storing water.

0444 ▲
Swan St Residence
Re-interpreting older residential buildings with an extroverted quality responding to contemporary ideas for dwelling. The role of the plasma screen is challenged by a dynamic engagement of interior and exterior.

0445 ➤
Perth Zoo orangutan enclosure
Assisting with the preservation of a species while responding to unfamiliar patterns of use (tree dwelling).

© Peter Bennetts

© Shannon McGrath

0446

Gidgegannup

A delicate line in the landscape that minimizes impact to the place.

0447

Florida Beach house

Intensifying the relationship of the occupant to the ocean and challenging building design guidelines.

0448

Meares Residence

Redefining societies understanding of the aesthetics of a sustainable dwelling. A sequence of pavilions are orchestrated on an abstract concrete platform.

0449

Information PODs

A brief moment of clarity and legibility in a context of visual chaos. Extra-small projects can have a large impact.

0450

Innocent Bystander winery

A shifting scale of experience to engage with a small scale town, exposing the wine making process, "re-constructing" the vineyard plantations (in paint) and the texture and fine grain of re-cycled jarrah timber.

J. Mayer H. Architects

Bleibtreustraße 54
10623 Berlin, Germany
Tel.: +49 (0)30 644 90 77 00
www.jmayerh.de

0451 ➤
Property development group Euroboden is building a unique apartment house at Johannisstraße in Mitte, Berlin's downtown district.

0452 ▼
Sonnenhof consists of four new buildings with office and residential spaces.

◄ 0453
The sculptural design of the suspended slat façade draws on the notion of landscape in the city, a quality visible in the graduated courtyard garden and the building's silhouette and layout. Plans for the ground floor facing the street also include a number of commercial spaces.

0454 ➤
The units' varying floorplans and layouts indicate a number of housing options. Condominiums are organized into townhouses with private gardens, classic apartments or penthouses with a spectacular view of the old Friedrichstadt.

0455
Spacious, breezy transitions to the outside create an open residential experience in the middle of the city that, thanks to the variable heights of the different building levels, also offers an interesting succession of rooms.

0456
The generously sized apartments will face south-west, opening themselves to a view of the calm, carefully designed courtyard garden.

0457
Located on a consolidated number of smaller lots in the historical center of Jena, Germany, the separate structures allow for free access through the grounds.

0458
J. Mayer H. Architects' design for the building, which will soon neighbor both Museum Island and Friedrichstraβe, reinterprets the classic Berliner Wohnhaus with its multi-unit structure and green interior courtyard.

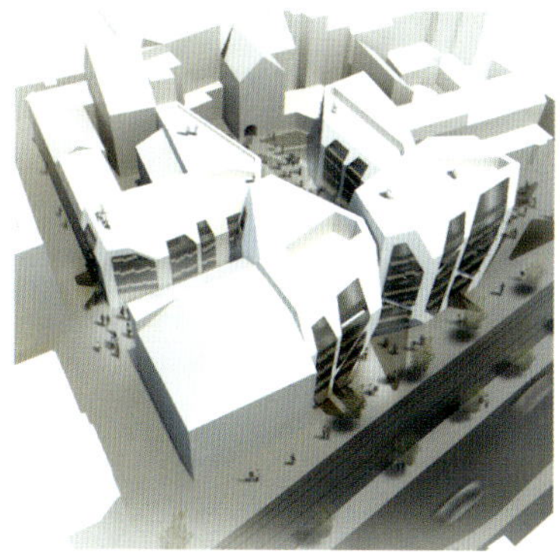

0459
Their placement on the outer edges of the plot defines a small-scale outdoor space congruent with the medieval city structure. Its outdoor facilities continue the building's overall design concept past the edges of the lot.

0460
The planned incorporation of commerce, residence and office enables a small-sectioned and flexible pattern of use that also integrates itself conceptually into the surroundings.

Johnsen Schmaling Architects

1699 N. Astor Street
Milwaukee, Wisconsin 53202, USA
Tel.: +1 414 287 9000
www.johnsenschmaling.com

0461
Smaller is better
Minimizing the footprint of a building limits the area of site disturbance as well as impermeable surfaces. For the Stacked Cabin, we organized the program components vertically, reducing the footprint by 50% over the horizontal configuration found in traditional cabin compounds.

0462
Reinvent and re-use
Re-using the bones of an old or obsolete building saves resources, embodied energy, and cost. The Ferrous House is the reinvention of a dilapidated suburban house. Leaving the existing foundations and most of the perimeter walls intact, the inside was entirely re-organized to accommodate a contemporary lifestyle.

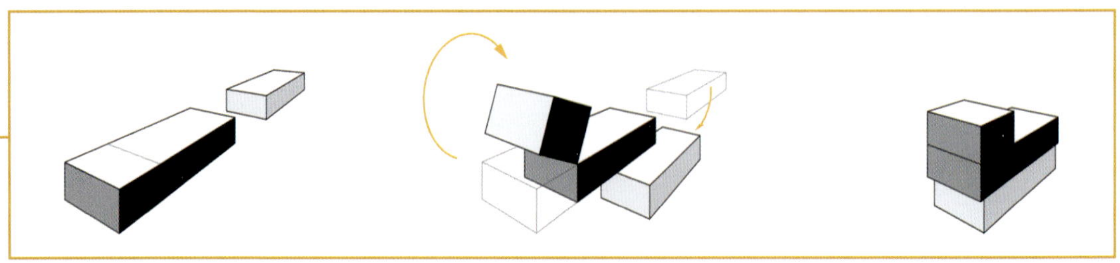

◄ 0463

Waste no space!

In order to minimize the size of the building, use every square inch intelligently. Built-ins may help utilize little corners that would otherwise be wasted space. In the OS House, we designed a built-in desk at the top of the stairs, offering a usable work surface in an area that would normally be impossible to use efficiently.

◄ 0464

Let it rain!

Instead of gutters and downspouts, which are usually connected to a municipal sewer system, use rainchains – they are easy to maintain and direct stormwater from roofs to a rain garden or gravel bed, where it can percolate into the ground and replenish groundwater resources.

◄ 0465

Good insulation pays for itself

Use formaldehyde-free expanding foam insulation, which creates an airtight envelope with superior insulation characteristics. In the OS House, we used foam insulation made from agricultural by-products, thus eliminating the need for petroleum-based insulation products.

0466 ►

Green roofs

Green roofs reduce stormwater runoff by retaining it instead of feeding it directly into storm sewers. They minimize urban heat islands and increase the insulation properties of a roof. Using sedums instead of simple grass creates durable and low-maintenance plant covers that can survive even the harshest climates.

0467 ➤

Camouflage

Visual pollution is as destructive as that caused by fossil fuels. When designing a building in the countryside, allow it to blend in with its natural setting. At the Camouflage House, we pixelated images of the surrounding forest and transformed it into a panelized façade system that echoes the hues of the deciduous trees.

0468 ➤

Use recycled and recyclable materials

It is important to consider the origin of materials as well as their possible afterlife. Therefore, building materials should be recyclable and we should use recycled resources. We used steel panels for the Composer's Studio. The panels contain 80% recycled steel. At the end of the building's life cycle, the material will be fully recyclable into other steel products.

◄ 0469

Natural light

Maximize the amount of natural light that penetrates the building in order to minimize the use of electricity. North-facing clerestories with translucent glazing, like the one used in the Ferrous House, flood the interior with an even level of natural light, literally eliminating the need for artificial illumination throughout most times of the day.

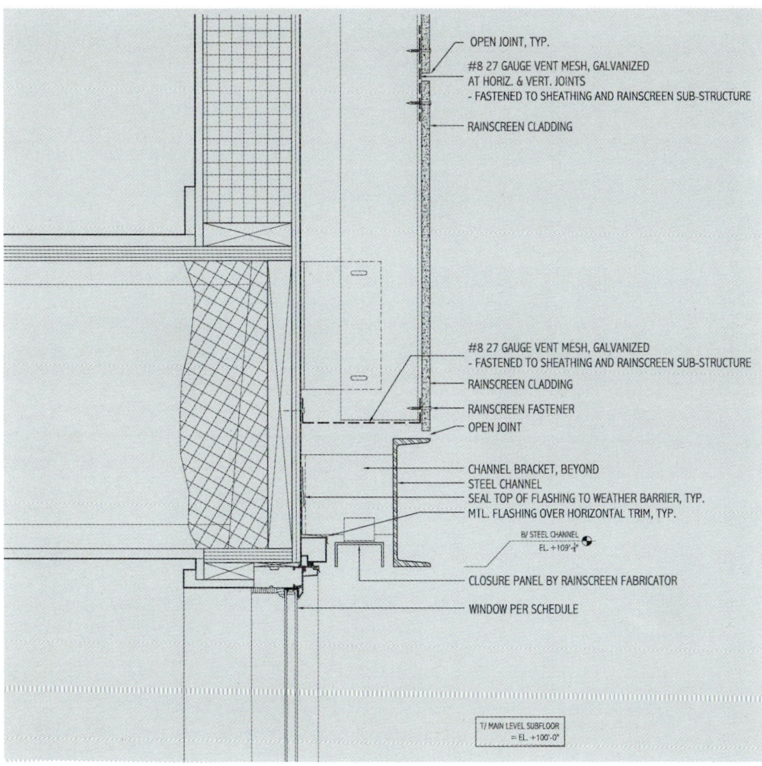

◄ 0470

Rainscreen façdes

Rainscreen façades are sophisticated alternatives to single-layer façade systems, offering superior thermal performances and thus reducing heating and cooling costs. The rainscreen's open air cavity between the insulated wall and the exterior cladding facilitates constant air movement between the two layers, eliminating the potential for trapped moisture or overheating.

Kendle Design Collaborative

6115 North Cattletrack
Scottsdale, AZ 85250, USA
Tel.: +1 480 951 8558
www.kendledesign.com

0471 ➤
Earth, as in the soil used for rammed earth or adobe block construction, is possibly the most readily available, most indigenous and most sustainable material available. It provides thermal mass for storing heat during cooler months and deters heat-gain during warmer months. And it roots a structure to its site like no other.

0472 ▼
Consider strategies which allow a home to "breathe." Placing window and door openings at opposite corners across interior spaces to enhance cross-air movement provides for passive cooling. Place operable windows low and high in order to facilitate a chimney affect evacuating warmer air during the hotter months.

0473

Rain is something to be celebrated and cherished in the desert. In this example, Kendle uses folded roof planes in dramatic form to collect rather than shed rain water, allowing it's targeted distribution to surrounding desert plants.

0474

Fire should not be used merely for its decorative beauty, but placed to foster the use of indoor and outdoor spaces unassisted by mechanical climate control. Used within a thermal mass such as rammed earth its warmth can be retained and distributed to surrounding living spaces.

0475

Water is a scarce and precious resource in the desert. Placing it where it not only adds visual beauty but established a micro-climate of cooled and humidified air can enhance both indoor and outdoor comfort. Here Kendle has positioned the pool to cool the air before it is drawn throughout the interior of the home, turning an amenity in to a necessity, a demonstration of passive cooling.

◄ 0476
Shade can be a desert dweller's best friend. However, properly designed indirect day-lighting reduces the need for electric light, lowering energy consumption and bathing interior spaces in an ever changing tapestry of light.

0477 ▼
The secret garden. Orienting interior spaces about a garden not only enhances the bond between man and nature, but allow those spaces to benefit from the micro-climate established through retained moisture within the planting area. Here Kendle uses a semi-enclosed garden to cool air falling from the adjacent mountainside before it is drawn through the interior spaces of the home.

0478 ►
Outdoor living areas designed as an extension of the interior volume expand the sense of spaciousness, blurring the line between interior and exterior spaces. This often allows for the reduction of interior conditioned volumes and expands the use of non-mechanically climate controlled living.

0479 ➤
Natural materials, left in their natural state, create a timeless and sustainable pallet. Concrete, rammed earth, copper and sustainably forested or reused wood are best expressed without secondary finishes, such as stucco or paint, and require little maintenance reducing the use of chemical cleaners.

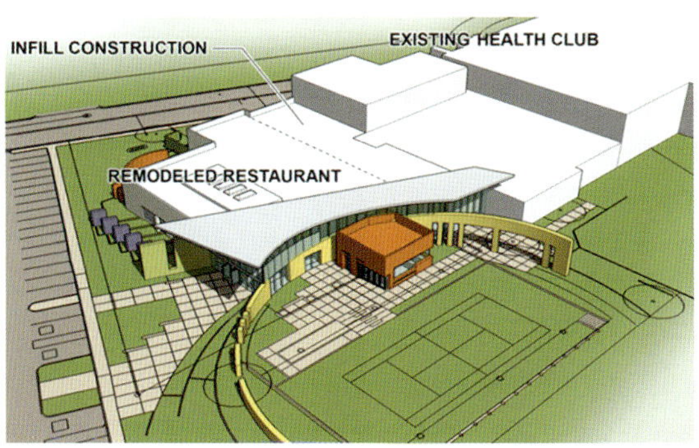

◄ 0480
Reuse, re-purpose. Always consider reusing existing structures in a new way before discarding them for new. Here a defunct restaurant is remodeled and repurposed as a spa and addition to an existing health club.

Kirkland Fraser Moor

Hope House
1 Stocks Barns, Stocks Road
Aldbury, Herts HP23 5RX, UK
Tel.: +44 (0)1442 851933
www.k-f-m.com

0481 ➤
Beaufort Court is considered to be the first historical building to be refurbished for commercial purposes without any pollutants.

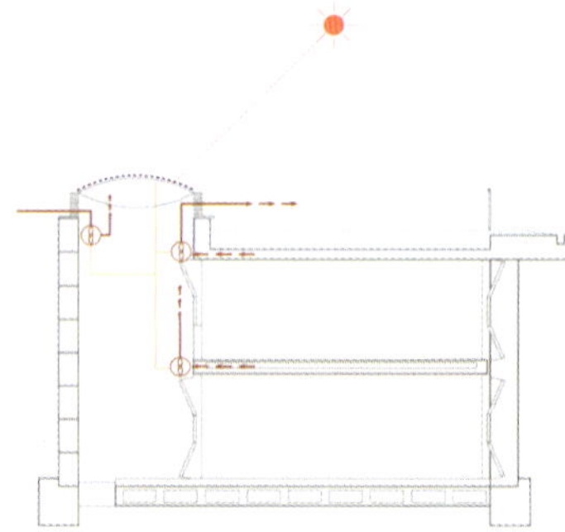

Ventilation section

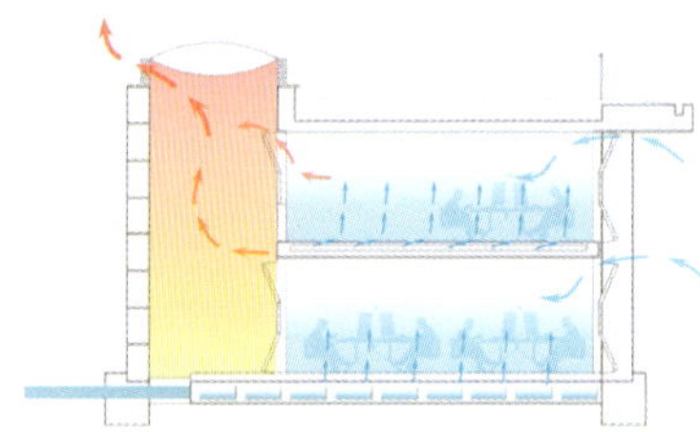

PV section

0482 ▲
The orientation of the complex, characterized by neutral carbon emissions, along with other passive strategies, was taken into account when developing the project.

◄ 0483
It is an historic example of the integration of renewable energies generated from the systems located on the site complex.

0484 ➤
The project includes a solar panel array, a biomass boiler, a heat store, a borehole with natural cooling and a 165 ft sq wind turbine.

Green section

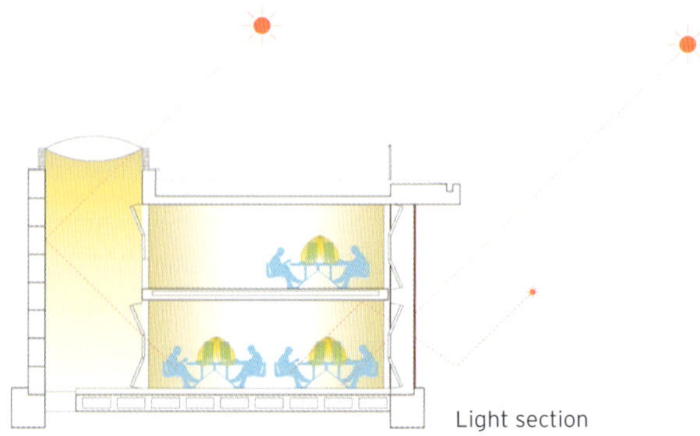

Light section

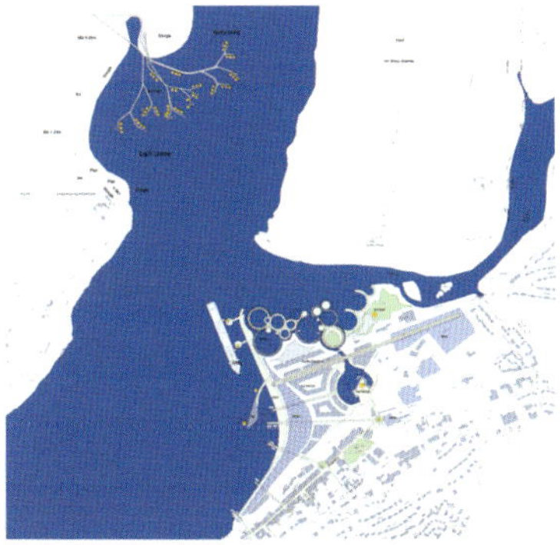

0485
The town of Fort William lies in the most strategic point of the West Highlands of Scotland.

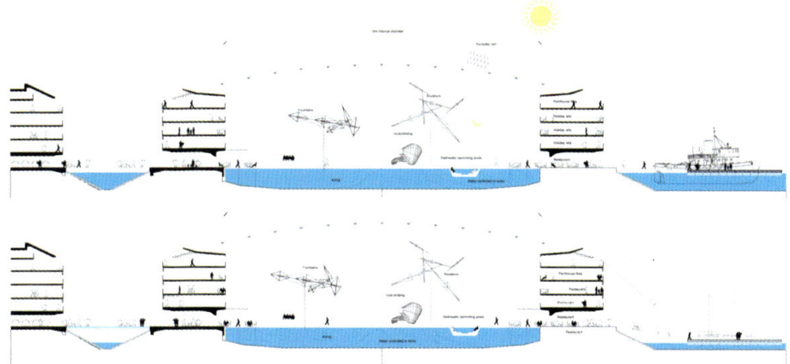

0486
It has a striking circular shape, enabling a microclimate to be created to allow it to be used all year round despite the low temperatures outdoors.

0487
The intersection of routes to the Isles, the proximity to Glencoe and the tidal waterfront create a leisure opportunity unmatched in Britain.

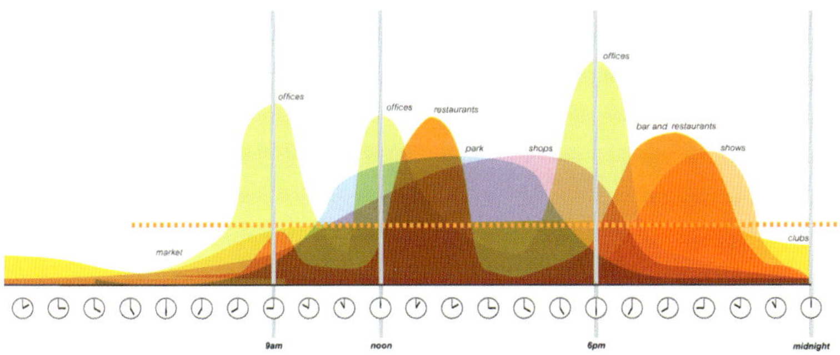

0488
Graphics about culture versus profit.

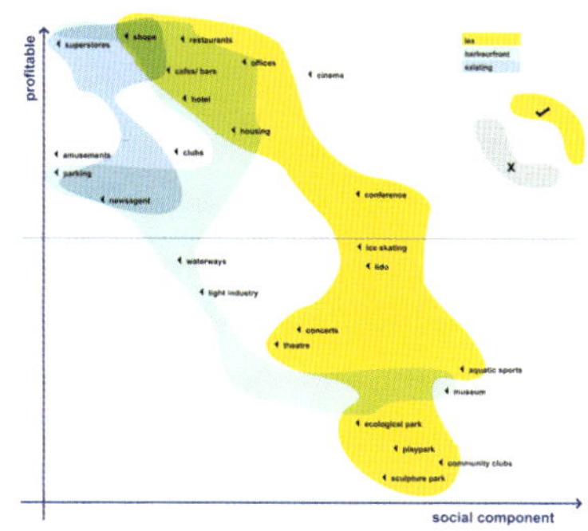

0489
Land is reclaimed from the substantial tidal flats along the waters edge. The power consumed by this compound is obtained from the tides.

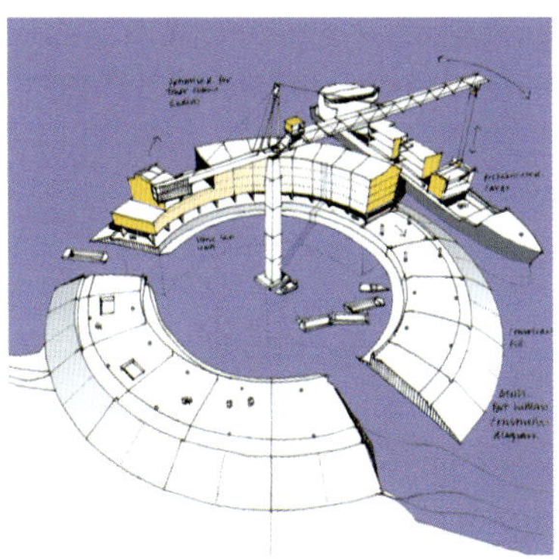

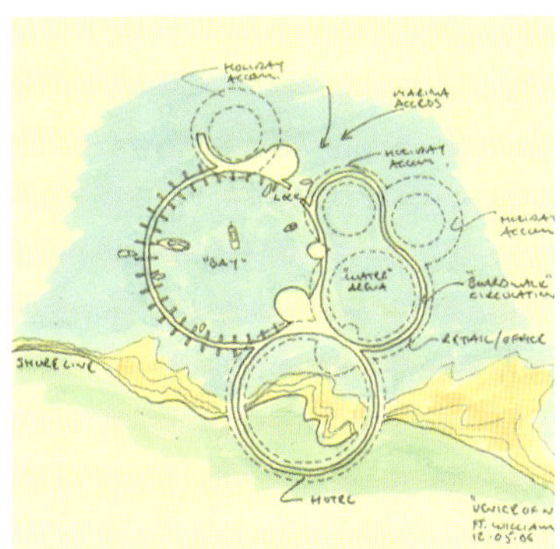

0490
The project includes plans to build hotel, offices, shops, cultural centers and housing.

Living Homes

2910 Licoln Blvd.
Santa Monica, CA 90405, USA
Tel.: +1 310 581 8500
www.livinghomes.net

0491 ➤
To reduce water usage in your home use low flow fixtures in your kitchen and bathroom. Installing a gray water storage and recycling system reclaims water from sinks, showers, and washing machines and can be used for irrigation in the surrounding landscape.

0493
Chose materials that are reused from existing projects, biodegradable, contain recycled content, and/or available locally.

0492
Use Energy Star rated appliances to reduce plug loads.

0494 ➤
Use alternative materials for insulation, such as cotton denim, which does not contain harmful chemicals or irritants.

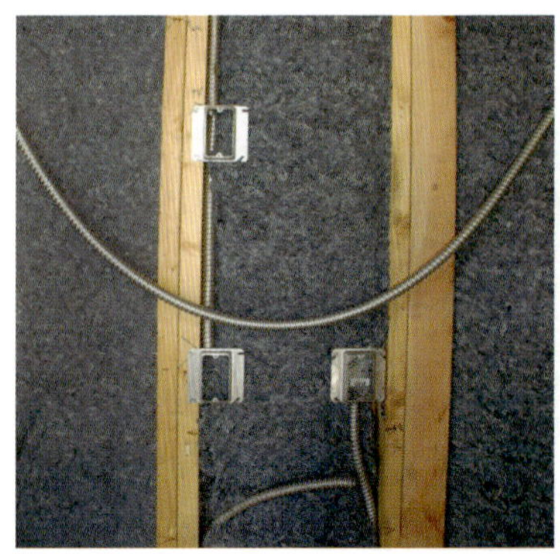

0495
Traditional paints contain VOCs (volatile organic compounds) that can cause irritation, nausea and even cancer. Low- or no-VOC paints and stains minimize off-gassing.

0496
If using wood, seek FSC certified wood. FSC is a non-profit that certifies forestries that practice responsible harvesting practices.

0497
Low-emittance (Low-E) insulated glass doors reduce heat loss and heating costs, keeping you warmer in the winter and cooler in summer.

0498
Radiant heating floors are a more efficient way to heat and they do not release contaminants into the air the way conventional forced-air systems do.

0499
Create clean energy from the sun by using photovoltaics.

0500
Employ modular construction to reduce construction waste.

LMN

801 Second Avenue, Suite 501
Seattle, WA 98104, USA
Tel.: +1 206 682 3460
www.lmnarchitects.com

0501

Building elements can be used to provide protection from the elements through natural shading, insulation, and water retention. The City College of San Francisco Performing Arts Center's roof incorporates a deep overhang to shade the transparent public lobby while also providing 30,000 sq ft of living roof which mitigates the solar exposure, reduces stormwater runoff, and provides a habitat for local wildlife.

0502

Unwanted solar gain and discomfort can be avoided by careful siting and use of existing trees to provide shading. PACCAR Hall was intentionally located on a campus infill site in order to define public spaces and routes while maximizing the use of mature trees. Trees that could not be saved were reused within the project as part of featured furniture pieces.

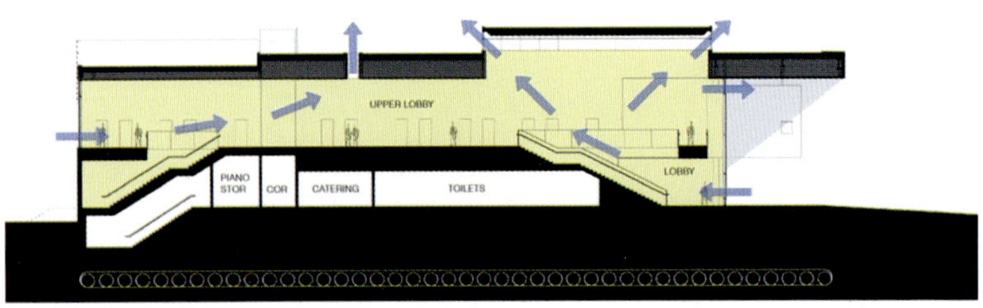

◄ 0503

Glazing systems should be designed to prevent unwanted solar heat gain. Marion O. McCaw Hall - home to Seattle's opera and ballet - incorporates a triple-height glass wall which connects the lobby to the exterior promenade. The high-performance double-layer wall system uses automatic blinds and vents to remove excess solar heat during the day and provide stunning drama at night.

◄ 0504

Building elements can serve multiple functions. The City College of San Francisco Performing Arts Center's internal spine acts as the lobby for three performance halls, as a venue for informal performances, as a common circulation space to encourage mixing of faculty, students, and audience members, and as part of the natural ventilation strategy.

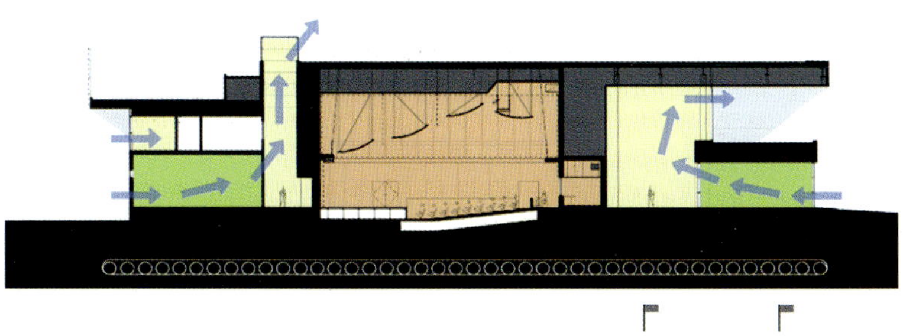

◄ 0505

Complex buildings require a complex mix of mechanical systems for optimum performance. This hybrid strategy is implemented in the LEED Gold targeted City College of San Francisco Performing Arts Center, which uses natural ventilation, radiant ceiling panels, radiant floors, and displacement ventilation to condition a wide variety of rooms ranging from classrooms to large auditoria.

0506 ➤
Buildings should improve their environment. Vancouver Convention Centre West is built on the site of an extensively contaminated industrial and rail yard and is 40% over water. In addition to remediation of the soil, the project's foundation creates a 1,500 ft long artificial reef built in consultation with marine biologists to restore the natural shoreline and enhance the marine ecosystem.

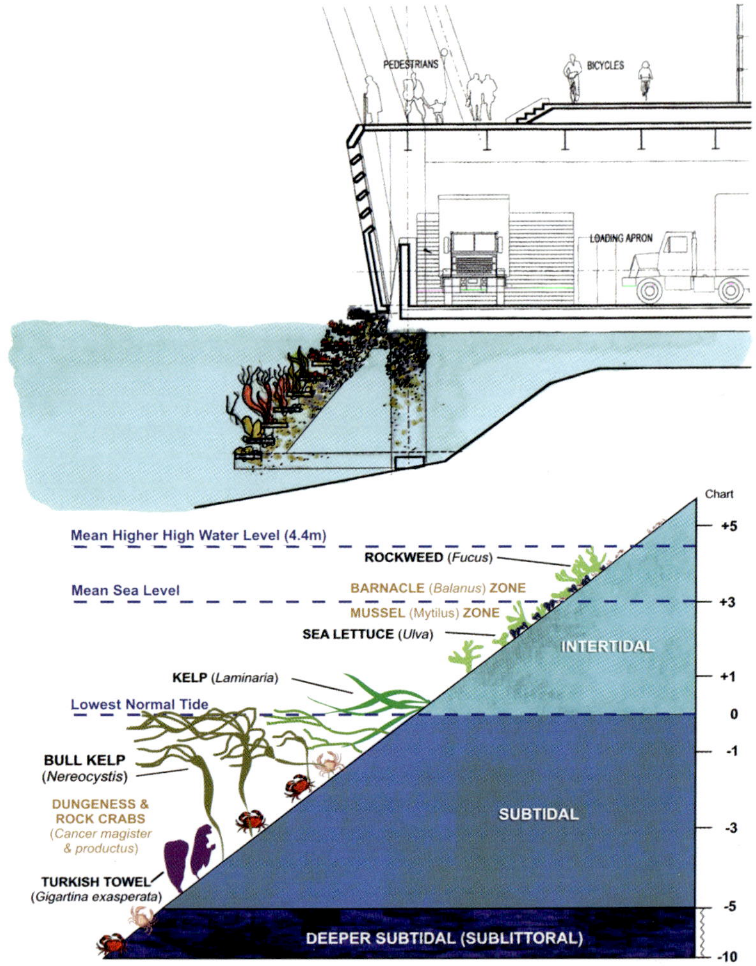

◄ 0507
Modern buildings can bring greenery back into our cities. The LEED Platinum Vancouver Convention Centre West incorporates an iconic 6-acre living roof which extends Vancouver's waterfront park and provides a low-maintenance habitat for birds and insects - including a colony of 60,000 bees, which provide honey for the center. The roof is watered with an ultra-efficient treated blackwater irrigation system.

0508

Materials should be local and renewable. Vancouver Convention Centre West makes extensive use of locally-harvested timber, including 165,000 linear feet of Douglas fir Glulam beams and over 2-acres of hemlock cladding, which evokes the Vancouver waterfront's timber industry roots and the region's natural resources.

0509

Buildings should be designed as places for people. Vancouver Convention Centre West includes 400,000 sq ft of walkways, bikeways, and plazas, as well as 95,000 sq ft of retail space, and is Vancouver's first major civic gathering space at the water's edge. The building allows users and casual visitors to enjoy outstanding views and connect with the natural setting of Coal Harbor.

0510

Internal atria can dramatically reduce the area of external envelope for a building while providing significant natural daylighting. Careful skylight design can create a large impact with minimal amounts of glazing. These strategies are implemented at PACCAR Hall, the new LEED Gold home of the University of Washington's Foster School of Business.

Luis de Garrido

Blasco Ibáñez, 114, 7-9
46022 Valencia, Spain
Tel.: +34 93 356 70 70
www.luisdegarrido.com

0511 ➤
Beardon Eco-House, Torrelodones, Spain
It is 100% sustainable and self-sufficient, powered by solar and geothermal energy. The house looks like a plant sculpture as its entire exterior skin is green (walls, roofs and sloped roofs). A plant wall-curtain has been used for the first time, capable of integrating vegetation with other faces and glass on the façades.

0512 ▲
Green Box, Barcelona, Spain
Considered as the symbol of sustainable architecture, and the best global reference, the house appears as an extension of the ground, as its sloping roof garden has a very slight gradient - it is a natural extension of the ground and invites you to go for a stroll.

◄ 0513
Green Box, Barcelona, Spain
This home is 100% sustainable, bioclimatic with zero consumption and zero emissions. It is self-sufficient in terms of water, energy and food. It has an infinite life cycle, as all components are assembled together easily, so that they can be recovered, repaired and used as many times as necessary.

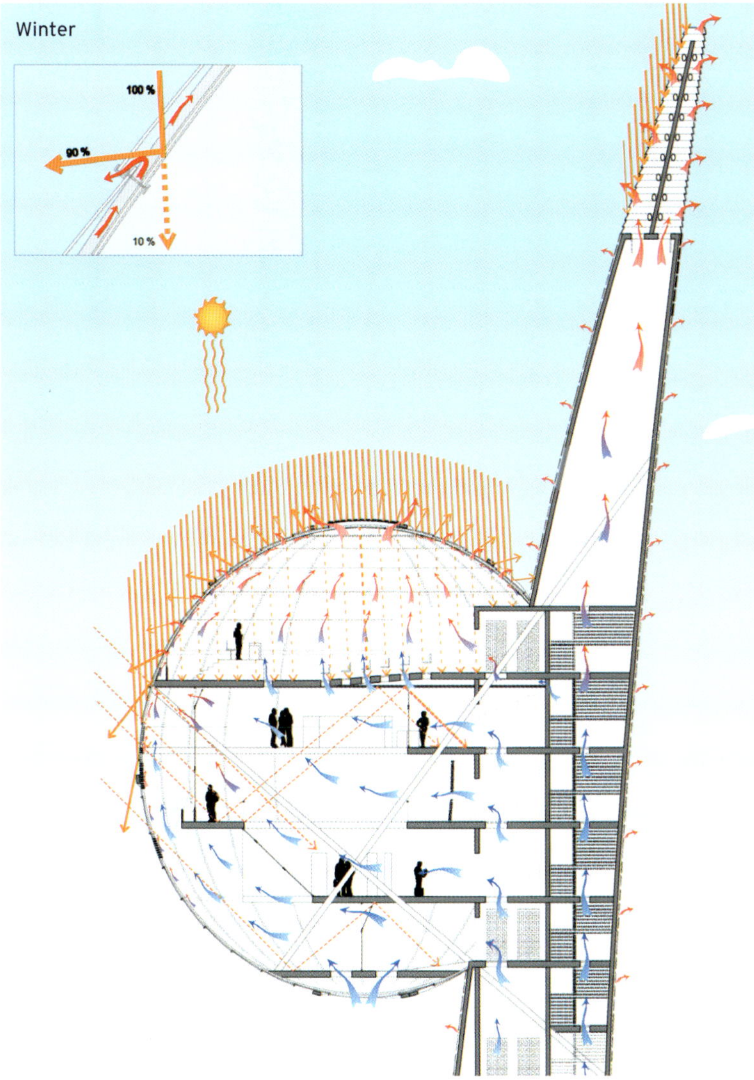

0514

Berimbau, telecommunications tower for the Olympic Games of Rio de Janeiro, Brazil

It is inspired on the ancient Brazilian musical instrument berimbau and dance of capoeira, as it wants to become a reference in Brazil and move all Brazilians. The building is 100% sustainable, bioclimatic with zero consumption and zero emissions.

0515

Geoda 2055, self-sufficient city, Mondragón, Spain

The city is self-sufficient in terms of water, energy and food. The most characteristic feature is that the water cycle has been expressed in a sculptural form, creating a cascade of water in which the buildings float as if they were crystal geodes.

0516

Green2House, Shoeburness, UK

This is a sustainable home for a prestigious English writer. It is self-sufficient in water and energy, with zero energy consumption and with a high level of bioclimatic treatment. It is shaped like an open book, a tribute to its owner, and also because it is a perfect architectural style that allows a high level of bioclimatic treatment.

0517

Eye of Horus Eco-House, Sedir Adasi island, Turkey

It is a house constructed for Naomi Campbell in one of the most beautiful islands in the world: Sedir Adasi. The home is bioclimatic with zero energy consumption, zero emission and it is self-sufficient in terms of energy, water and food. Finally, all of its components are prefabricated and removable.

0518

Lliri Blau ecological housing development, Massalfassar, Spain

It is Spain's first ecological housing development. It contains 129 low-price, bioclimatic and ecological houses. In its construction materials only environmentally friendly and healthy materials have been used. The whole design is very unique and offers an important bioclimatic level so that the houses are self-heating.

0519

VitroHouse, Barcelona, Spain

The only house in the world built exclusively with flat glass. The housing is intended to illustrate the fact that true sustainable construction should be based on standardized and prefabricated industrial elements, assembled together.

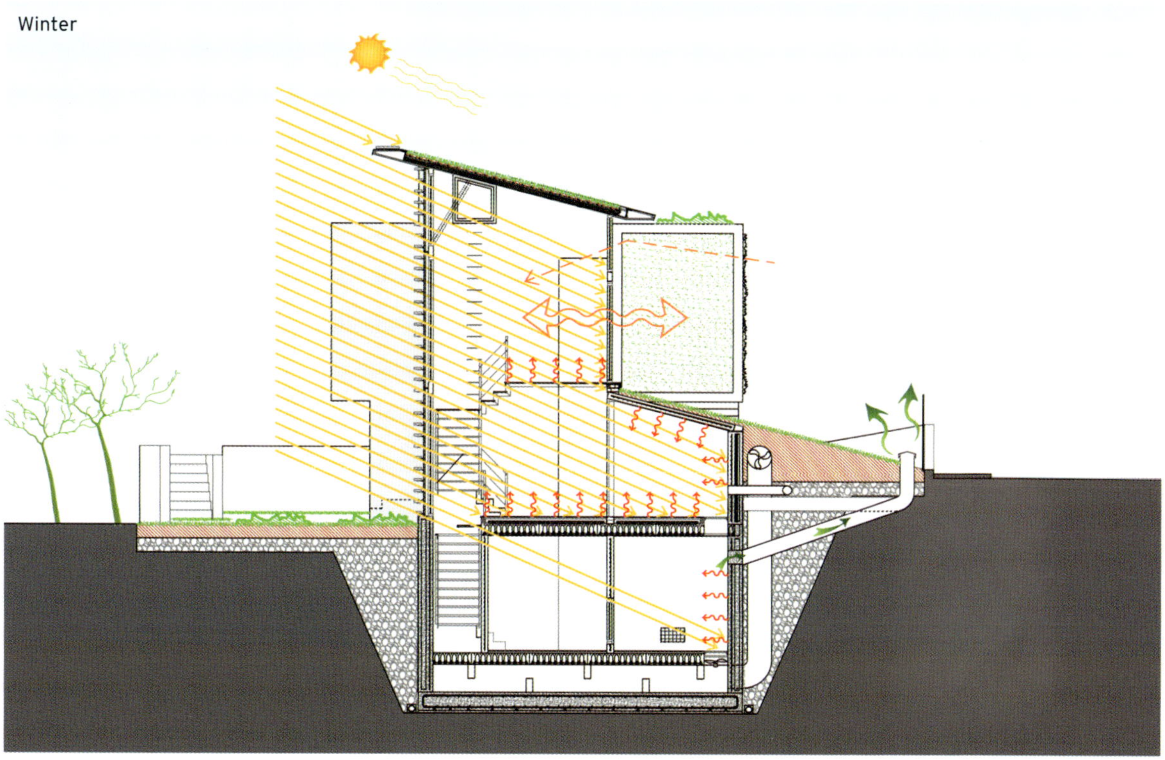

0520

Unique design, high bioclimatic level

One of the most important features of the work by Luis de Garrido is that all buildings have a perfect bioclimatic performance due to their special design and care. Luis de Garrido has been laying the conceptual foundations of a new paradigm in architecture for over 20 years.

Manasaram Architects (Neelam Manjunath)

No 7, Aditigreenscapes,
Survey No. 20, Venkateshpura, Sampigehalli Road
Bangalore, 560064 Karnataka,
India Tel.: +91 080 22792658
www.manasaramarchitects.com

0521 ➤
Rejuvenate the site. The project site was a filled lake bed. Though not included in the project brief, we proposed the buildings along with a comprehensive lake rejuvenation scheme. Educate your clients on environmental issues with easy solutions - they will definitely accept it.

◄ 0523
Always feel a material before using it in your buildings, listen to it, and then you can make it work the way you want.

◄ 0522
Try applying Indigenous systems to modern structures. It involves simple technology and high science and gives economic sustainable solutions.

0524

Any project design should start with in-depth analysis with several system maps drawn to understand the relationships. All these maps should lead to some conclusions, and that should give you the concept or the starting point of the design solution.

0530

Local materials and building technologies are easy to source, easy to work with, weather well in their climate, and are economical; hence they produce effective and sustainable solutions.

0525

Stone, mud and bamboo/wood and other such natural materials are going to be the main building materials of the future. In the cities, waste or recycled waste could be the future, with large building and infrastructure projects being undertaken with rise in urbanization.

0528

Understand who your real clients are? Center your design on them.

0527

Building a glass box or such unsustainable building, and then installing mechanical systems, such as air-conditioning, for comfort and light does not lead to a zero carbon building. Try making your building zero carbon and not the mechanical systems. That is "sustainable architecture design."

0526

Each geographical region in this world has suitable building materials and construction system for that particular region. It is Nature's way of giving solutions to us. Look for it, listen to it.

0529

Local solutions to global problems is sustainable development, and not global solutions to local problems. They are always energy intensive, uneconomical, difficult to execute and hence unsustainable.

Mario Cucinella Architects srl.

Via Barozzi 3/A
40126 Bologna, Italy
Tel.: +39 051 6313381
www. mcarchitects.it

0531 ➤
The SIEEB building is a platform for the bilateral cooperation between Italy and China in the fields of energy and environmental preservation efforts. It is also a showcase building for reducing CO_2 emissions in the construction sector in China.

© Daniele Domenicali

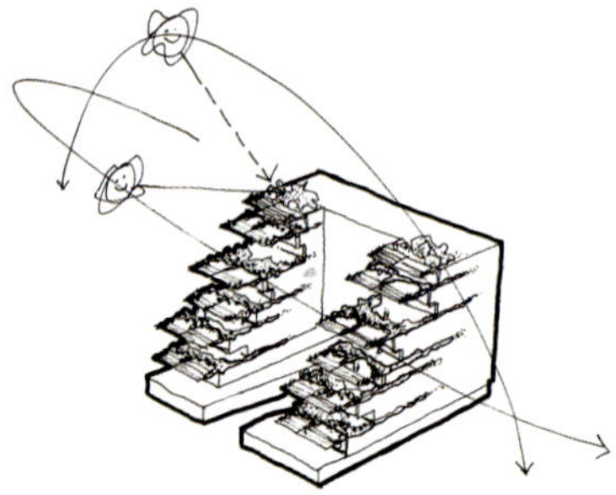

◄ 0532
The design incorporates passive and active strategies in its form and skin to control external environment and improve interior air quality.

© Daniele Domenicali

◄ 0534
The offices and laboratories located on the upper floors have terraced gardens that also use cisterns. Together with overhanging structures, where the photovoltaic panels are located, they act as sunshades for the floor directly below.

0533 ▼
The building features a bioclimatic design. It combines the use of glass for natural lighting with renewable energies and rainwater collection by means of roof cisterns.

© Daniele Domenicali

0535 ➤
The north-facing façade is closed and highly insulated, given that the cold winter winds come from this direction. The façade becomes more transparent toward the south. On the east and west sides, sunlight and radiation are controlled through the double glass skin.

© Daniele Domenicali

0536 ➤

These sustainability efforts enable the SIEEB to emit around 550 short tons of CO_2 per year, compared to the average of 30,860 short tons emitted by a conventional building, with a 50% saving on air-conditioning usage and costs.

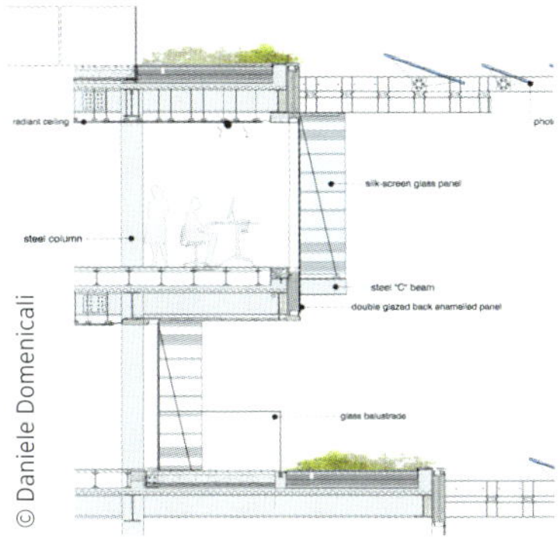

0537 ◄

This residential building was designed for the 2008 exhibition Habiter Ecologique, held at the Cité de l'Architecture in Paris. The building is 19,160 sq ft over six floors and is located in Boulogne-Billancourt, just outside Paris.

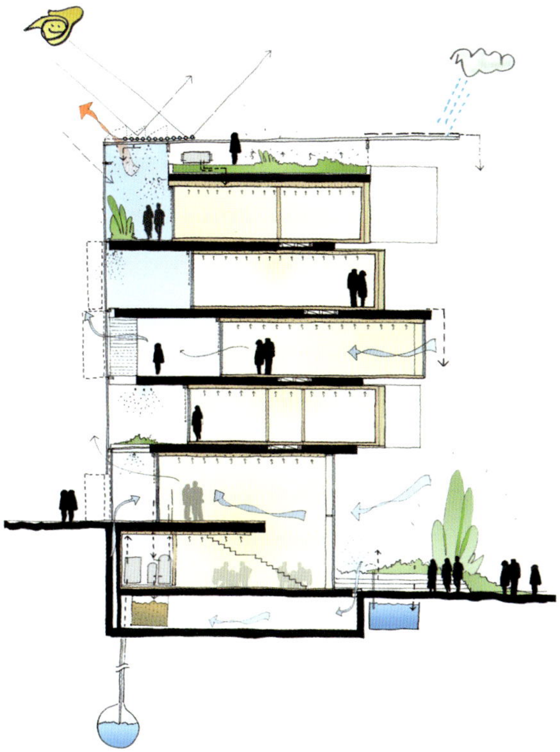

0538 ➤

Shared services are on the ground floor, such as the kindergarten, the restaurant and the bar. On the roof there is a garden shared by all the inhabitants.

0539 ▲

The environmental strategies employed, such as photovoltaic panels, materials and insulation, have allowed a building that is energy positive, producing 6kWk/m^2 per year - more than it consumes.

0540 ➤

It is conceived as a series of overlapping timber layers. One façade has protruding "boxes" that create a dynamic elevation with private protected terraces. The opposite side is calm and ordered. The spaces flow into one another and link the two sides of the building.

Mark Kingsley Architects

Piccadilly House
London Road
Bath, BA1 6PL, UK
Tel.: +44(0)1225 326442
www.kingsleyarchitects.com

0541 ➤
Environmentally responsive architecture needs to work in synergy with its site context. Form and the arrangement of function respond directly from a topographical understanding of site and its available natural resources.

◄ 0542
Obtain a thorough understanding of the macro- and micro climate issues associated with a site. Utilize the natural environmental strengths of a site to inform a design. The resultant architecture should then reflect and work in harmony with these strengths.

◄ 0543
Urban environments offer the opportunity to insert environmentally responsive architecture which is in keeping with the architectural grain of the local town or cityscape. Reduce the urban heat island effect and improve biodiversity by designing in green roof and wall systems.

0544 ►
Sustainable architecture requires appropriate levels of financial investment. Additional investment over and above a basic build cost model in time, quality and durability. This investment will then result in financial user savings during the life of the building (typically 50+ years) along with other brand, community, wellbeing and environmental benefits.

0545

High levels of natural daylight should be designed in and positioned to prevent overheating from summertime solar irradiation. Stack ventilation should also be included to allow a building or dwelling to stay naturally cool, by none mechanical means, in its summertime mode.

0546

Utilise space, transparency and views in designs to enhance lives. Specify and build with as many locally sourced natural (non-synthetic) materials as possible, which are renewable, durable, of low environmental impact and recyclable.

0547

In northern hemisphere countries adopt a fabric first design approach. A highly thermally efficient and airtight external fabric will require very little energy to heat. A low-energy ventilation strategy should then be adopted, type depending on use and an occupant's thermal comfort requirements.

◄ 0548
Challenge conventional design norms to reduce the resultant environmental impact of architecture and environments. Question perceived requirements and how they could be rethought requiring less or no energy.

0549 ▼
Existing or period architecture can be successfully refurbished or retrofitted to enhance user comfort and reduce its environmental impact without needing to be demolished.

0550 ▲
Question how, why and where we live. Is it for socio-economic reasons we live the way we do? Why is the design of our habitats and dwellings so constrained by society? How could we live in a manner which is more in harmony with nature?

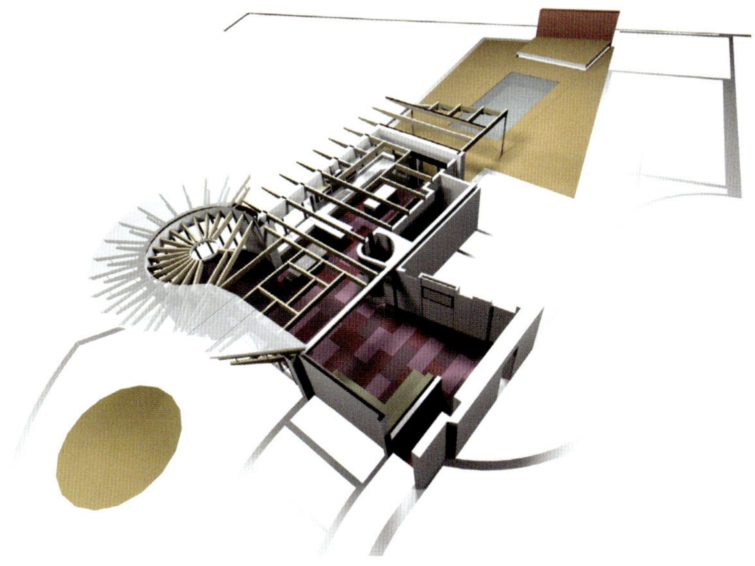

Mark Merer

Welham Studios
Charlton Mackrell
Somerton TA11 7AJ, UK
Tel.: +44 0 1458 223341
www.markmerer.com

0551 ➤
Climate, orientation, position on the plane,t from a geographical and cultural point of view, should be the starting point of any design. It should embody the spirit of a place and time.

0552 ➤
How we place a building in the context of a site is one of the most important aspects of the design process and is a reflection of our attitudes. Look for one's own relationship to the surroundings.

0553 ▲
Gardens need very little lighting. Make use of what is available. To see the night sky requires very low levels of illumination and the night sky can be far more evocative than artificial light.

0554 ▼
Light is one of the most important aspects of a design as it informs us of the space. It can provide passive heat while keeping us connected to the outside.

◄ 0555
A truly sustainable building is not just about energy consumption and responsible materials. The design itself has to aim at an aesthetic quality to ensure its existence in the future.

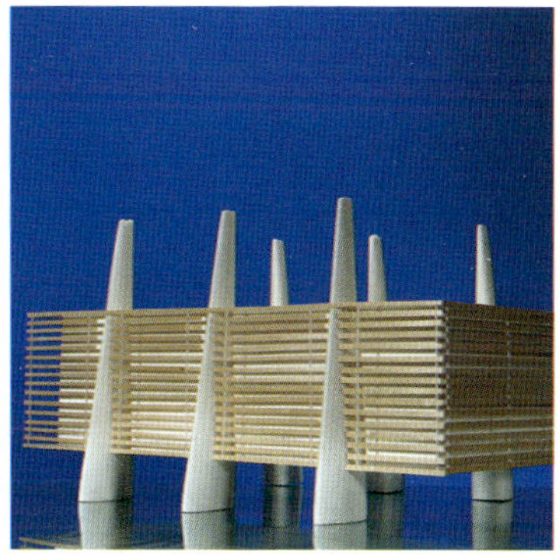

0556
Always materialize the idea in model format as soon as possible.

0557
Place faith in the design process and use drawing as an essential tool. Not for presentation but for exploring the ideas.

0558
Nature has many examples of the union of object and environment which can often help us find solutions to how we build within different contexts.

0559
I see no boundaries between any three-dimensional construct and spend my time observing land use, construction and development. I find the three dimensions a universal tune, a conduit that enables us to see the physical world in more than scientific truths.

0560
Local culture and traditions are vital considerations. And when using traditional formats be careful not to just supply clichés. That will only make a mockery of the heritage.

Max Pritchard Architect

ABN 91 090 808 815
PO Box 808
Glenelg, SA 5045, Australia
Tel.: +61 8 8376 2314
www.maxpritchardarchitect.com.au

0561 ➤

Preserve and respect the local environment

A 655-ft-long structure of 21 luxury resort suites steps down to follow the slope of the land with minimal land and vegetation disturbance. A continuous ramp connects the suites.

0562 ▼

Collect and use rainwater

Over 264,000 gallons of water is stored from roof collection for use in this luxury tourist lodge to reduce dependence on central services.

0563

Minimize disturbance of the land

A "touch the earth lightly" approach where the house is supported from the ground at only four points. Construction can be largely prefabricated off site.

© Trevor Fox

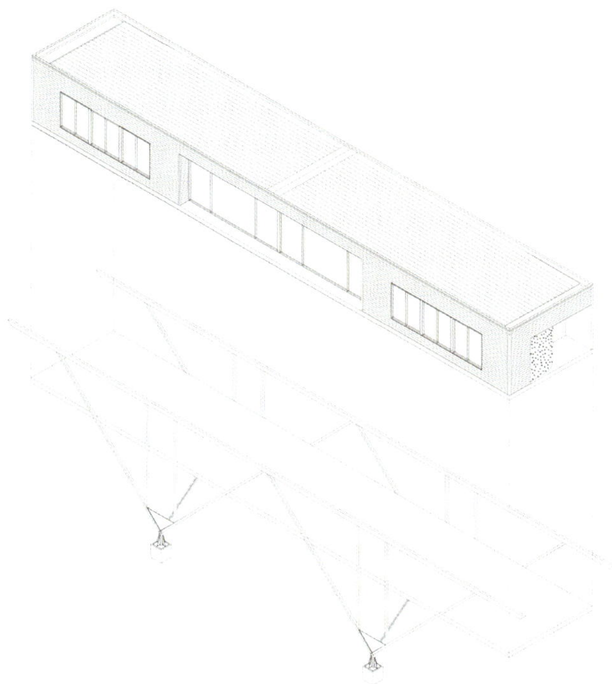

© Sam Noonan

© Ben della Torre

© Ben della Torre

0564

Use local materials

Stone is collected on the site and incorporated into the building to form walls, fireplaces, etc. The timber framed structure is sourced from local plantation pine.

◄ 0565

Maximize sun access for winter heating

Orientating all living areas to the North (southern hemisphere) allows the low winter sun to penetrate inside and provide most of the winter heating. The daytime heat is absorbed into the dark concrete floor and reradiated at night. Well-insulated walls and windows help maintain comfortable conditions naturally.

0566 ►

(Re)Use existing structure and materials

An 26-ft-diameter and 20-ft-deep concrete rainwater tank was constructed 60 years ago for supplying the city's water. It has been adapted by building another level on top and cutting openings in the tank wall to form an economical family home.

0567 ▼

Use vegetation for economical but attractive summer shade

Deciduous vines climb over a light structure providing shade in summer but allowing winter sun to penetrate indoors.

0568

Connect the inside with the outside

In many climates, outdoors is often the most pleasant environment, as long as shade wind rain protection is provided. Even in dense cities, courtyards can provide a natural oasis. Give people a chance to open a door or window before they reach for the air-conditioning remote.

0569

Design for the climate

Sited on a hill with expansive sea views, the house is buffeted by winds from many directions. Creating multiple outdoor spaces means there is always a sheltered outdoor option.

0570

Plan efficiently

A small house designed as a three-level tower fits amongst existing trees with minimal land disturbance. Design multiple use space and maximize views. Sliding doors and large windows allow relatively small spaces to appear expansive as well as encouraging appreciation of outdoors.

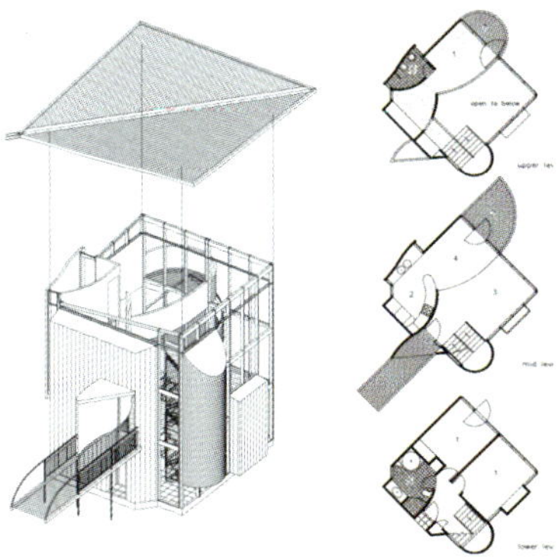

Leddy Maytum Stacy Architects

677 Harrison Street
San Francisco, CA 94107, USA
Tel.: +1 415 495 1700 x 302
www.lmsarch.com

0571 ➤
Pushing to net zero energy
Vai Avenue case study, Cupertino, CA.

© Bruce Damonte

© Tim Griffith

0572 ▲
Transforming historic resources
Bay School, Presidio of San Francisco, CA.

© Richard Barnes

◄ 0573
Adaptive reuse and harvesting built resources
California College of the Arts, San Francisco, CA.

0574 ▼
Buildings that teach
Nueva Hillside Learning Complex, Hillsborough, CA.

© Tim Griffith

0575
Fostering biodiversity and rebuilding native habitats
California Shakespeare Theater, Orinda, CA.

0576
Preserve history and place and sustainable transformation
Cavallo Point – Lodge at The Golden Gate, Sausalito, CA.

0577
Connecting to the rhythms of the day and the seasons
Homer Center for Science and Student Life, Atherton, CA.

0579
Synergy between universal design and sustainable design
Ed Roberts Campus, Berkeley, CA.

0578
Social sustainability: building a just and sustainable future for all
Plaza Apartments, San Francisco, CA.

0580
Biophilic design: making abstract connections to nature's forms
Climateworks, San Francisco, CA.

Michael Jantzen

www.humanshelter.org
mjantzen@me.com

0581
The project will be approximately 150 ft high, 250 ft long and 120 ft wide.

0582
The pavilion is designed to celebrate the return of the sun's rays every day to the surface of the earth.

0583
The structure will consist of 12 precast concrete rectangular columns, symbolizing the rays of the sun.

0584
The design of this winery explores ways to integrate alternative energy collection and storage systems into commercial architecture.

0586
The steel arches and horizontal supports would be covered with glass panels that open and close automatically, coated with photovoltaic material to control natural ventilation.

0585
The pavilion should be erected on a site in a temperate climate, and could function as a winery, wine-tasting center or a venue for special events.

0589
The Eco-Tower is a conceptual design for a public meeting place with a special Wi-Fi network that might be located on a university campus or in a public park.

0587
The structure can be constructed using prefabricated glass and steel.

0590
The tower would have seven platforms, six of which would be accessed via a spiral staircase in the middle. Finally, on top of the roof there would be a wind turbine.

0588
The observation structure would have an approximate height of 120 ft and could be built of concrete and steel.

Minarc

2324 Michigan Ave
Santa Monica, CA 90404, USA
Tel.: +1 310 998 8899
www.minarc.com
www.mnmMOD.com

0591

Enjoy life

Spend family time together at home, i.e. playing crocket is both healthy for your mind and body and very sustainable.

0592

Layering

Try to avoid layering. No additional layering of decorative materials like paint tiles carpets are needed. They only add unnecessary chemicals and waste.

0593

Recycle

Give something a second chance is good for the soul – try it sometime!

0594

Simplicity – simple is beautiful

Easily deconstructed, and recycled parts at the end of building life cycle. Zero waste, diverting all materials from the landfill. Design a very energy efficient building envelope by selecting external wall system and door window package with high R and U value.

0595

Use what you have

Design environmentally and economically sensitive structures: "If a building's orientation, massing, window area/shading, insulation arrangement, and air tightness are not properly optimized, no amount of mechanical system makes the building a 'low-energy' building. And if it is not a low energy building, it is not a sustainable building."

© Art Gray

0596 ➤
Be responsible and put in practice your ability to respond
Sustainable building is a social responsibility to reduce the building carbon footprint. Selecting green materials, systems, and technologies that are sustainable.

0597 ▼
Functional
Chairs that have their own space in the island. Time is valuable, making our environment functional is very sustainable. It safes us time, effort and frustration since it gives us more valuable time with family and less waste of time.

0598 ➤
Change is good
Use alternative construction methods. Thermo mass reduces the mechanical load, energy use and cost.

© MNM|Mod

0599 ⮟
Life style choice
Should not have to be a downgrade version of lifestyle. There is a rather easy solution – i.e,. is there anyway you can live close to work? It saves time and energy. Preferably where you can beat traffic on a bike. That would give you workout and transportation at the same time. Can you put waterfilter on your faucet to eliminate carrying of plastic bottles? Make your own sparkling water.

© David Lena

0600 ⮝
Common sense
Use passive and active design principles.

MVRDV

Dunantstraat 10
3024 BC Rotterdam, The Netherlands

Postbus 63136
3002 JC Rotterdam, The Netherlands
Tel.: +31 (0)10 477 28 60
www.mvrdv.nl

0601 ➤
Spijkenisse public library
The program consisted of building a public space that incorporated intelligent, low-energy environmental technology while not requiring an overly large investment.

◄ 0602
Spijkenisse public library
The building has a timber frame with glass walls. The floor is fitted with radiant floor cooling featuring cold water flows to offset the heat accumulating through the entry of sunlight and body heat. This system operates by releasing cold air under shelves.

SUMMER

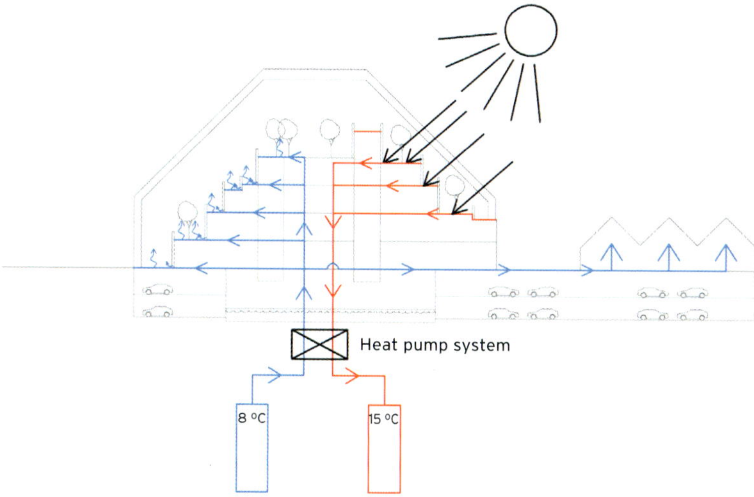

WINTER

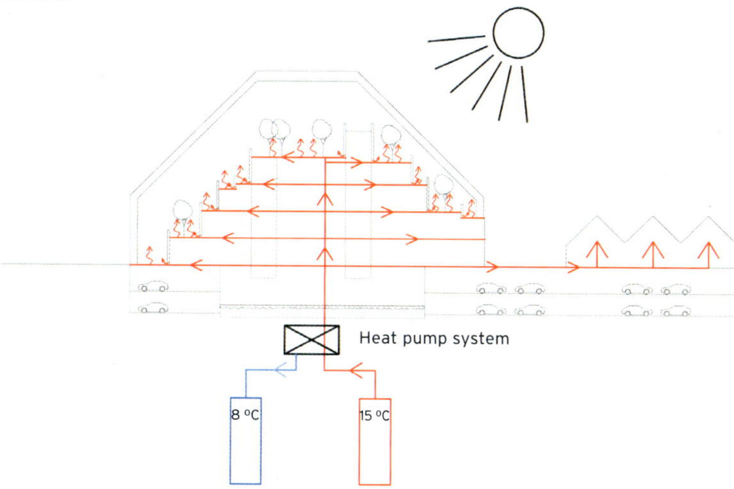

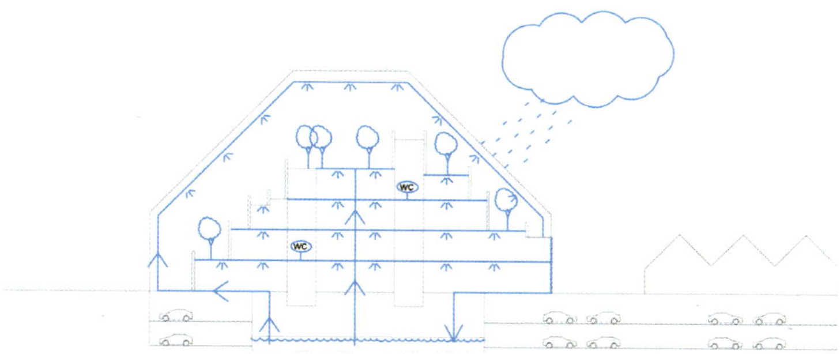

0603

Spijkenisse public library

The cool exterior is heated in summer by the adiabatic effect. The system sprays water into the interior air, cooling it. This cool air enters the heat exchanger and extracts heat from the incoming air. Additional cooling of incoming air in summer is provided by the cold accumulated in the underground collector.

0604

Spijkenisse public library

The façades have automatic sun protection systems and a ventilated second skin formed by sunshades. This system filters 90% of solar radiation, preventing excess heat. The roof collects rainwater, which is used in toilets, watering plants, fire protection, and the adiabatic air-conditioning system.

0605 ➤

Ecociudad Montecorvo, Logroño, Spain

In 2007, MVRDV together with the Spanish office GRAS joined a competition for a sustainable urban extension area of Logroño, a medium-size city of approx. 130,000 inhabitants, in the wine region of La Rioja in the north of Spain.

0606 ▼

Ecociudad Montecorvo, Logroño, Spain

The 138-acre site, just in northern Logroño, on the two small hills of Montecorvo and la Fonsalada, has a lot of potential to create a new neighborhood. Besides the fact that the hills provide a beautiful view over the city, the slopes are orientated to the south, thus solar energy is easily generated.

0607 ▲

Ecociudad Montecorvo, Logroño, Spain

The program consists of approximately 3,000 social houses and its complementary program: schools, social buildings, sports facilities – all developed in a sustainable way. By producing on site all the energy needed, the new neighborhood achieves a CO_2 neutral footprint.

0608

Gwanggyo Power Centre (site)

The Gwanggyo Power Centre site is situated 22 miles south of Seoul. It is part of a major development for a new mixed city. Two centers will be realized in this development. One of these will be the new Power Centre; the other is the new Central Business District.

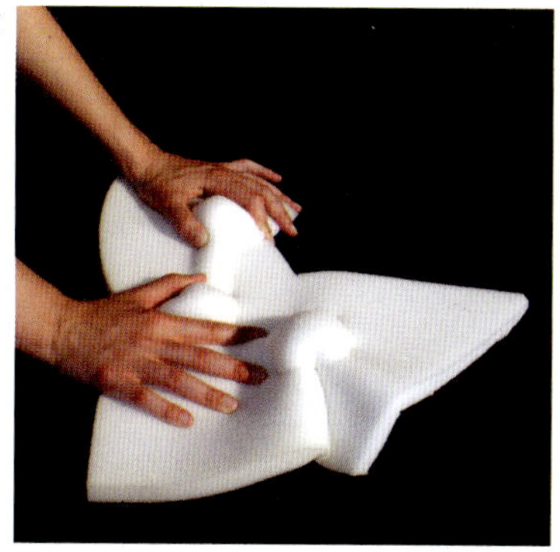

0609

Gwanggyo Power Centre (grottoes)

This shifting of the floors, causes, as a counter effect, hollow cores that form impressive empty grottoes that are open to the bottom. Here they form lobbies for the housing and offices, plazas for the shopping center and halls for the museum and leisure functions.

0610

Gwanggyo Power Centre (The Green Power Centre)

Maybe we can create a landscape on top of the new program that enlarges the green qualities and that links the surrounding parks. It thus turns the site into a park itself. This park can form an aquatic and energy buffer. It can hold the water for cooling. It can cool the buildings reducing the energy demands.

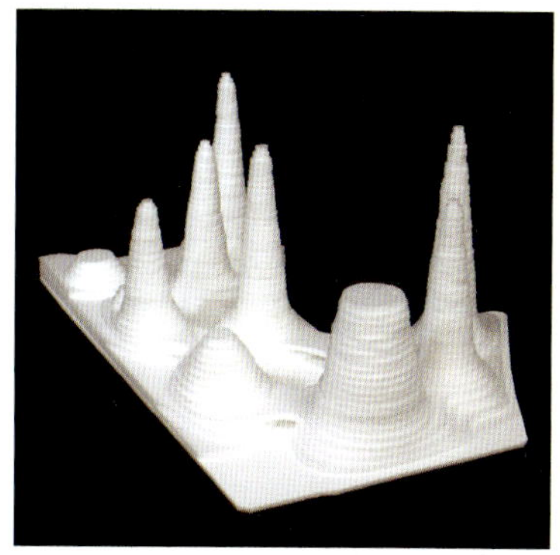

Nicholas Burns Associates

Tel.: +65 6738 0064
nb@nicholas-burns.com
http://www.nicholas-burns.com

0611 ➤
Every element should have multiple functions
A screen provides shade, creates privacy, allows cross ventilation, and is powerful design element and light filter.

0612 ➤
Adaptability
Factor in possible future functions and allow for others that you haven't considered by making the building dynamic.

© Earl Carter

◄ 0613
Authenticity of materials
Design using durable and recycled materials that evolve and improve over time. This increases the usable life span of the building without the need for renovation or repair.

0614

Passive is better than active

Use passive means first: block summer sun, allow winter sun, optimize thermal mass, accommodate cross ventilation.

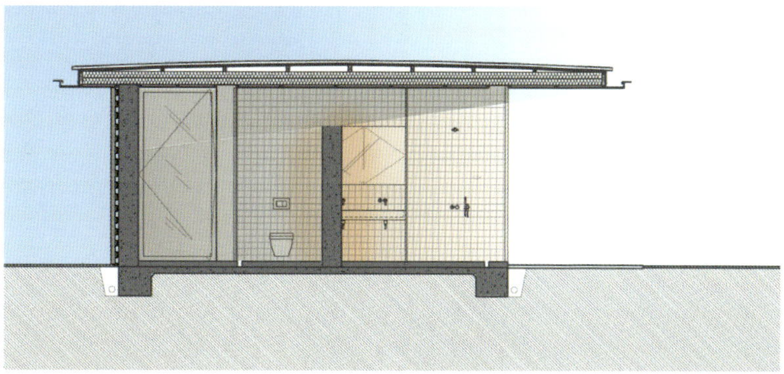

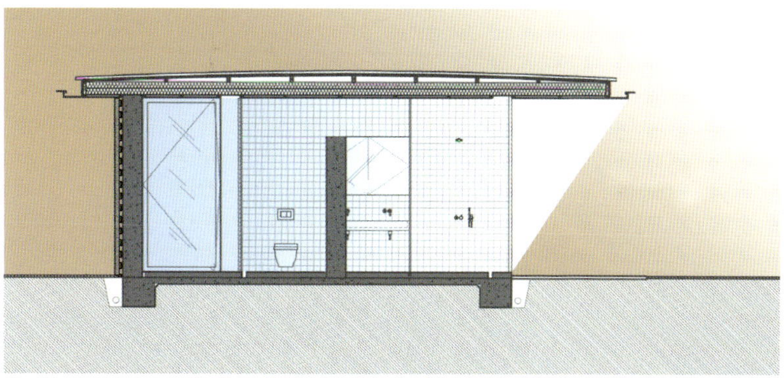

0615

Don't rely on insulation

Thermal mass complements insulation and stabilises internal climate.

0617 ➤

Reuse

Look at ways to improve the functionality and climate response of older buildings.

0616 ▼

Learn from the past

Look to indigenous cultures. The way they adapted to the landscape and climate is a great resource.

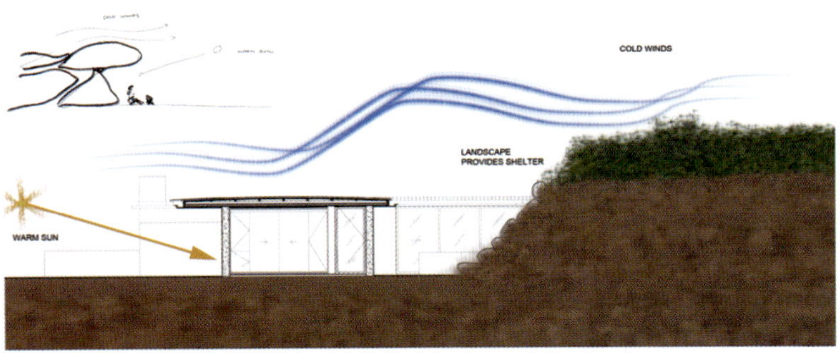

© Rupert Singleton

◄ 0618

Engineering

Avoid engineers that use a cut and past methodology. Buildings are often over engineered by up to 30%, increasing the embodied energy of the project unnecessarily. Find engineers that work and think hard, calculating structural loads for all elements of each individual project.

0619 ➤
Grow food in small courtyards
Roof space and even a balcony can provide meaningful quantities of produce, connecting to seasonality, increasing diversity and health whilst reducing your carbon footprint.

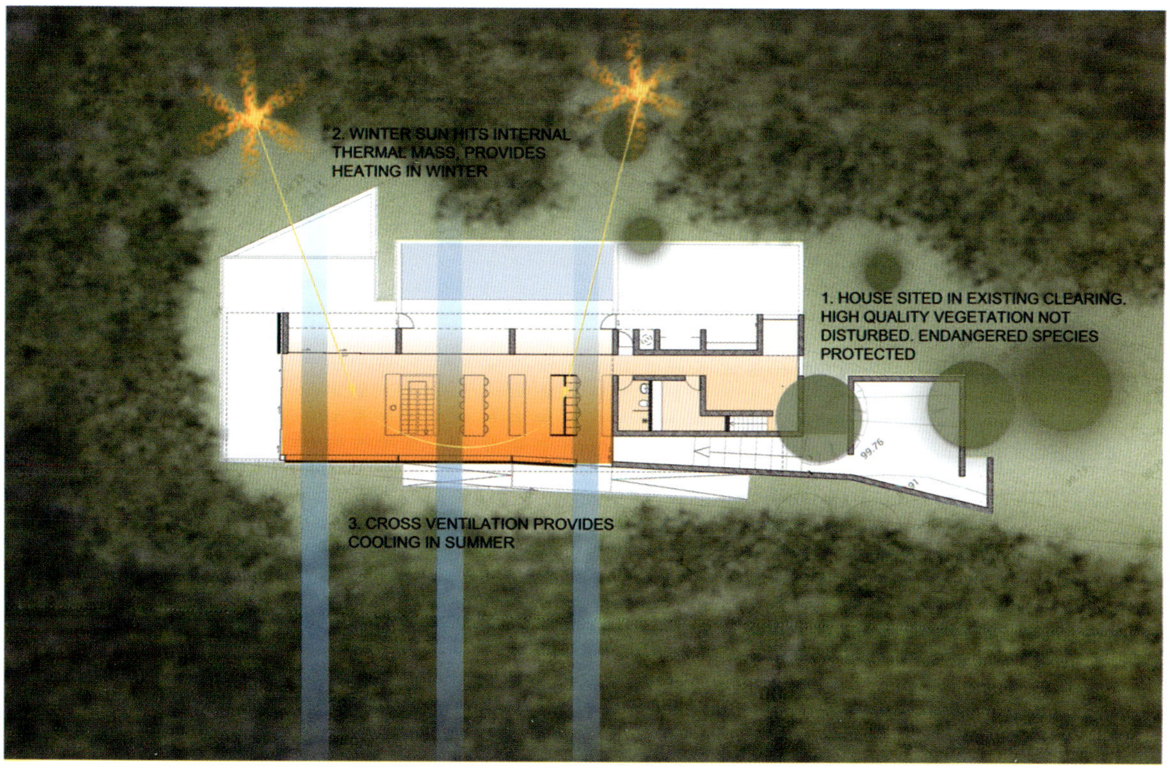

◄ 0620
Site
Start with a detailed site analysis, use the landscape to your advantage. Capture the sun and cooling breezes, look for areas with opportunity to build with minimal disturbance to flora and fauna.

OFIS Arhitekti

Tavcarjeva 2
1000 Ljubljana, Slovenia
Tel.: +386 1 4260084
www. ofis-a.si

0621 ➤
This cabin is located in a small village that is part of the Triglav National Park. There are very strict building rules in this area, particularly to prevent deterioration of the natural landscape.

© Thomaz Gregoric

0622
The house, measuring 20 x 36 ft and with a gabled roof at an angle of 42 degrees, has the same dimensions and materials as the original.

© Thomaz Gregoric

0623
The materials, including stone and timber, are locally sourced and used in a way that is consistent with the local style of architecture.

© Thomaz Gregoric

© Thomaz Gregoric

0624
The residence has a logical interior layout. The staircase wraps around the central fireplace, which provides heat for both floors.

0625
Urban growth and suburban expansion is causing the rural towns around Ljubjana to merge with the capital. This development of single-family residences attempts to maintain the typical layout of rural settlements with small branching streets connected by paths.

© Thomaz Gregoric

0626
The temperature is regulated by this fireplace and passive systems, such as the windows being oriented toward the sun, and the placement of black foil behind the wood to absorb heat and conduct it to the interior.

© Thomaz Gregoric

0627

Rainwater is also collected by means of vertical pipes inserted into the wooden posts.

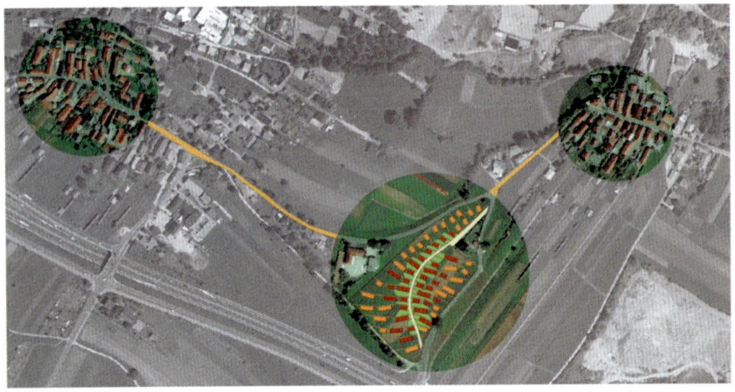

◄ 0628
One of the first ideas was to use the orientation of the houses and their openings to create cross ventilation.

0629 ▲
The materials are locally sourced, and the finishes are water based and non-toxic. The water used for watering the green areas is harvested rainwater.

◄ 0630
Natural light was also used, particularly in winter, although the overhanging features protect the interior from excess exposure to the sun in the summer.

Office of Mobile Design by Jennifer Siegal

1725 Abbot Kinney Blvd.
Venice, CA, 90291, USA
Tel.: +1 310 439 1129
www.designmobile.com

Collaborators:
Taliesin Design/Build Studio,
M.P. Johnson Design Studio

0631 ➤
Ninety years ago, Frank Lloyd Wright introduced a pioneering plan to build houses with prefabricated parts: precut structural frames, mass-produced furnishings, etc. The First World War frustrated the project and only a handful of houses were built.

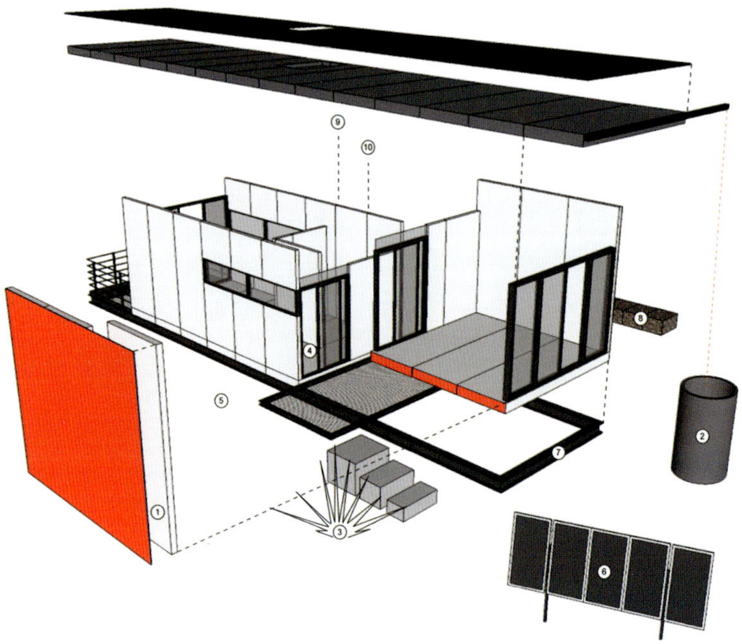

0632 ▼
The Taliesin Mod.Fab prototype is an attempt to follow in the path of the great architect and is seen as an example of a simple, elegant, and sustainable home.

© Bill Timmerman

© Bill Timmerman

0633 ▲
This home was built using structural insulated panels, which make the production and assembly processes fast and economical.

0634 ➤
It can also function off-grid, taking advantage of natural ventilation, photovoltaic panels in the garden, rainwater collection, and gray water reuse.

© Bill Timmerman

0635
All of these features demonstrate the feasibility of sustainable architecture that makes good use of the resources offered by nature.

0636
The photovoltaic array in the garden provides electricity to meet the occupants' needs.

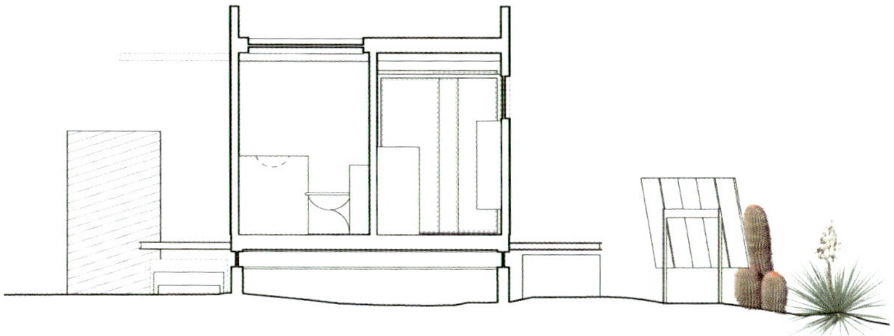

0637
Additionally, most of the materials used follow sustainability criteria. The paints are free of volatile organic compounds (VOCs) and the adhesives are non-toxic.

0638
The glass is low-emissivity, which prevents infrared radiation from passing through and heating the interior in summer. It prevents heat loss from the interior in winter.

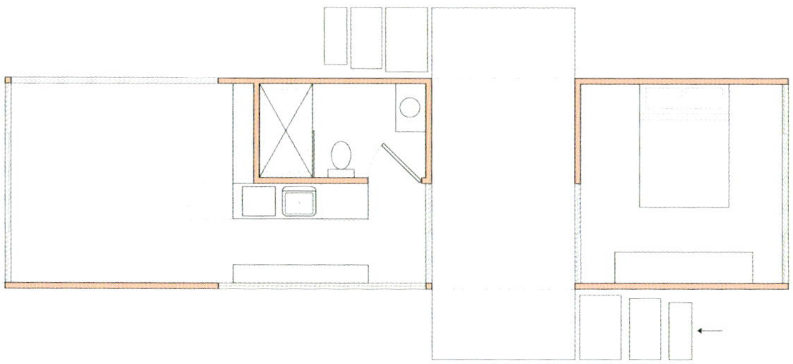

0639
Two of the façades are exposed, while the rest are more enclosed and private.

0640
The roof cantilever creates a porch area that offers shelter and shade. The glass wall let natural light in for most of the day.

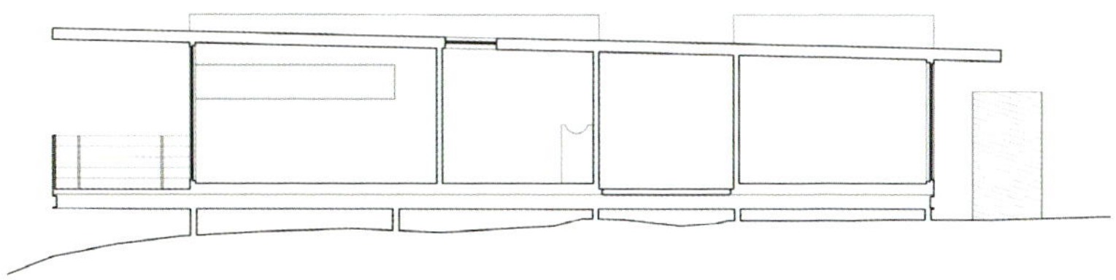

OLGGA architectes

14, rue de l'Atlas
75019 Paris, France
Tel.: +33 01 42 40 08 25
www.olgga.fr

0641

The Stadium du Littoral, built at Grande Synthe, France, is the first facility north of Paris that brings together five sporting disciplines under one roof. This sports venue has stadium seating capacity for 617, two club houses, locker rooms, a multi-purpose hall, and administration offices.

0642

The project was designed as a single rectangular block in response to the unique program and thermal load specifications laid down by the clients.

0643

Our sustainable approach, combined with the clients' wishes regarding ecological impact, led to the creation of a building that is at the cutting edge of environmental friendliness. The Stadium du Littoral has very low consumption and achieves significant energy savings.
The stadium makes use of durable materials and was built in compliance with French Très Haute Performance Energétique (THPE 2005) energy performance standards. Reinforced insulation, two condensation boilers, and a double flow ventilation system prevent heat loss. Low energy lighting was installed in the interior.

0644 ▼

Vertical section

1. Wall construction: round log construction, halved, maritime pine, processed in an autoclave, diameter 6 in.
   Sub-construction: scots Pine vertical lathing, 1.2 in sealing; solid wood panel larch 5-ply crosswise-glued, 4 in.
2. Roof seal.
3. Laminated glass comprised of 0.01 x 0.17 in.
4. Scots Pine glass strip 0.8 in.
5. Acacia cross beam, 5.9/5.9 in.

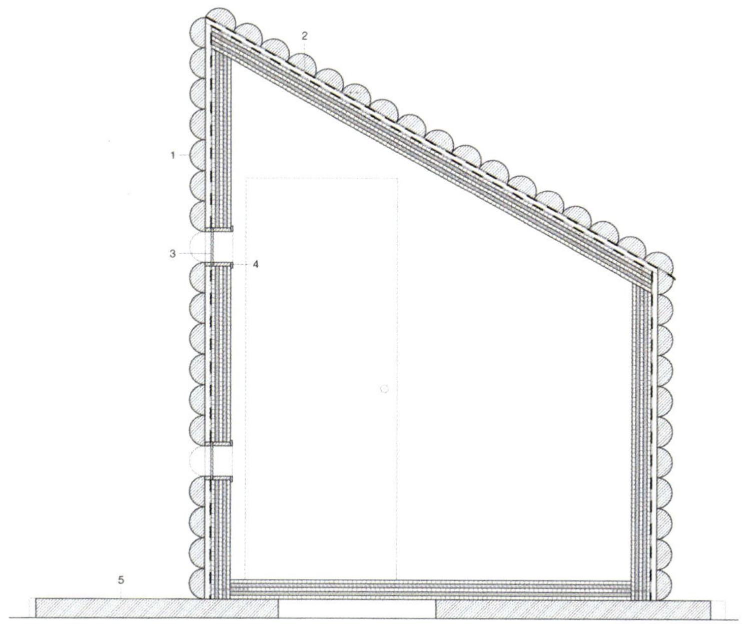

▲ 0645

Flake House, a nomadic dwelling complying with standards for road transport, was designed to embellish whatever place it is set up and to turn the scene into a singular one. The house is split into two parts to establish a radical spatial boundary between living and functional areas, while creating an unexpected entry sequence. The interior finishes were purposefully pared down with a smooth appearance to contrast with the traditional look of the exterior log siding.

0646 ▼

Building program for 100 student homes in Le Havre, France, using metal shipping containers according to the clients' specifications.
Certification: French high energy performance THPE 2005 standard and EcoCampus certification.
Clean site, solar hot water, reinforced insulation, and rainwater capture.

0647 ➤

EvolutiV' is a design for a modular ecological house with a timber frame. The model is based on energy consumption of 48kW/m²/year. Energy performance is guaranteed by different systems:

1. South facing outlook that enables solar radiation to heat the house in winter.
2. A heat pump, combined with heat exchanger, provides an ideal ambient temperature.
3. Solar panels on the roof produce sanitary hot water.
4. A rainwater capture tank installed inside the wood pile feeds the toilets, washing machine, and faucets for watering the garden.
5. Wood wool insulation.

◄ 0648

Our management and environmental goals led us to design a complex of 21 low energy homes in Beuvrages that offer an alternative to the typical layout of suburban housing developments. We used an innovative construction system: timber frame and brick facing. This system takes advantage of the building and thermal qualities of wood in combination with the durability of brick. Low energy certification. Solar hot water, wood burning stove for thermal inertia and gas condensing boiler, R-20 7.88-in thick wood wool insulation, water-saving appliances.

0649 ▲

Program for the construction of 100 residential units, and commercial spaces in Caen, France. Certification: Effinergie low energy label and French H&E certification Level A. Polystyrene panel external insulation on vertical walls with systematic correction of thermal bridges. Installation of high energy performance aluminum and wood window joinery (U = 1.4W/m^2 °C).

◄ 0650

This business incubator in La Rochelle, France, specializes in renewable energy companies. The main façade is comprised of solid wood slats that create a filter to protect the interior from the sun. These wood slats are stacked some distance away from the largely glass building front. This distance, combined with the spacing between the slats, enables solar incidence to be optimized in summer without obstructing solar incidence in winter. Low energy certification. Passive solar strategies, double flow ventilation, geothermal gas heating, rainwater capture and green roof.

Paratelier (Leonardo Paiella, Monica Ravazzolo)

Rua São Mamede 8A
1100-582, Lisboa, Portugal
Tel.: +351 218822075
www.paratelier.com

0651 ➤
Let the nature be the source of inspiration and a starting point of a design. In the case of Guest House, it was the pine wood, the sand dunes of the Atlantic ocean, and the local climate that set the direction of the design and conditioned the architecture.

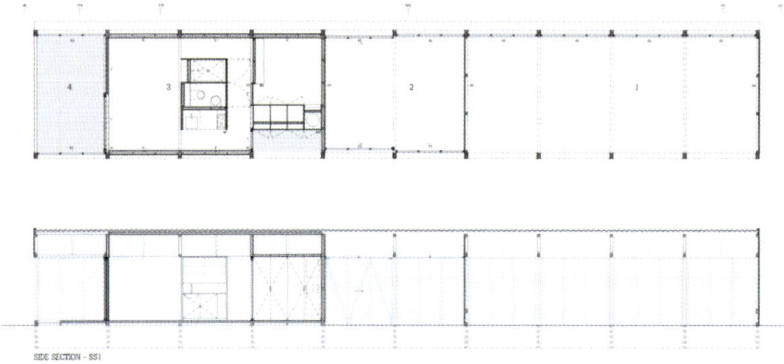

0652 ▼
To enhance the vivid colors of the surrounding nature, architecture is made transparent, semi-transparent and opaque, with the ability to transform itself, depending on the needs and the current weather conditions.

◄ 0653
The architecture, entirely made of the local pine wood, is designed as a light and simple construction that, beside considering the Portuguese architectural culture, respect the natural environment in the most sensitive, aesthetic and creative way.

0654

Everything matters. Along with the wood, other organic materials, such as cork and Eco-paint, were used to create this highly adaptable, sustainable and recyclable architecture. Self-ventilating walls in this work represent another way of interaction between the architecture and the nature, paying the respect to the importance of the environmental sustainability.

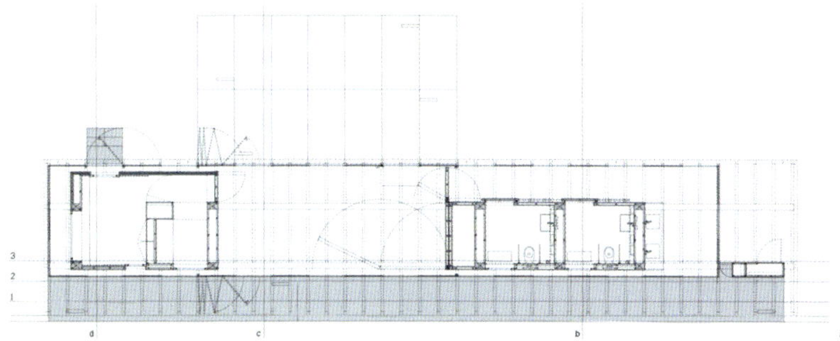

0655

In the case of Pavilion of Almada, sustainability was also searched through the sociocultural context which is necessary to achieve the holistic environmental balance.

0656

Flexible and foldable, the pavilion integrates in the park environment as a semi-transparent structure, where full is void, where inside is outside.

0657

The pavilion was exclusively realized in eco-compatible material. One unique material used – wood. Rough, not treated, rugged, plain and full in the outside, it is transformed into a surface more and more defined and refined. The bands are made from local pine, left raw to limit visually their environmental impact in the external prospectus.

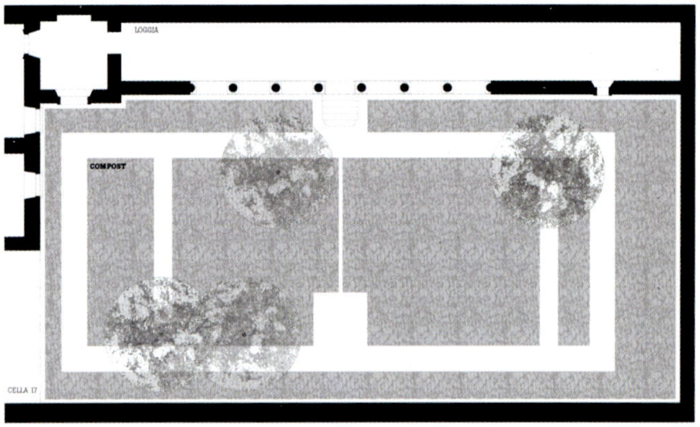

0658

Use the creativity to demonstrate the natural processes that are crucial for the functioning of the earth system. The project Ortus Artis rises from the desire of subverting the common idea of "garden = green," and suggests new sensations and images by reinterpreting the issue.

0659

The core of the project is the level difference used to donate the sensation of walking through paths excavated under hypothetical surface of the garden and putting the feet on soft earth as it was just stirred. In reality there is no a real excavation, but a lifting of the present level through 6.5 fthigh moulds of fine net.

◄ 0660

Conciseness of human being as an integral part of the natural processes is one of the keys of the ecological thinking. In the center of the project area, still surrounded by the "walls" of compost-earth, there is a basket full of apples: an invitation for the visitor to eat them and throw the rest in the moulds of compost.

Paterson Architects

Six Darnaway Street
EH3 6BG Edinburgh, UK
Tel.: +44 0131 220 1088
www.patersonarchitects.com

0661 ➤

Less is more I

Why use a dozen materials when one might do? The simple act of building in timber retains CO_2 for the life of the building. Use screws and not nails, and the timber can be re-used indefinitely. Managed forestry replaces felled timber with new planting so the balance is maintained indefinitely.

0662 ▼

More is more I

Who can predict the future for a building? In a Victorian tenement, you might find young or elderly single people, couples, families, an accountant's office, a dentist's surgery, an online retailer – the list is endless. In a new build apartment block in Scotland you will find single people and couples. It's not just developers who like it that way, so do our city planners.

◄ 0663

More is more II: loose fit

Our house plans are always flexible to allow for long term adaptability. One of our key aims is to create lifetime homes. We also incorporate space to recycle, space for bikes, space for things you don't need now, but might need later.

◄ 0664

Less is more II

Existing buildings by their longevity alone are already sustainable. They have stood the test of time and taste. Huge windows, large rooms, high ceilings, period detail, "character," often on sites on which it would now be impossible to obtain permission to build. However, they often no longer perform or function as well as they might, either in layout or thermal performance. Re-use, re-furbish and adapt.

0665

More is a bore I

Good, functional and appropriate design lasts a lifetime. Our aim is to always keep it simple. Our design solutions always derive from the site. In our project Three Seton Mains the living accommodation is elevated for the view, as this diagram clearly shows. The resultant house is configured around this key design principle.

0666

More is a bore II

"Product" has limited lifespan. Photovoltaics, wind turbines, water wheels, boilers, heat exchangers, etc., will fail or become obsolete. Invest in insulation and air tightness, in high performance windows and durable sustainable materials. Invest in good, appropriate, site specific design.

0667

Design I: natural light

All our projects seek to maximize the amount of natural light to the interior habitable spaces, something we believe is imperative in our part of the northern hemisphere. We undertake sun path diagrams to help decide on window locations. Clients have commented favorably about not having to put their lights on during Scottish daylight hours.

0668

Design II: orientation

All our projects pay particular attention to their orientation. Our project House on a Hill is a good example of this. Large south facing windows light the principle spaces. East and west facing windows light the bedrooms for morning and evening sun. In the Scottish tradition, rooms on the north elevation are ancillary with much smaller windows.

0669

Design III: landscaping

We believe that landscaping should be indigenous. The garden planting at our own house, Three Seton Mains, is mainly grasses and succulents, plants that are native to the house's coastal location. Species were chosen for growth so the garden was established relatively quickly. We also specifically chose low maintenance plants, which is an ecological virtue for a busy family.

0670

Design IV: site layout

Our Cupar houses are carefully located to maximize sunlight and daylight penetration with all primary accommodation facing south. Deep window reveals provide shade in the summer and allow sunlight penetration in the winter. The project successfully adopts the language and density of the Fife vernacular with environmentally responsive homes designed for life time occupation and the changing needs of modern family life.

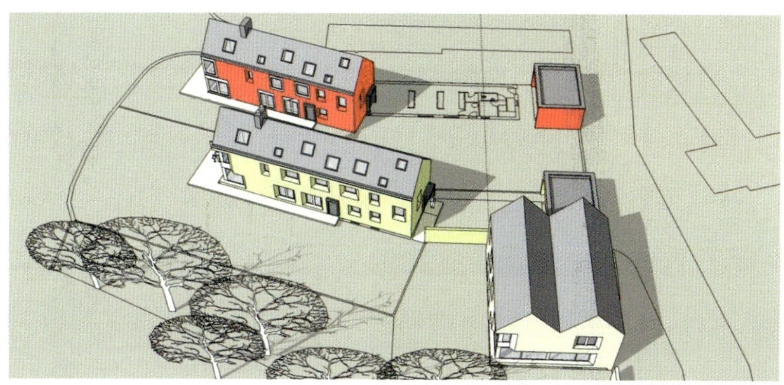

Patrick Nadeau

45, Av. de la République
75011 Paris, France
Tel.: +33 (0)6 07 06 38 17
www.patricknadeau.com

0671 ➤
The movable and adjustable garden unit is a large teak and stainless steal cabinet standing on four legs 35 in above the ground. When the four sides of the box are opened and placed horizontally, they are transformed into greenhouse tables. Plants grow in the thick trays, drawing liquid nutrients from the channels filled with coconut fiber.

0672 ▼
A mixture of garden and events space, this terrace is distributed into several areas.
An esplanade features mobile gardens with a spatial layout that adapt to the life of the company. A small thicket is formed by bushes planted in the ground in leather bags.
The main façade reinterprets the Vuitton chessboard with plants and light.

◄ 0673
Halfway between a garden and an urban square, this space is built using objects and furniture in Ductal®, Corian®, and stainless steel. Two units resembling bookcases contain the plants. Combined with public benches and Holm oaks in tubs, they form the boundaries of micro urban spaces designed as many small gardens that intrude on the square.

◄ 0674
This 1,400-sq-ft home nestles under the wave formed by a timber hull. Entirely "greened," the wave-house is a piece of the landscape lightly raised above the ground. It borrows from industrial greenhouse construction in its use of a double polycarbonate skin over a glass façade. The green roof optimizes thermal insulation.

0675 ▲
A sheet of silvery glass winds its way through a field of red poppies. Out of the presles (aquatic plants) emerge slabs of frosted glass over which lightly ethced motifs float. The hydroponic irrigation of the roots appear through the transparent surface. Standing tubular aluminum structures enable plants to be suspended.

0676

Plant bags and plant sacks are entirely made of textile. They allow interior spaces to be greened in a number of ways: they can stand on the floor, hang from walls, or be suspended from ceilings. Their design responds to the requirments of plant growth. An interior pocket in water-retaining felt and a water reserve make caring for plants easier and reduce water consumption.

0677

This installation is made up of epiphytes - Spanish moss - hanging from structures made in Corian®. Spanish moss is native to the forests of South America. They live above the ground, hanging from tree branches and feeding only on the humidity in the air.

0678

At a workshop, horticulture students met designers and proposed new garden designs. Horticultural techniques and materials, and accessories and tools were used to create contemporary forms that combine plants and manufactured articles.

0679

Between utopia, fiction, and reality, Green Waters embroiders a theme of water and plants. The project illustrates the implementation of the latest advances in ecodesign in bathrooms (economy, natural capture and filtration of water by plants).

0680

This project proposes research into the new typologies of objects that incorporate plants. Tables, pots, shelves, and green walls offer a view of domestic spaces that is both landscape and landscaped.

Paul McKean Architecture Llc.

2505 SE 11th Ave.
Portland, OR 97213, USA
Tel.: +1 503 784 3236
www.pmckean.com

0681 ▼

Reduce the amount of products in the project by getting double use from your materials

In this house we used concrete floors that act as structural as well as durable finish flooring. They also provide an excellent base for radiant floor heating.

0682 ➤

Separating a building from its site can have its advantages

In this case, a raised design protects the house from wild fires and flooding.

© Stephen Tamasie

© Stephen Tamasie

0683

Don't under estimate the 8 ft ceiling

With the proper window and room proportions, an 8-ft ceiling can feel tall. This simple move will save on materials, labor and operational expenses.

© Dan Kvitka

0684

Pay attention to the common details that get replicated across the entire building

These simple details can raise the quality of design across the whole project.

0685

Have spaces serve multiple purposes for planning efficiency

This canoe loft also serves as an acoustic separation between the main cabin and guest quarters.

0686

Don't under estimate how much you can transform an existing building

Before considering demolition, fully evaluate the potential of the existing building. Most structures have construction or design value that can be optimized in a renovation.

© Dan Kvitka

© Dan Kvitka

0687

Design for flexibility

This display wall was built using an adjustable museum fixturing system that allows for infinite variations in the shelving layout.

0688

Make it smaller

The best way to decrease the environmental impact of a building is to minimize its footprint. Careful study of use patterns, storage and circulation will lead to more compact designs, and leave more room in the budget for higher quality finishes and systems.

0689

Add to existing structures successfully by having a strong concept for integrating the new and the old

In this master suite renovation, we detailed the new construction as temporary cabinetry, providing deep reveals at the connections.

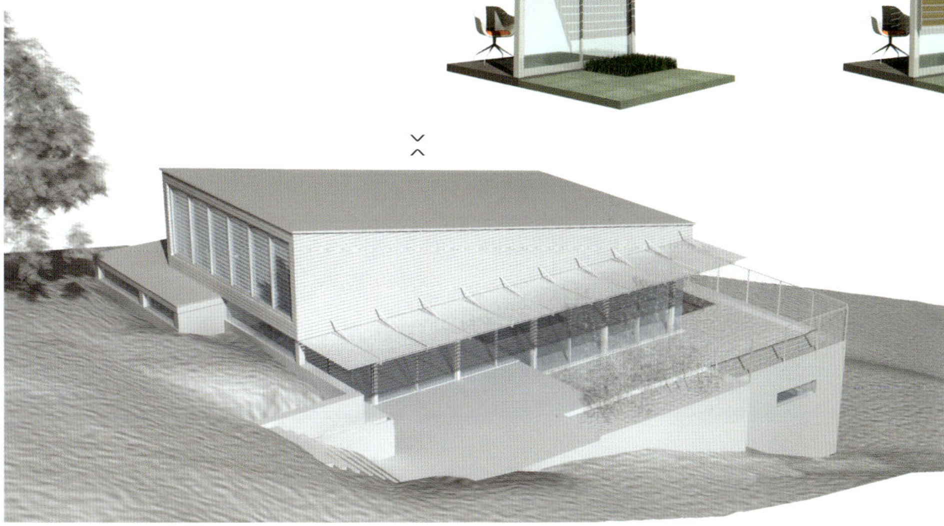

0690

Use a planning module

Most building products work more efficiently on a 16-to-48-in on-center dimension. Working within these constraints can maximize the abilities of sheathing, formwork, framing and finish panels. This method will also substantially decrease waste.

Paul Morgan Architects

Level 10, 221 Queen Street
Melbourne, VIC 3000, Australia
Tel.: +61 3 9605 4100
www.paulmorganarchitects.com

0691 ➤
Harness the natural load-bearing capacity of timber found in the region by utilizing bifurcations, or tree forks.

© Peter Bennetts

0692 ▼
Get your structural engineer to complete structural optimisation testing on the proposed bifurcations, ensuring maximum load bearing efficiency with the minimum amount of timber.

© Peter Bennetts

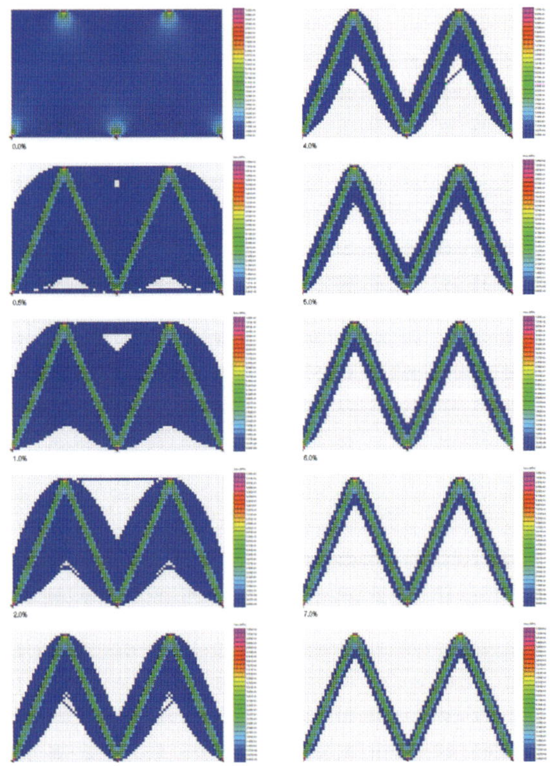

0693 ▲
Ensure the bifurcations are continuous, forming a truss-like frame around the entire house.

© Peter Bennetts

0694 ➤
Make sure the structure is continuous, applying internally as well as externally.

0695 ➤
Fix the lining boards, which have moved no more than 165 ft from removal to fixing.

0696 ➤
Achieve a six-star energy rating through the use of double glazing, extensive insulation, cement floor slab and overhanging eaves.

0697 ➤
Minimize the carbon footprint. Remove six trees to make way for the cabin. Mill the trees into lining boards with a mobile milling machine brought on site. Season the lining boards on site.

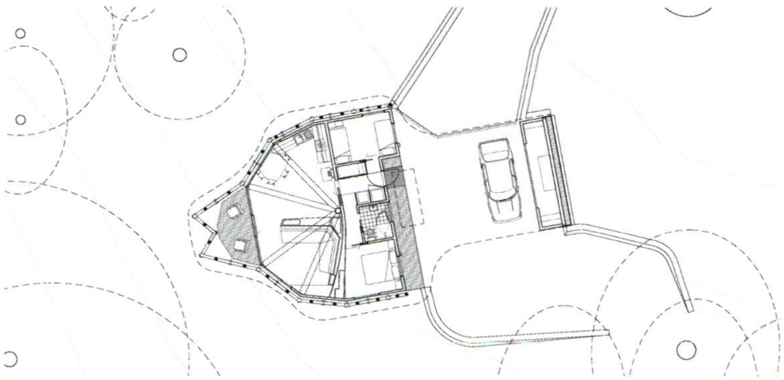

➤ 0698
Ensure additional lining panels and floor boards are sourced from plantation timber.

0699 ➤
Harvest the rainwater and store in tanks.

➤ 0700
Investigate the ecological drivers of a region – the study of the relationship between organisms (trees) and their environment has driven the formal and technical design response in this project. Michael Hensel and Achim Menges have coined the term "morpho-ecology," which relates "a biological paradigm ... with issues of higher level functionality and performance capacity."

Peter Kuczia

Osningstraße 34
49082 Osnabrück, Germany
Tel.: +49 163 929 50 50
www.kuczia.com

0701

The best and least expensive method of developing sustainably is, of course, not to build, which is neither satisfactory for future home owners nor for myself as architect. The second best solution is to create only as much built space as is really required. Economical layout and compact shape save resources, energy and money.

0702

When possible, reuse existing building substance. Spaces with old or vintage construction elements have particular spirit and charisma.

0703 ➤
When it comes to chemical-based coverings, a little goes a long way. Sometimes a few accents are all it takes to make a lasting color impression.

0704
Use local, natural materials such as wood, e.g. in the form of timber cladding for facades.

0705
Many roofs can be greened. Not only good for microclimate, green roofs insulate and protect the roofing materials from UV rays and extreme temperature fluctuation.

◄ 0706
The sun is the most important source of energy on Earth. Make use of it in every possible form, e.g. for passive heat by creating winter gardens...

0707 ►
... or by installing solar heating panels for hot water, heating, or even for cooling (also possible).

0708 ▼

Plenty of natural sunlight saves on energy required for lighting, and it is good for your psyche.

0709 ▲

Loam has a very low embodied energy. Use it for the walls inside. It collects surplus of humidity from the air and releases it when the interior is too dry.

◄ 0710

Reuse building elements: in this way you can conserve resources, reduce waste and save money.

PopovBass Architects

Level 3, 2 Glen Street
Milsons Point, NSW 2061, Australia
Tel.: +61 2 9955 5604
www.popovbass.com.au

"Our aspiration is to leave the world in a better state than when we found it."
Brian Bass on sustainable design

0711 ➤
An architectural language that respects the site.

0712
Light-filled open spaces that give joy to its users.

0713
Economic construction methods including the use of modular components and pre-fabricated construction.

0714
Adaptation of regional architectural typologies, such as "the verandah," to modern planning (this second skin wrapping around the house creates sun protection, privacy and frames views).

0715 ➤
Selection of sustainable materials. Sustainable materials do not only pertain to recycled and low carbon products. Sustainable also means low maintenance, robust and timeless, making the building last longer.

0716 ▼
Façade systems controlling views, sun and privacy.

0717 ▲
Cross flow ventilation.

0718 ▼
Orientation and creation of overhangs to control natural daylight.

0719 ▲
Low-energy lighting.

0720 ➤
Application of environmental technologies such as solar power, integrated heating systems, and rain water collection and recycling.

Prodesi|Domesi

Husitska 36
130 00 Prague 3, Czech Republic
Tel.: +420 283 853 424
www.prodesi.cz
www.domesi.cz

0721 ➤
A passive house doesn"t have to look like a science lab.

0722 ▲
We use the leftover cuttings from construction to create furniture.

◄ 0723
We always minimize the dimensions of a house.

0724
Our goal is to reduce the impact on the scenery.

0725
The interior of the house is furnished by local suppliers and finished by a local carpenter.

0726 ➤
To pursue the idea of environmentally conscious architecture, we avoid using exotic woods.

0727 ➤
A house in the countryside should give you the impression it has stood there since time immemorial.

➤ 0728
A modern wooden house does not have to be just a weekend house in the mountains. Wooden houses are also a part of the confident, clean, urban architecture of today.

0729

A huge terrace should stand next to the main and compact body of the house – we lose so much heat by biting out the building's bulk.

0730

Combining the traditional, the contemporary and the surroundings should be the way of thinking in modern architecture.

R&Sie(n)

rsie@new-territories.com
www.new-territories.com
http://www.new-territories.com/blog

0732
Dustyrelief / B_mu

1. Random relief calculated by particles and pixelisation for a pure grey ectoplasm under the lightning grey sky of Bangkok.
2. Collecting the dust (particles of carbon monoxide) of the city by an aluminium envelop and electrostatics system.
3. Exacerbating the skyzo climate between interior (white cube and labyrinth in an Euclidian geometry) and exterior (dust relief on topologic geometry).

0731
Aqua Alta 2.0
Water bar pumping directly the polluted, disgusting water of the Laguna for the French Pavilion, on a Vaporetto, for sharing substances and psycho-physiological repulsion.

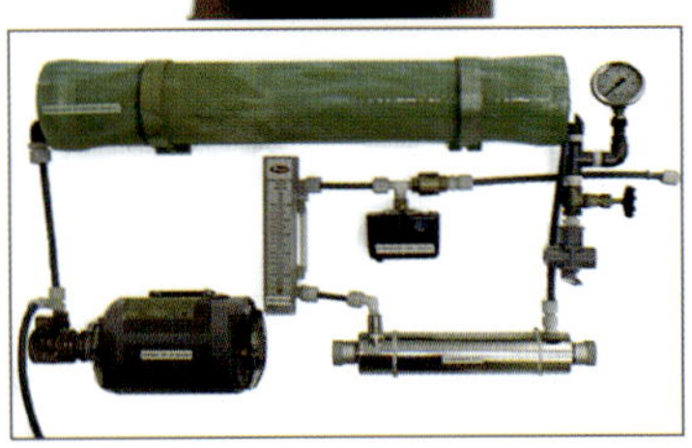

0733
heShotmeDown
Design of a multi-purposes house, including private house, dancing center, shop, restaurant, children museum...

◄ 0734 ▼

i'mlostinParis

1. Design of a private laboratory as duck blind cabana.
2. 1,200 hydroponics ferns.
3. 300 glass beakers "blowing" components for bacterial culture; production of *Rhizobium* bacteria to increase the nitrogenize percent without chemical manure; extra light through refraction.
4. Collecting raining for watering plants with individual mechanical drop by drop system.

0735 ▼

Hypnosischamber

Experiment of hypnosis individual cession in the research and exhibition "I've heard about."

1. Enter in a "heterotopian" cognitive room.
2. Let you dive secondly in a "wake up dream," filled by vocal information on "I've heard about" urbanism.
3. Feel yourself as a nerve termination inside the organic and self-determination growing structure.
4. Keep the speculation and experiment alive as a possibility of transformation of your own biotope.

◄ 0736

Hybridmuscle

Construction of a work and exhibition space that would generate its own electricity and thus be "unplugged" from the power grid. Private commission.

0737 ➤

Olzweg

Design of a museum for experimental architecture. The courtyard of Frac is smeared and aggregated of glass stick in order to generate a gluing, a smearing of the existing building as a potential of a "body without organ" (a "going to be done" and unachieved process of construction), and inside the thickness of the glass a labyrinth walkway and accessibilities. A scattering script is written to develop the aggregation.

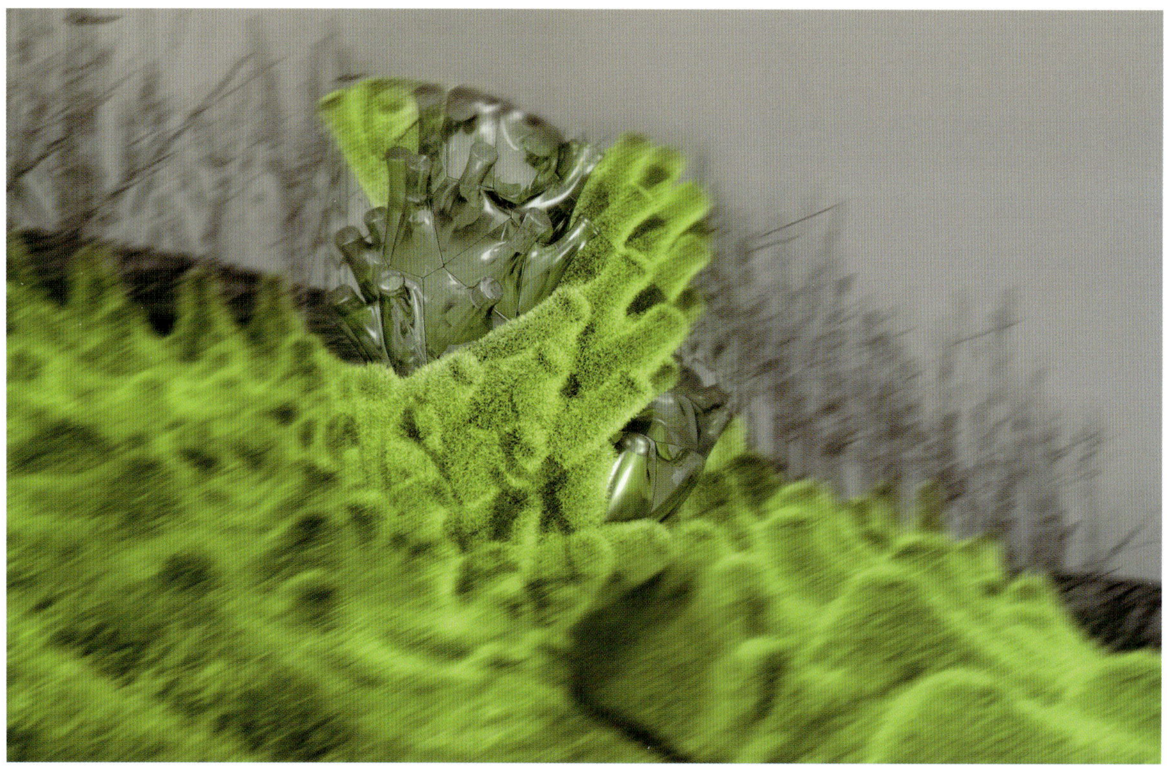

0738 ➤

symbiosis'Hood

How to blur the boundaries between two properties (as a Proudhonism request – property is theft !)

0739

theBuildingWhichNeverDies

Construction of a laboratory of light to test both "the dark adaptation" to reduce urban light pollution and "the melatonin effect" with Oled lamp to test the human metabolism circadian cycle and the UV pathologies from the Ozone weakness evolution.

0740

waterFlux

1. Digitization of the envelope of a traditional habitat.
2. Scooping out hollows within this volume as if it were an ice cavity, but in full wood by a five-axes drill machine.
3. Water states and flows vary according to the seasons.
4. Exacerbation of the winter climate by artificial snow (17,657 cu ft).

Ray Kappe

715 Brooktree Road
Pacific Palisades, CA 90272, USA
Tel.: +1 310 459 7791
www.kappedu.com

0741 ➤
Living Homes is a company specializing in prefabricated homes that uses a steel structure allowing for a multitude of different layouts and finishes.

0742
The firm seeks to create smart buildings based on passive designer systems, such as a natural heat-monitoring system harnessing the house's orientation, thermal mass, etc. In addition, it also incorporates some active systems, such as photovoltaic panels.

0743
Energy savings amounting to more than 36% of the standard ratings have been made thanks to the measures implemented to achieve a reduction of the impact on the environment, air quality inside the building, savings in energy made from thermal insulation, solar protection, and renewable energy systems, for which it has earned the category of LEED Gold rating.

0744

The association of the manufacturer with recycling companies will enable 76% of the materials used in the construction and assembly of the building to be reused when it reaches the end of its useful life.

0745

The house will therefore be dismantled instead of being demolished, which generates far more waste.

0746

Amongst its objectives, the firm seeks to reduce the environmental impact, work with natural materials and preserve and reuse natural resources.

0747

The prefabricated modules have been mounted on top of reinforced concrete blocks of cement, which are good thermal mass materials.

0748

Rochedale House is a perfect example of integration of architecture and mass construction. The architectural firm is strongly committed to the ideals of energy efficiency and environmental responsibility.

0749

Since it is a prefabricated building, the structure of this house can be erected in just three days. Apart from this new assembly system, the levels of environmental quality achieved have been recognized by the LEED rating system.

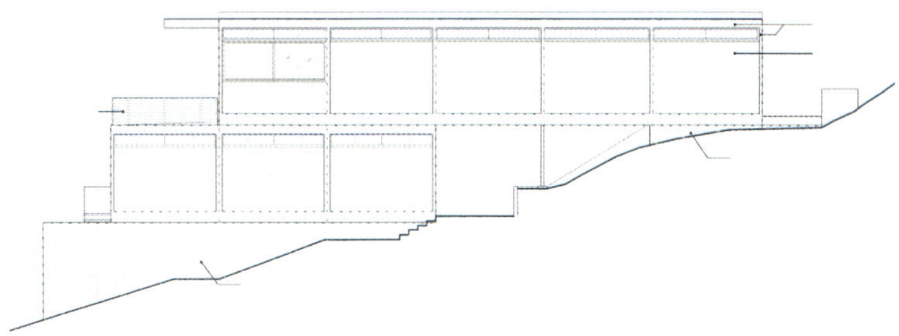

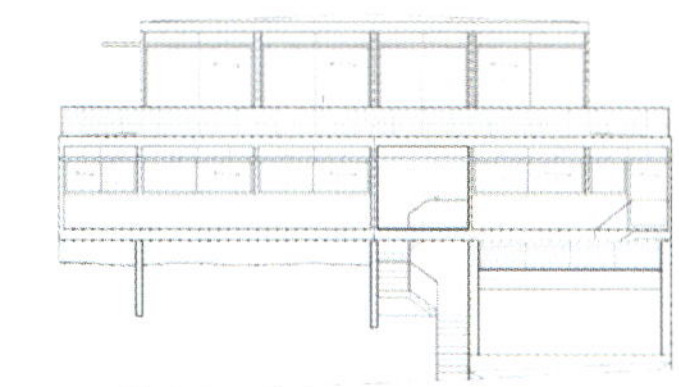

0750

The sections show the interior spaces of the house and the different levels. The elevations present openings and windows with low-emission glass and certified wood cladding.

Resolution: 4 Architecture

150 West 28th Street, Suite 1902
New York, NY 10001, USA
Tel.: +1 212 675 9266
www.re4a.com

0751 ➤
This prefabricated house combination was designed as the best solution for a three-bedroom, two-bathroom house.

0752 ➤
The sustainability of this home is determined by a number of features: the company that manufactured the prefabricated pieces has its own waste management and material recycling programs.

◄ 0753
The photovoltaics panels on the roof and the use of geothermal energy turn the house into a power plant that also supplies the local grid daily.

0754

The main volume is protected by warm-hued cedarwood, while another part of the exterior is covered in cement.

0755

Prefab construction requires shorter work times, which lessens the environmental impact on the site. Plantings do not include non-native varieties, the lawn are is limited, and drought-resistant plants have been used.

0756

This orientation offers the house the maximum hours of light. Openings are larger on the south façade, where there is also a large deck and glass-encased porch.

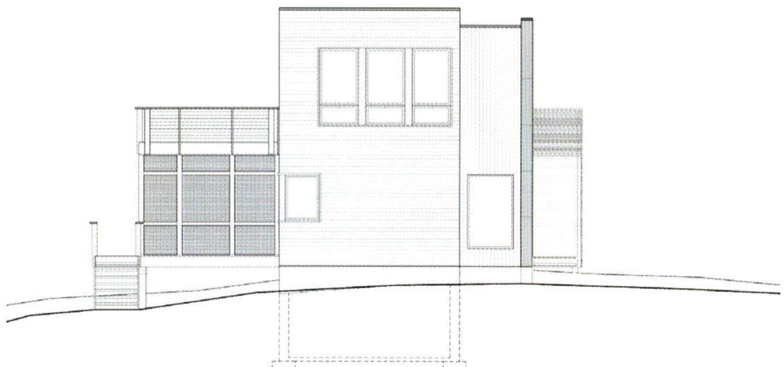

0757

The kitchen is at the heart of the upper level and separates the living area from the dining area and the bedroom. The electricity used comes exclusively from photovoltaic panels and geothermal energy.

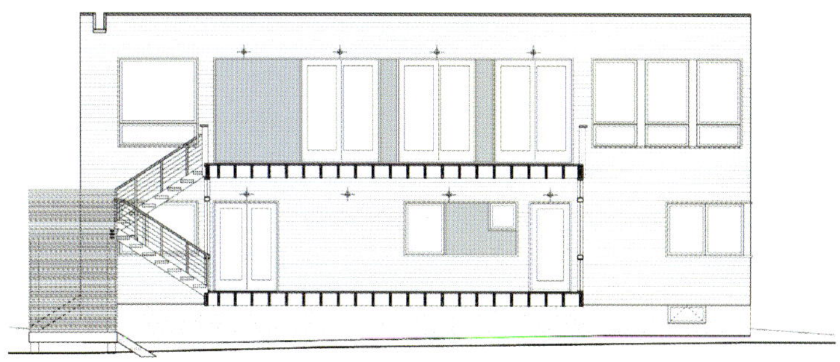

0758

A concrete base was built on which factory-made modules were positioned. The house is off-grid; any electricity required is produced by photovoltaic panels.

◄ 0759
This prefabricated house is located in a small town in the state of Vermont. Nearby is a state park crossed by the West River and Hamilton Falls. Prefabricated houses involve less impact on the land and lower CO_2 emissions as building times are shorter.

0760 ▼
Radiant floor heating keeps the house warm in the coldest months. Different types of materials were used: recyclable materials, such as the corrugated-metal cladding, and other natural materials, such as cedar, used on the exterior and the bamboo flooring inside the house.

> <

Rintala Eggertsson Architects

Stavangergata 46a
0467 Oslo, Norway
Tel.: +47 22230006
www.rintalaeggertsson.com

0761

Narrative

Buildings are not monuments for architects, but tools of communication between the inhabitants and the outside world. It is therefore an important part of a design task to communicate a story, and connect people with one another. Buildings are like language – they describe our understanding and place in the universe.

0762

Physical engagement

Buildings are extensions to our bodies as shields for protection and sensorial membranes. There will always be a physical connection which should activate our bodies and sensitivity towards the environment.

0764

Compact living

Compact living is good for the wallet and the environment, as it reduces the need of building materials, saves construction time, costs and, consequently, the CO_2 footprint.

0763

Energy saving

Saving building volume is an efficient way to save energy for heating or cooling down the living spaces, which in turn reduces the negative impact on the ecosphere.

◄ 0765

Four dimensions

Understanding the environment is to recognize time as the 4th spatial dimension, which gives room for all kinds of changes to a given situation. In an age of global transformation, climatic, demographic, and geo-political changes have to be taken into account.

0766 ►

Anchoring

Most of our physical environment has been occupied by other human beings in past history, for cultivation, breeding animals or hunting. Preserving a link to these patterns of the past is saving valuable information about the cultural landscape for future generations.

0767 ▲

Site specific

The use of local building materials is an obvious way to establish a visual connection with the surroundings. However, beyond the visual, there is also an important connection to local building traditions which have sustained people in climatically harsh areas around the world for millenniums.

◄ 0768

Orientation

In critical climatic situations, directing the building towards a specific cardinal direction can reduce the need for external heating and air-conditioning to a minimum.

◄ 0769

Social awareness

Sensitivity towards the physical environment is not the only way to make beautiful buildings. Awareness of social factors is important in order to achieve a well working relationship between a built structure and the group of people who are going to use it.

◄ 0770

Thermal mass

Indigenous people have always taken into account the physical features of building materials when shaping their surroundings. One important feature is thermal mass, which differs from one material to the other and makes it possible to establish a good microclimate in a building.

Rob Paulus Architects

990 E. 17th St., Suite 100
Tucson, AZ 85719, USA
Tel.: +1 520 624 9805
www.robpaulus.com

0771 ➤
Location efficiency
Location, location, location - location is key to any successful business, but, as it turns out, an urban location also has the advantage of being a more efficient way to live and work. Transit-oriented urban density provides substantial savings in energy efficiency, with the added benefit of direct exposure to the creativity of living within an urban setting.

© Liam Frederick

© Ross Cooperthwaite

0772
Responsible density
Responsible density is vital to creating walkable, mixed use cities. Not only is this a good thing for the environment, but it also allows better chances for the financial success of a project while providing amenities and goods within a short distance of home or office.

0773
Reuse/Re-purpose
The most sustainable building is one you don't have to build. Re-purposing old structures with new uses gives new life and density to a community without using up as many precious resources. Everyone loves a good story, and authentic historic buildings come with their own tale, which can keep evolving and be in step with the new use of the structure.

0774 ➤
Be optimistic
A healthy dose of optimism is necessary to be able to think clearly to take on creating environments that respond to man and nature. We owe it to our children to be vigilant and create the best possible built environment for their future.

© Rob Paulus

© Ross Cooperthwaite

0775 ➤
Make it sexy
An important element of design that is not talked about enough is the notion of creating something that is both functional and delightful. In other words, creating something sexy that evokes both intellect and intuition. As complex as we humans are, there is also a simple, child like appreciation and gut reaction to our built environment that defines great design.

© Brad Wheeler

© Liam Frederick

0776

Loose fit

Buildings should be designed with simplicity and adaptability in mind to provide a loose fit to allow for future generations to retrofit and occupy the structures we design today.

0777

Passive first, then active

Building design needs to first acknowledge passive approaches before incorporating active technologies. The basic tenants of natural light and ventilation, as well as designing for the region and climate, are a solid starting point.

© Liam Frederick

© Brad Wheeler

0778

Healthy habitats

A naturally-based environment, with day lighting, fresh air and non-toxic materials, makes us happy and healthy and leads to a more productive lifestyle that is in tune with the daily and yearly cycles of nature.

© Ross Cooperthwaite

© Brad Wheeler

0779

Water

Water is the new oil. Almost one-fifth of the world population lives in areas of water scarcity. All design should acknowledge water conservation and use this precious resource for inspiration in the creation of buildings, landscapes and cities.

0780

Humanistic approach

Good design must embrace our existence on this fragile planet we call home and acknowledge our connection to our natural environment to live in balance with Mother Nature.

Rongen Architekten GmbH

Propsteigasse 2
41849 Wassenberg, Germany
Tel.: +49 24 32 30 94

Glockengasse 31
99084 Erfurt, Germany
Tel.: +49 36 15 61 57 70
www.rongen-architekten.de

0782

Sustainable architecture is part of the nature. Passive House Standard is a worldwide-acknowledged standard for energy-saving building. The amount of energy consumption for heating and cooling is around 20% of the amount of a conventionally-built building, which is the actual standard for new buildings in Germany.

0781

Sustainable building also means to take into account the urban environment. The design does not stop in detail.

0783

Passive houses offers its residents all the way best living comfort. Its pleasantly warm in cool winter and pleasantly cool in hot summer. Architecture should always be clean and clear and thereby necessarily true.

0784

Overhanging floors and balconies can replace movable sun protection and thereby further increase the energy efficience.

0785

Sustainable building also means to take nature into account. Passive houses save energy resources, and contribute to reduce CO_2 emission into the atmosphere and to protect climate. For our Mother Earth there are no spare parts.

0786 ➤
Photovoltaic panels can replace sun protection and produce green power concurrently.

0787 ➤
Sustainable building also means to take into account the site place to build with the nature.

0788 ➤
The design with all its details and also the building construction should always be done very neat and tidy.

><

0789 ➤
Sustainable building also means to use renewable building materials.

0790 ➤
Sustainable building also means to take into account space saving building.

SAAI. Sustainable Architecture Advisors International

SAAI has offices in eight countries (UK, Australia, China, Costa Rica, Thailand, Greece, Mexico and Spain)
www.saa-i.com

0791

Use of skylights to improve daylight quality

Compact buildings and deep plans can compromise daylight availability due to the excessive distance from windows to the central core. This is counteracted by the use of skylights, which can provide a more homogeneous daylight distribution, avoiding sharp contrasts and reducing the need for artificial light.

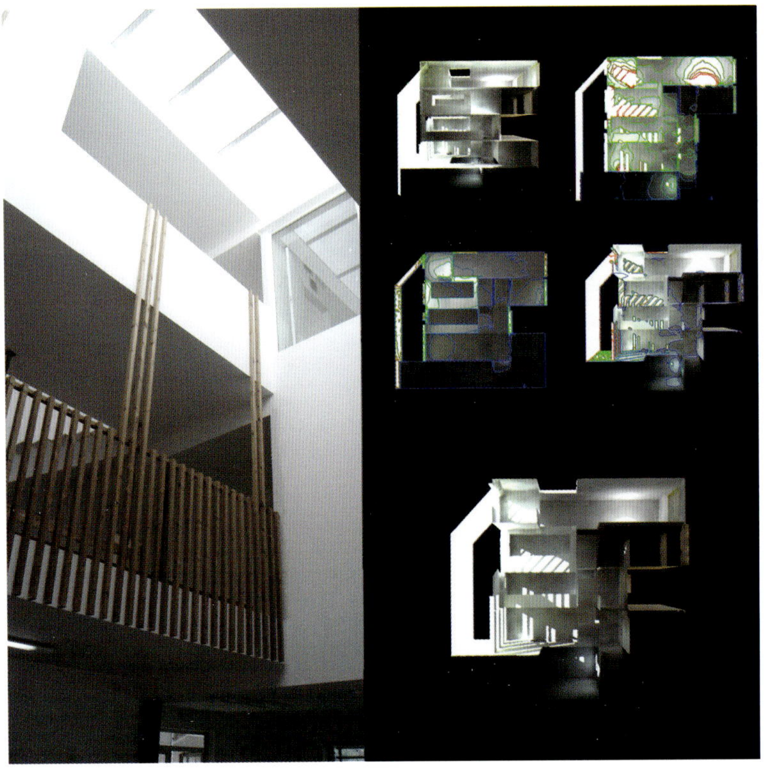

0792

Transitional spaces

The indoors-to-outdoors transition can be softened with the use of buffer zones, which have an undefined character but a great potential for casual usage. In this cultural center located in northwest Spain a timber structure mitigates the effect of solar radiation during the warm season while allowing useful gains in winter.

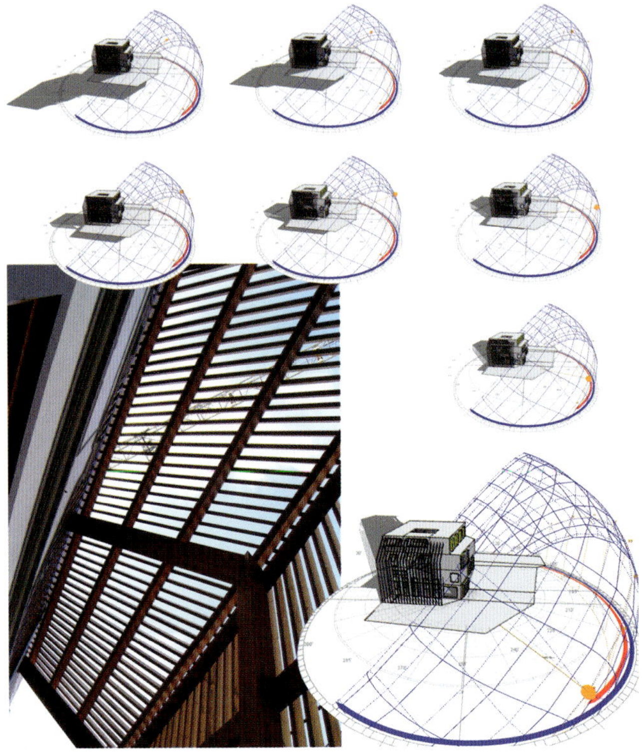

0793

Ventilation

Buoyancy-driven ventilation is based on the different rate of air pressure reduction to different temperatures, since air pressure decreases with height, and warm air is less dense. This allows incoming bottom level and outgoing upper level air flows to be enhanced when indoor temperature is warmer than the outdoor.

0794

Materials: timber

As a natural material, and provided its responsible sourcing, timber has a relatively low environmental impact. In this cultural center, the potential of timber to provide architectural expression has been explored in various ways. Its different configurations respond to the specific needs of each orientation and the functions behind the façade.

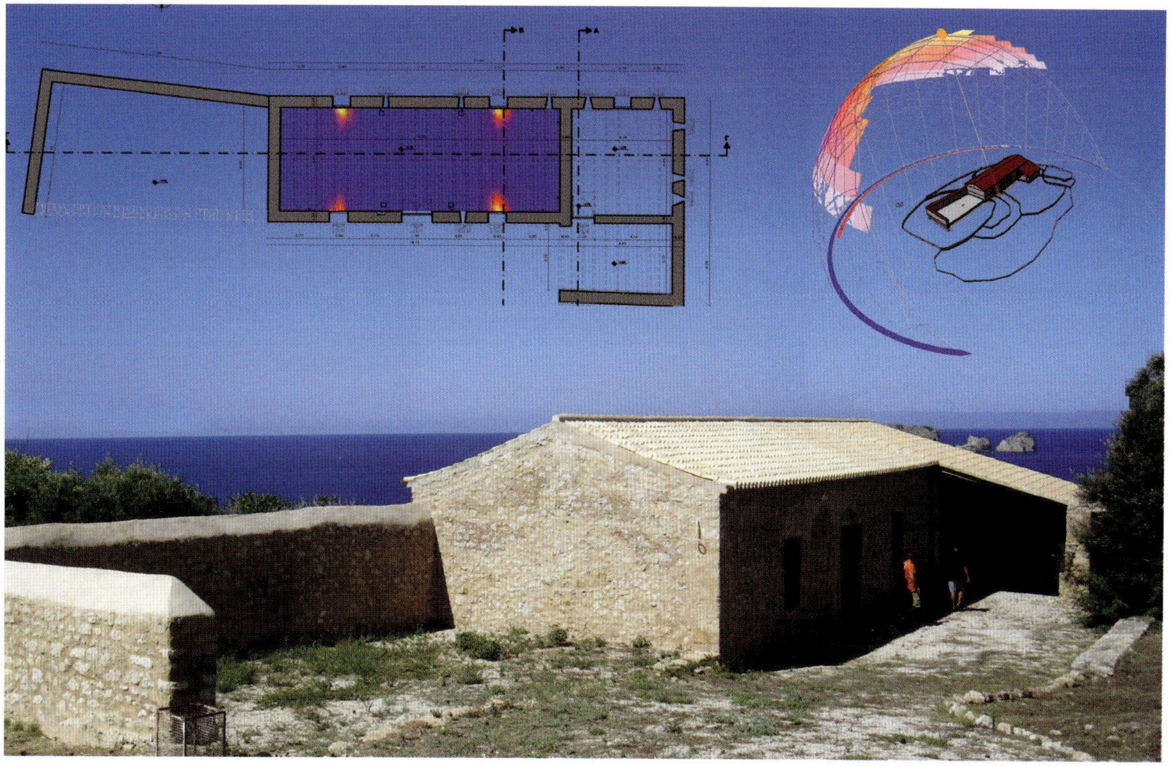

"All year round residence" occupancy scenario simulation results for the three spaces (cell, living room, bedroom)

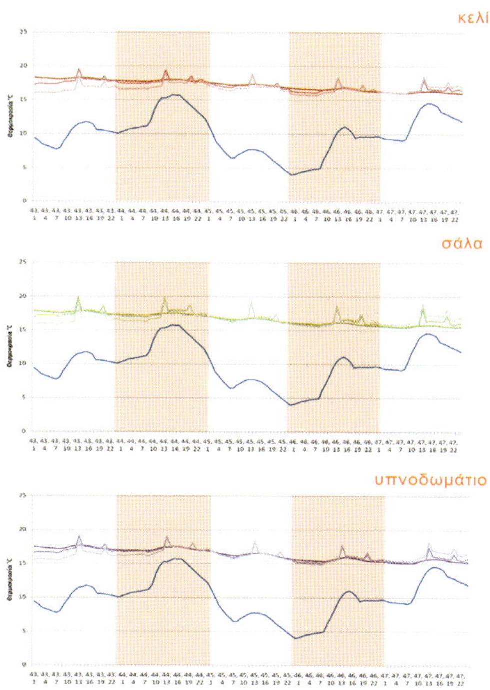

0795

Transitional spaces

In the Museum of Underwater Antiquities of Pylos in Greece, a transitional space allows visual adaptation of the visitors.

0796

Materials: stone

Heavy mass stone walls are ideal for Mediterranean climate as it ensures stable temperatures. Moreover, stone is an easy-to-find building material in most places, as it was the case of this restoration project in Paros, Greece.

0797 ➤

Local vernacular

Application of concepts from the Greek vernacular architecture has been applied on the design of this resort in Paros island. Given its prevailing summer use, heavy construction is optimal to provide stable internal temperature, with small openings for less solar gains and visual comfort, and white roofs, shading elements, and village-like configuration to allow ventilation.

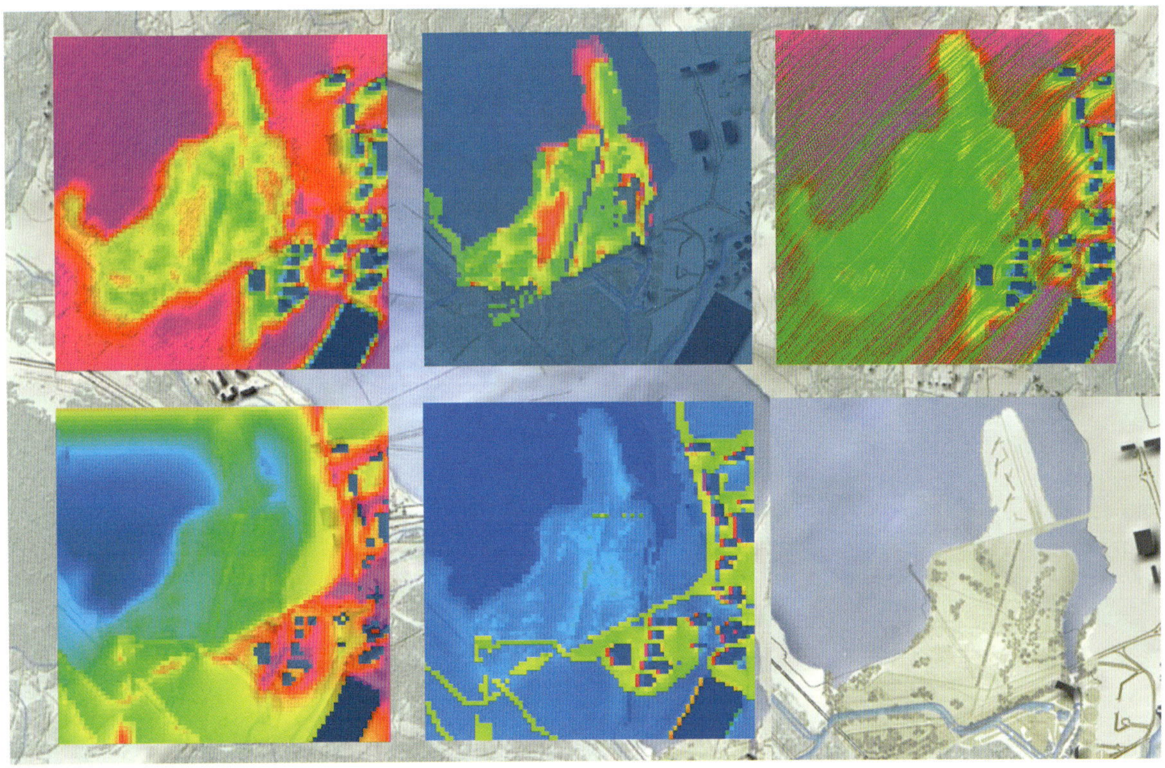

◄ 0798

Sustainable landscapes

Understanding of the elements that trigger and influence natural processes is essential to ensure the correct evolution of the place. The regeneration project of an old quarry in northwest Spain started with a detailed study of climatic and microclimatic factors, including prevailing winds, deposition ratio, thermal flows and soil properties.

0799 ➤

Local vernacular

Elements from vernacular have been also applied to this housing project in Porto Rafti, Greece. The small size of the openings and the carefully designed shading devices respond to the specific characteristics of the Greek bright daylight. A projected overhang is a good shading solution for South orientation in seasonal climates, as it allows sun penetration in winter when the angle is lower.

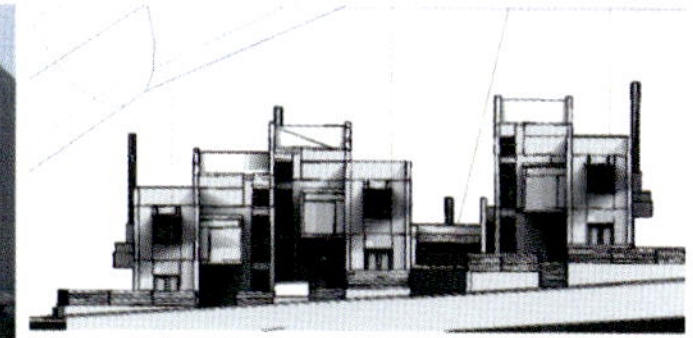

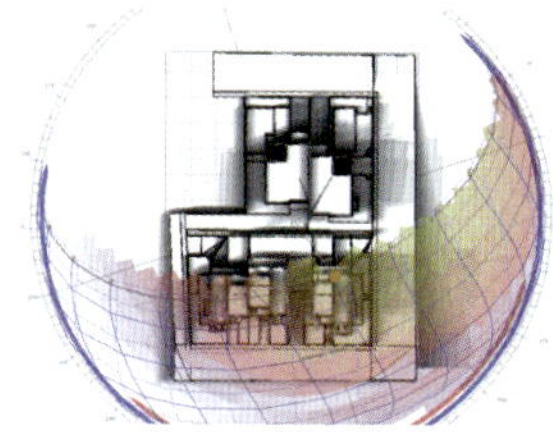

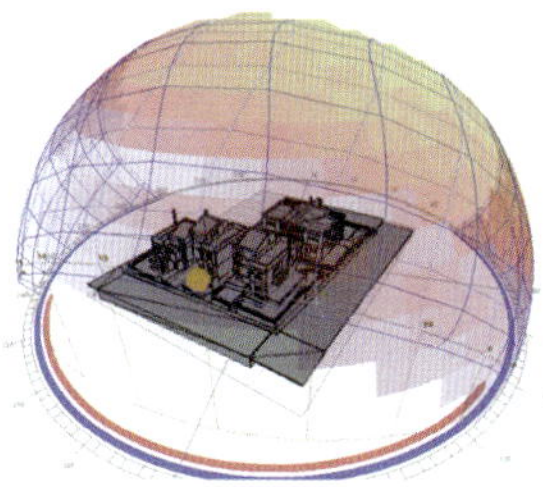

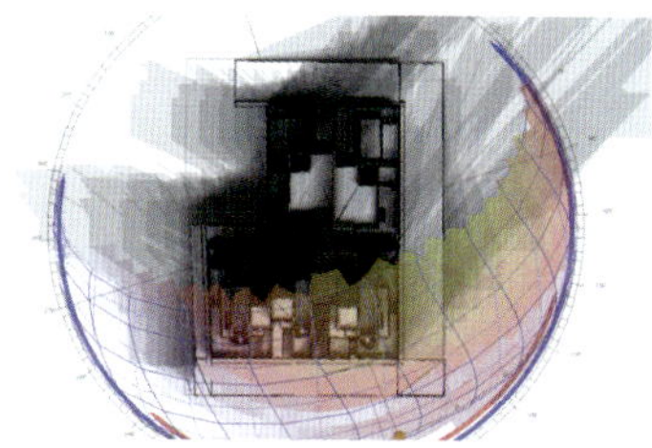

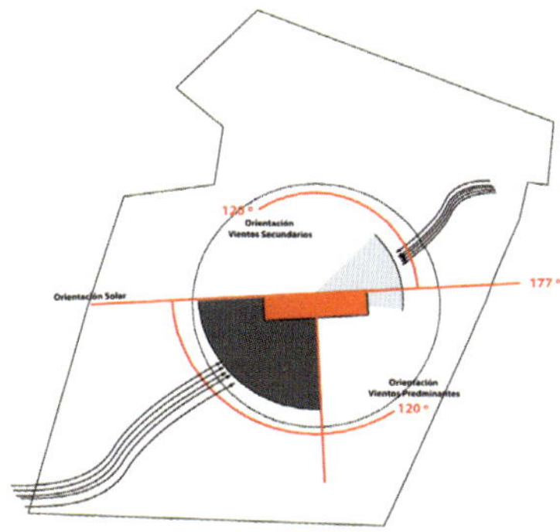

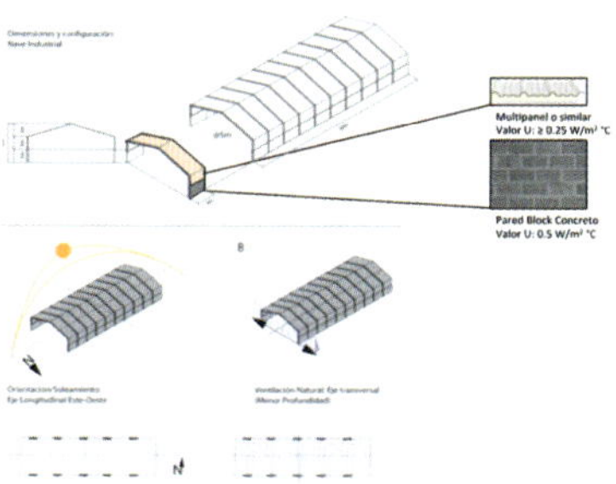

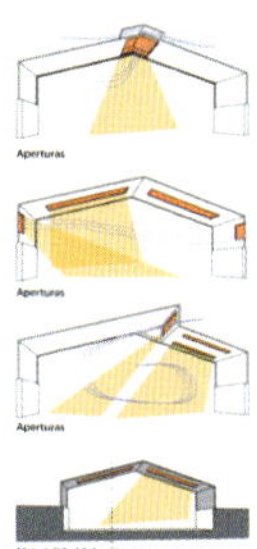

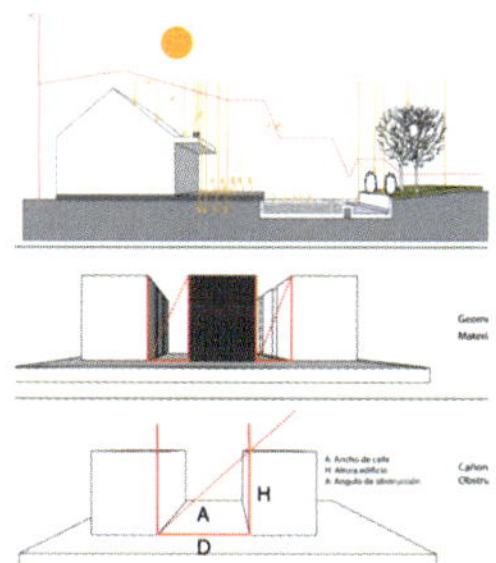

0800 ▲

Wind corridors

In this small community near Bangkok, Thailand, permeability through fragmentation was the key strategy to allow sufficient air movement in and around buildings. In warm and humid climates, ventilation becomes a fundamental strategy to achieve comfort.

Samyn and Partners, Architects & Engineers

Chée/Stwg op Waterloo,
1537 B-1180 Brussels, Belgium
Tel.: +32 2 374 90 60
www.samynandpartners.be

0801 ➤
Care first for the sun path – its trajectory rhythms space hour after hour, day after day. Sun penetrates through east and west openings and through the glazed roof to light the cotton fabric diffusing daylight in the classrooms of the Architecture School of Lubumbashi. Termitarium-like structural form cares for the natural ventilation and thermal comfort.

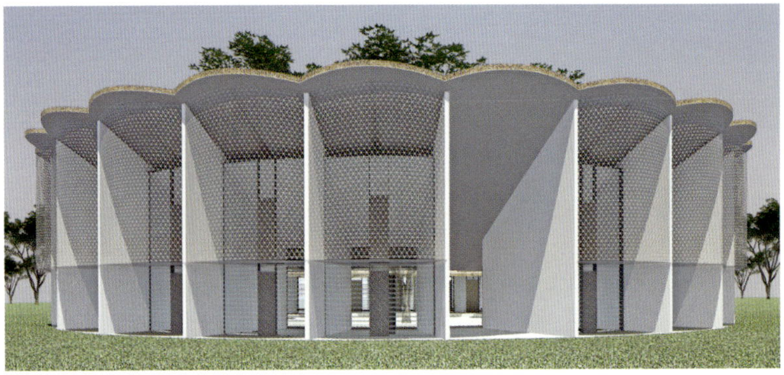

0802 ➤
Care for dimensions and quotations. Their force proportions, rhythms and orders of magnitude are to architecture what "music theory" is to music. Simple volumes and window dimensions rhythm the campus of the Sans Souci Psychiatric Hospital.

◄ 0803
Analyze the *genius loci* – it fosters or tempers the great aspirations of the sponsor and feeds your quest. Cultural diversity and unity of Europe are expressed through the patchwork façade of the new European Union Council headquarters, made of reused oak windows from all its region. The project is anchored in an historical building and in Brussels city pattern.

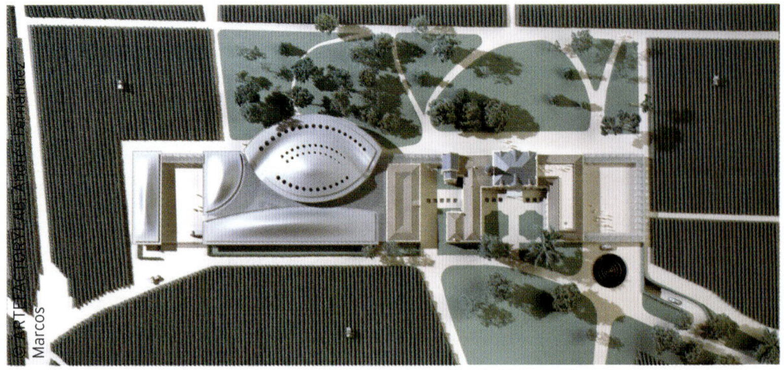

0804

Realize that geometry is the most powerful tool of the architect, and drawing is its vector. At Château Cheval Blanc wiey in Saint-Émilion, the conical stainless steel tanks are arranged like organ pipes. Their perforated extensions support the wooden roof shell and filters day light, while providing safe access to the tanks tops (preliminary design).

0805

Think about space, the voids between solids, as it is the only matter specific to architecture. A large open space for the public is sheltered by the Alibaba headquarters in Shenzhen, in contrast to the classical artificial commercial compound so common in Asia (competition entry).

0806

Study the art of construction – it disciplines the conceptual dream. Invite artists to the game. The former Eastman Institute in Brussels is enlarged to house the future Museum for European History. The colorful extension by artist Georges Meurant expresses youth and interculturality. The exhibition spaces are all naturally lit with three sets of mirrors (competition entry).

© Polygon Graphics cvba, Stijn Stragier

0807 ▲

Accept that matter dictates form. The large wicker huts at the Ngozi cultural center in Burundi are suspended to a knitted aramide net spanning between the old eucalyptus trees. This allows for large volumes, as their structures aren't any more in compression, avoiding buckling. (design stage).

0808 ▼

Ask for lightness, as the art of engineering is to reduce material consumption. The canopy of the Leuven train station is designed for ultra lightness while providing a gently protected space.

© Andrés Fernández Marcos

0809 ▲

Design lovable spaces - they will be loved. A small nursery for a residential neighborhood in Brussels got its rounded plan from the gentle curved movements the teachers used to explain the cocoon atmosphere they were looking for (on hold).

© Jan de Coninck, Marie-Françoise Plissart

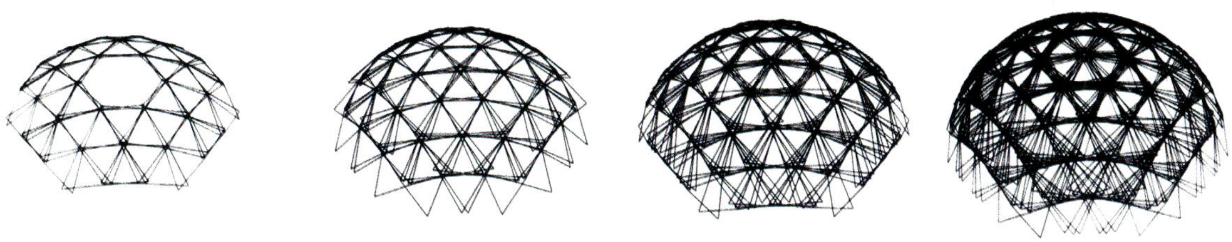
© Samyn and Partners, Architects & Engineers

0810 ►

Dream, think and realize. This dome is the result of the repetitive unfolding of the equilateral triangles within the central regular hexagon.

Sander Architects, LLC

2434 Lincoln Blvd.
Venice, CA 90291, USA
Tel.: +1 310 822 0300
www.sander-architects.com

0811 ▲
Horizontal shade fins protect the south-facing translucent wall from solar infiltration in summer months while allowing plenty of natural daylight. In winter, the lower angle of the sun allows more solar penetration and more natural heating of the space. The wall is constructed with multi-cell translucent material that has twice the R-value of insulated glass and provides excellent insulation.

0812 ►
Eco-friendly recycled blue jean insulation is layered over a thin "space blanket" of foil insulation to double the normal R-value of the walls and roof. This allows the house to be heated or cooled with less energy. In this room we exposed the blue jean insulation, keeping it in place with a fine wire mesh, so that it doubles as an acoustical layer.

0813 ►
A reflecting pool provides natural cooling. Inside, high windows on the far wall allow rising hot air to escape. This creates a natural convection that sucks the air in from an awning window at pool level: air passing across the pool is naturally cooled, it enters through the low poolside window and passes through the house lowering temperatures inside.

0814 ►
Recycled steel frames provide the structure for our trademark Hybrid House: our "part prefab, all custom" building style uses warehouse frames as the basic structure and then completes the building with standard construction techniques. This way waste is reduced, costs are lower and construction time is shorter.

0815 ▲
Using translucent materials for interior partitions allows light to penetrate to all areas of the house. This way, the house is lit using natural light rather than electric light. Daylight spaces not only use less energy – they have been shown to have a positive effect on mood.

0816

Careful siting of a building allows existing landscape features to remain undisturbed and can provide an interesting design feature. In this case, the external entrance stair to the house is situated to preserve three 100-ft Beech trees on the property. The stairs then cantilever out to capture a view of a seasonal stream before returning to the front door of the house.

0817

This recycled aluminum staircase is a prime example of using a client's skill set to enhance their home. In this case the client, a lighting designer, had access to a metal fab shop used for building lighting grids and they fabricated the staircase using our design. The recycled metal pulls material out of the waste stream and repurposes it in an interesting way.

0818

An exterior skin made of recycled steel panels, manufactured with fewer alloys to reduce impact on the environment, are installed in a staggered pattern that echoes the rocks of the distant butte. Time will rust the metal, increasing the resemblance and avoiding the need for costly maintenance.

0819

Reusing old structures preserves history and provides an eco-friendly option to creating a new building. In this case, a 300-year-old cotton storage warehouse becomes residences for a group of scientists. Ancient stone walls were all that remained of the warehouse so the firm inserted modern structure using local materials and recycled steel frames.

0820

The double-height entry staircase in this project captures daylight and fresh air as well as providing a heat chimney for hot air to ascend through the house and escape through vents in the roof. Exposed recycled structural steel creates a sculptural entrance that combines functionality with drama.

Sau, Taller d'Arquitectura S. L.

Paseo García Faria 21-23, bajos
08005, Barcelona, Spain
Tel.: +34 93 308 6551
www.sausl.com
sautallerarquitectura.blogspot.com

0821 ➤
Can Guetes walkway in Ripoll
Collective memory and nature. Recovering the historic identity of a site with an industrial past while integrating it into the natural landscape is compatible.

0822 ▼
Train depot in Ribes de Freser
Designing with light, reflections and textures of the environment makes it possible to integrate large volumes into organic and delicate landscapes.

0823 ▼
Colonized Fields in Kirchheim
Architecture as an open system. Architecture should be capable of resolving the current needs using the minimum resources. The system can be enlarged or reduced without a trace to meet new needs.

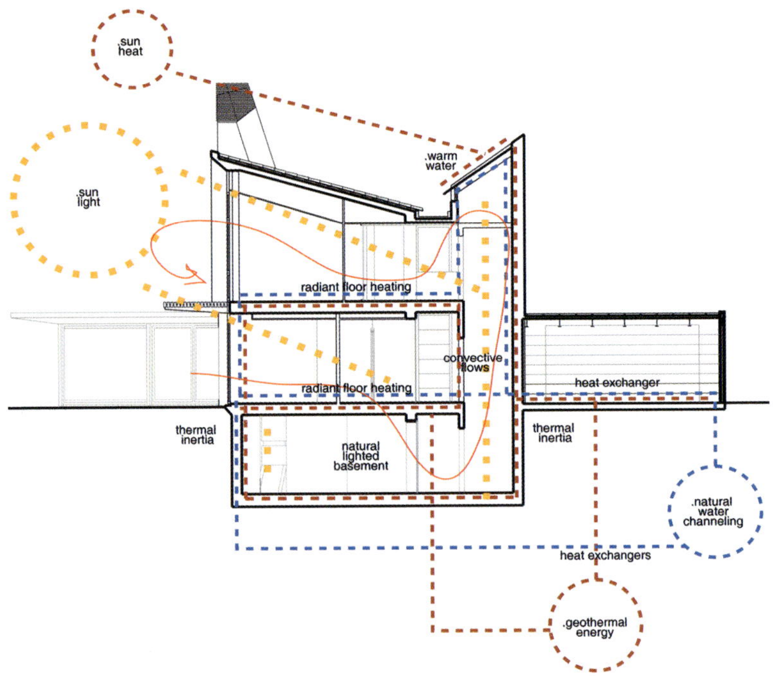

0824 ▲
Roser Square in Sant Joan de les Abadesses
Minimum physical intervention. At times, making an existing scenario accessible is sufficient; users will take charge of the rest.

0825 ➤
Cases de l'estació in Sant Joan de les Abadesses (with the collaboration of architect Agustí Vilà)
The city, a changing system in continuous evolution. Town planning, studying and designing the city to be in force throughout its evolution, at a social and energetic level.

© Adrià Goula

0826 ▲

La Cabanya kindergarten in Torelló

Lights, textures and scale. Transfer the characteristics of the exterior and filtrating energy to an interior space to achieve spatial sense of the former and the living conditions of the latter.

0827 ➤

Xemeneia House in Torelló

Integrate architecture, understood as an energy system, into the environment and generating exchange flows. Makeuse of the existing potential as key to come closer to energy self-sufficiency.

0828
Wooden table
Having knowledge of the mechanical capacities of the materials and using them transparently is a fundamental tool to optimize resources.

0829
La Cabanya kindergarten in Torelló
Permeable architecture. Interactive architecture. Architecture that lets the environment and light penetrate the interior. Architecture that relates with people. Architecture that relates people with the landscape.

0830
Train depot in Ribes de Freser
Reversible systems. Energy collector integrated into the landscape during the day. At night, an architectural landmark that lights the project area by removing the need for additional systems.

Schlyter / Gezelius Arkitektkontor AB

Brännkyrkagatan 91
118 23 Stockholm, Sweden
Tel.: +46 0 708 18 54 35
www.schlytergezelius.se

0832 ▼

Use small local contractors and carpentry shops

Digital tools were used to design a handcrafted building by updating local building crafts with today´s digital manufacturing techniques and using local materials, a local carpenter shop and a local contractor. Use digital tools to calculate the use of building material in order to create a minimum of waste. All that was left for me as a keepsake was a small 6-in piece of façade panel!

0831 ▲

Use the conditions of the site with respect, and make as little impact as possible

This house was placed for optimal shelter from the wind and to obtain the best balance of sunlight to increase inflow of the sun and decrease energy losses of wind. No stone was blown up and no trees were felled. Don't forget the undercurrents of the water flow. Work with the natural conditions not against them!

◄ 0833

Integrate with what was there before

Memories in the ground and in people's minds. In this project an old stone wall was incorporated in the building and was used to equalize heat over time.

0834 ▼

Use green materials

All elements in this project are made by custom-made wood. From a carpentry in the neighborhood. We were all very happy when it was finished. It was a house that smells good.

0835 ►

Adjust the shape of the project to as many site specific conditions as possible!

This building was shaped by the terrain, adjusted to rocks, trees, wind conditions – as many site-specific conditions as possible. The forms in the landscape giving rise to the form of the building. My 3-D software is a great help when designing site specific.

0836 ➤

Convert large non-use buildings

This old hay loft was converted into an art capsule, a box that was been pushed right through the old building. Two large windows in opposite directions give the studio light. In the interior, white-painted hardwood floors and white walls make the light reflect. The shelves are integrated with the windows for storage. New entrance doors and windows are built in the old facade.

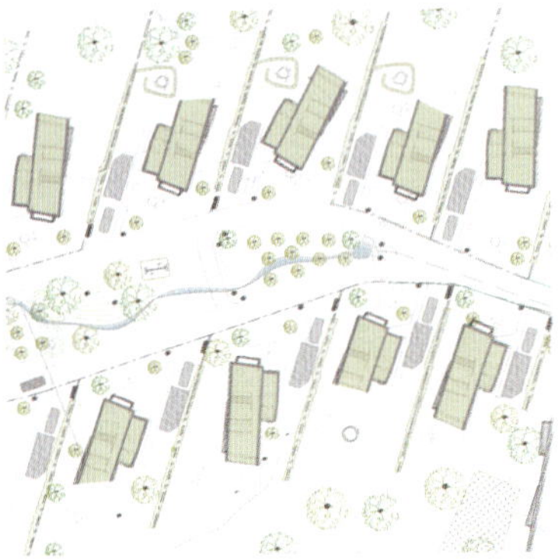

0837 ▼

Importance of details

By upgrading details and craftsmanship we can develop and enrich architecture. Details are the architectural alphabet, our building blocks. Without detail, there is no architecture.

◄ 0838

Reduce surface area

By reducing surface area and volume but not architecture we can achieve more architecture. We can use architecture to expand space, without expanding the physical space or physical volume.

◄ 0839

Use space to grow eatable plants and fruits

This garden was designed to supply fruit and vegetables for one family all year around. The garden contains free land growing space, a fruit orchard, an orangery and a greenhouse.

0840 ▼

What kind of society do you want to live in?

If we want to understand our global society, it is crucial to understand how our physical landscapes hang together. Because if we do not understand the physical landscape, how can we ever talk about a sustainable society?

Simon Winstanley Architects

190 King Street
Castle Douglas DG7 1DB, UK
Tel.: +44 01556 503826
www.candwarch.co.uk

0841 ➤
The house is located on a spectacular site overlooking the Solway Firth in southwest Scotland. The site is a steeply sloping, former quarry in a National Scenic Area which slopes in two directions from the quarry base that forms the only level ground access.

0842 ➤
The glazed pavilion is constructed with a steel frame and highly insulated timber infill panels clad in cedar and triple glazed windows.

◄ 0843
External walls, floor and roof are insulated to a high standard, and air infiltration is minimized. Triple glazed windows with warm edge spacer bars, thermally broken frames and inert gas filled to achieve a whole window U-value of 0.7W/m^{2}K.

0844 ➤
Heat pump using a borehole as the ground source for the underfloor heating and hot water system with a closed combustion wood burning stove as back up. Microgeneration of renewable electricity using roof mounted photovoltaic panels.

◄ 0845
Whole-house heat recovery ventilation system.

0846

The design intention is to create a contemporary single storey "long house" which is recessive in the landscape, sustainable in its construction, very low in energy consumption, and aiming for zero net emissions of carbon dioxide for all energy use in the house.

0847

The slope of the roof of the main living accommodation follows the slope of the hillside, with the roof of the rear accommodation meeting the main roof at a shallower angle to allow morning sunlight to penetrate the center of the house.

0848

The design uses lightweight but highly insulated steel and timber frame construction, clad in cedar weatherboarding allowed to weather to a natural silver grey color. The roof uses pre-weathered grey standing seam zinc. Windows and external doors are to be high performance timber, painted grey.

0849

The entrance to the house is sited on the northeast side of the house under the cover of the roof to provide shelter from the prevailing wind.

0850

It is proposed to achieve a zero-carbon house by using very high levels of insulation, minimizing air infiltration, heating using a ground source heat pump with solar hot water heating panels in the roof and generating electricity using a wind turbine.

SPGArchitects

127 West 26th Street, Suite 800
New York, NY 10001, USA
Tel.: +1 212 366 5500
www.spgarchitects.com

0851

Use green roofs

Not only are green roofs aesthetically pleasing, but they help cool the air through evapotranspiration, the natural process by which water is transferred from plants back into the atmosphere. Additionally, green roofs help provide cleaner air, are great insulators, and they require less maintenance than conventional roofs and have longer life than conventional roof.

0852

Build with renewable material

This small house located in Costa Rica is made distinctive by its soaring bamboo structure, a renewable building material that is economical and light-weight. The sculptural roof springs from the ground level, mimicking the rainforest''s canopy. This structure filters and shields the interior spaces from the sun and elements while providing views of the rainforest.

◄ 0853

Build as small as possible

This weekend house provides a dramatic rural haven in a very small footprint of 1,076 sq ft. The home's minimal material and resource demands make it a model for efficient living. The interior rooms look toward the views and visually expand the rooms to the landscape beyond.

0854 ▼

Use renewable energy source

The economics of photovoltaic HIP solar cells improves every year, especially when local tax and power company incentives are included in the calculations. This house is completely powered by solar energy for all of its domestic needs, including lighting, appliances, plumbing system, swimming pool pumps and other equipment.

◄ 0855

Use pervious paver materials

As an alternative to conventional concrete or stone walkways, the pavers used on the entry walk and the green roof allow the rainwater that hits these surfaces to percolate through the material into the ground. In turn, this allows the rainwater to reach the soil without contributing to soil erosion and allows these normally impermeable surfaces to contribute to the refilling of the local aquifer.

0856 ➤

Zone the house to save energy (program zoning)

Use layout that allows for certain zones to be shut down throughout the year when they are not needed. The energy demands of this house are decreased comparing to more conventional layouts. This house is heated and cooled by a geothermal system in three independent zones - the lower level or guest wing, the public living areas, and the master bedroom suite.

0857 ➤

Use energy efficient lighting

Using a combination of LED lighting, along with fluorescent, fiber-optic and low-voltage lighting, as well as solar-powered landscape lighting, greatly reduces the energy consumed in this house while still providing a beautiful atmosphere both indoors and out.

0858 ▲

Use white roof membrane

The highly reflective membrane roof provides significant energy savings as compared to conventional dark roof surfaces as it reflects the sun's rays and diminishes heat gain associated with the absorption of solar energy. In addition, it does not deteriorate due to exposure to the sun's ultraviolet rays.

0859

Use low-VOCs painting and wood finishes

To protect indoor air quality during the manufacturing process and in the home environment, use paints and wood finishes that are water-based and low in volatile organic compounds (VOCs) to prevent harmful out-gassing of toxic materials from harming the building occupants.

0860

Take advantage of natural ventilation

Maximizing cross ventilation in each room of this house has eliminated the need for air conditioning in this year-round tropical climate. Windows on at least two sides of each room allows the house to take advantage of natural convection caused by the cooling of the air as it moves up the hill on which the house sits.

Stuart Tanner Architects

City Mill
11 Morrison Street
Hobart, TAS 7000, Australia
Tel.: +61 3 6224 4377
www.stuarttannerarchitects.com.au

0861
Arm End House: humility and solitude, protection and openness.

0862
Goulburn Street Primary: place and context, linkage and unification. The new multi-purpose pavilion provides an alternate entry to the school, linking two large oak trees and revealing a broad vista of West Hobart toward the city.

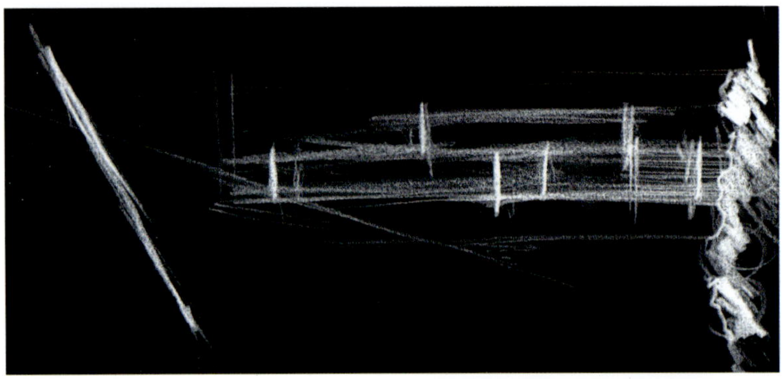

0863
The core principle of "building less" was fundamental to the project's sustainable characteristic. A humble presence on the site also lowered impact on the broader context.

0864
Millpond: shadow and light.

0865
Millpond: stillness and memory.

0866
Not only does this home offer unfettered visual connections to the flora and fauna flowing out of the park, but it protects that environment by minimizing its physical and environmental footprints.

0867
Pirates Bay House: structure and expression, perception of landscape.

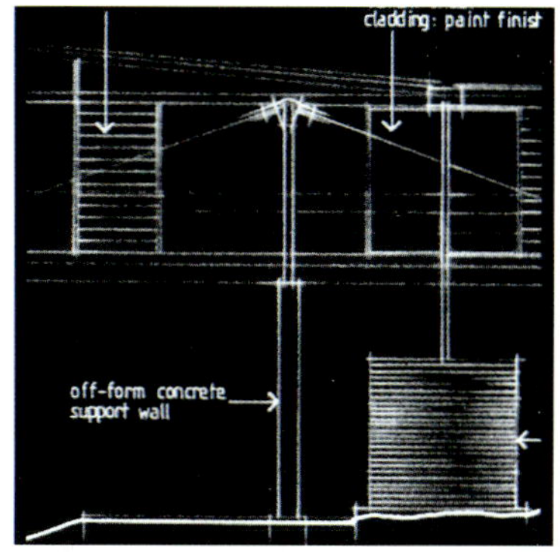

0868
Pirates Bay Pavilions: solid and transparent, interplay of components.

0869
Passive heating and cooling through cross ventilation, on-site waste water management, rainwater harvesting, and exterior sunscreens are some of the more impressive architectural components that make the project green, in addition to all of those little things we can all do, such as using low energy appliances, fixtures, and bulbs.

0870
Adjacent to the Pirates Bay House, you will find two small pavilions, nestled into the terrain, perfect for summer family use. Both buildings feature heavy and slender structures as well as solid and transparent planes, opening up to the breathtaking views of the bay below.

Studio 804, Inc. (Dan Rockhill)

Marvin Hall
1465 Jayhawk Blvd., Room 105
Lawrence, KS 66045-761, USA
www.studio804.com

0871 ➤
A narrow footprint positioned within the site maximizes passive strategies and takes advantage of a south face.

0872 ▼
A broad southern façade made up of electrochromic glass - a smart glass that assists in maintaining thermal comfort by mitigating solar heat gain through automated tinting technology - lets the sunlight in during the winter and keeps it out in the summer.

0873 ▲
Rainwater collected from the roof and diverted to an underground cistern helps reduce potable water demands and storm water runoff. The water can be used for exterior landscaping as well as interior uses, such as flushing toilets and irrigating living walls.

◄ 0874
Functioning as storm water detention and a way to decrease urban air temperatures, plant life helps insulate the building, reduce the heat island effects, and preserve the life of the roof.

0875

Helping to conserve natural resources and reducing the load on landfills, a variety of reclaimed/recycled materials can be incorporated into the design. It is also important to be responsible for waste generated on site. In this example, stone tailings were reclaimed for the façade and the site waste generated was used along the north side of the building as fill.

0876

A heavy skeletal frame enables much more insulation to be used in the cavities that exist between the frame materials. Insulating to Passive House standards reduces energy loss through the building envelope up to 90%.

0877

The visibility and accessibility of a building can influence the use of space to publically demonstrate the latest technologies in design. In this example, a touchscreen panel in the lobby displays real time energy consumption within the building.

0878

Most roofing materials are dark in color, but the industry trend to avoid the heat island effect is to use a light color to reflect heat in climates where air conditioning in the summer months is necessary.

0879

Providing priority parking and charging stations for electric vehicles, as well as on-site bicycle racks, help to encourage the use of alternative transportation.

0880

Implementing passive strategies of heating and cooling help to reduce energy loads. One example is a Trombe wall, a thermal mass which will absorb the sun's energy during the day and radiate the stored energy at night.

Studio of Environmental Architecture (David Hertz)

Tel.: +1 310 829 9932
www.studioea.com

0881 ➤

Automate

Windows and skylights can be optimally placed for passive natural convective cooling when they are controlled with a simple thermostat and humidistat to become self regulating. These windows open automatically to the prevailing breezes when the interior reaches a certain temperature and close when it gets too cool or moist out.

0882

Orientation

The McKinley house is situated on the farthest edges of its lot, leaving the center of the property open to the southern exposure and passive solar gain. Sliding doors and windows open common and private areas to the outside, with threshold less-continuous floor material blurrong the definition of exterior and interior. Exterior finish provides thermal mass.

0883

Expose

A large pre-fabricated monitor was added as an architectural intervention but also served three primary functions: to provide a flat roof for integrated photovoltaic roofing, daylight harvesting by using reflective roof and ceiling to bounce light into space (with integrated automated daylight sensors for lighting controls), and to provide for high operable thermostatically controlled windows for heat exhaust.

0884

Simplify

The Panel House uses aluminum-clad structural insulated panels that are typically used for industrial freezers. The high performance panels offer super insulation of R-50 instead of typical R-19 walls. Panels are pre-cut and the building's finished walls are put up in a matter of a few weeks not months, and require no additional exterior siding, paint or interior finishes, which simplify's materials and minimizes waste.

0886 ▲

Hidden use

The bathroom mirrors in this home slide open to the open up the view and reveal or conceal the living space below while providing expansive views from floor to ceiling windows and maintaining natural ventilation, where typically a wall would bifurcate the spaces.

0887 ▼

Re-purposing

The 747 Wing House is made from the wings of a retired 747 airplane, which have been re-purposed as its sculptural roof. Use of abandoned or underutilized structures or materials minimizes usurping primary raw materials from the lithosphere for new building materials and minimizes transportation and construction waste using conventional materials.

0885 ▲

Pre-fabricate

This house in Venice Beach uses pre-fabricated tilt-up concrete walls that were poured offsite and brought to the location. This greatly reduced cost in construction compared to poured in place walls that would require weeks of building plywood forms or conventional materials, which create construction waste. The thermal mass of the walls create an isolation to climate rather then insulation from climate.

0888

Natural light

Sometimes natural light is reserved only for main areas of the building. Smaller rooms and walkways are often overlooked and often require just as much lighting. This bathroom has an entirely glass ceiling and requires no light during the day. This provides natural light to the halls and rooms during the day as well as cross ventilation.

0889

Use the roof

The roof of the Mullin Automotive Museum is easily accessed by patrons via the main elevator and stair. The roof features a modular green roof of native grasses and plants as well as park style seating that affords opportunity to exhibit the solar panels and wind generators and creates space with access to the sun, views and ventilation not afforded a typical interior use.

0890

Use the sun:

These parabolic evacuated tube solar collectors capture solar radiation even on cold cloudy days and take up much less area than typical panels. This system is so effective it can produce enough hot water for domestic hot water and hydronic radiant heating needs for an entire family.

Studio Negri

Unit 87, The Academy Building, Parkwest Pointe,
Dublin 12, Ireland
Tel.: +353 86 8212674
www.studionegri.ie

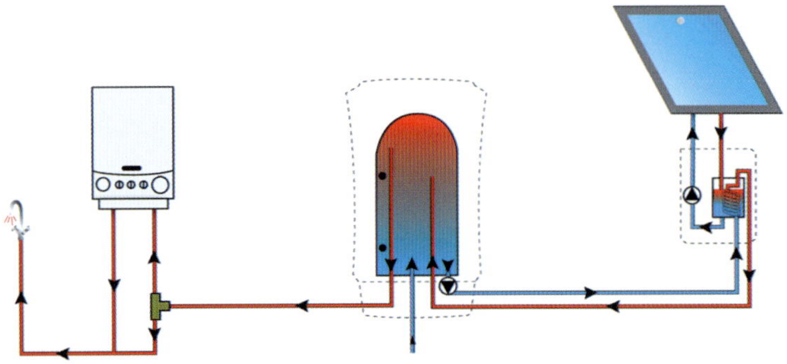

0893 ➤

Create an eco-corridor

Green Connections, a proposed artists center in Ballymun, Dublin, links the new built structures into the existing green spaces. All the trees and vegetation are linear, and even the green roofs of the new buildings blend into the public park. This creates an architectural eco-corridor and a less fragmented approach to designing eco-habitats.

0891 ▲

Combi-boilers and solar panels

This house in Dundrum, Dublin has a system that uses solar panels in conjunction with combi-boilers. The solar panel collectors feed into a buffer tank that directly heat the showers and hot taps, but if this water is not hot enough, a thermostatic valve diverts the pre-heated water to the combi-boiler, which boosts it to the required temperature.

0892 ➤

Maximize interaction with nature

This proposal for a social care center uses high-level windows and a courtyard in order to maximize natural light. The narrow plan and the forming around the courtyard also allow natural ventillation.

0894

Internal courtyards to maximize natural light

These dark circular walls are both tall and thick, and this maximizes the absorption of solar energy during the day. These Trombe walls have vents added to the top and bottom of the interior wall to allow heated air to flow via convection into the building interior.

0895

Roof garden with water retention tanks

This roof garden, on a house in Seafield in South Africa, not only allows optimized views and additional outdoor living space. It also provides resistance to thermal radiation and reduces rain run-off. By connecting the run-off to water retention tanks, this water is re-used in the garden and connected to flushing toilets.

0896

Low-maintenance and recycled materials

This attic conversion uses both zinc and recycled timber. Zinc is 100% recyclable, very long lasting and does not require maintenance. Recycled timber used internally can give a much better effect than new timber floor. Always analyse the embodied energy of a material. Try to find the sum total of the energy necessary for an entire product lifecycle.

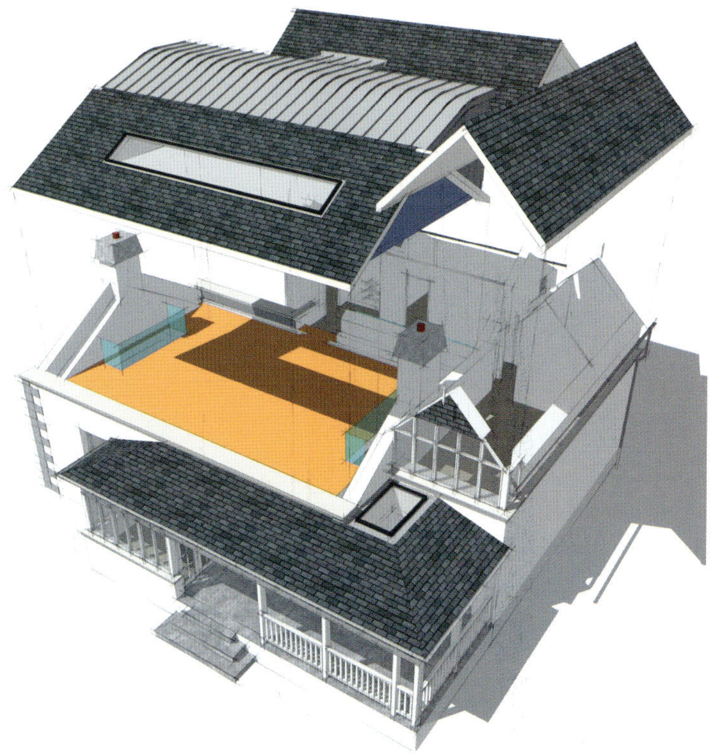

◄ 0897

Optimize south orientation with generous overhangs

This overhang is a shading device to reduce glare and net gain during the day and heat loss at night. For overhangs to be effective they must be carefully designed to be appropriate to location and orientation.

0898 ▼

Natural light

Electric lighting contributes to internal heat gains in buildings, which reduces the buildings winter heating load, but increases the summer cooling load. Introduce surfaces of high reflectance and maximize natural daylight, thereby reducing artificial lighting and associated capital costs. Natural light also allows internal planting to thrive as much as possible.

◄ 0899

Natural ventilation

The rate of ventilation required by the occupants of a space must be fully understood prior to designing. Natural ventilation works best in narrow spaces and 40 ft wide or less.

0900 ➤

Masterplan showing combined principles

As well as normal drawings and architectural masterplans, also try to explain by diagram all the eco-mechanisms and strategies. This is a proposal for a sports hall in Dalkey in Dublin. It contains a multitude of eco-solutions – solar energy, geo-thermal ducts, heat recovery systems and rain-water harversting.

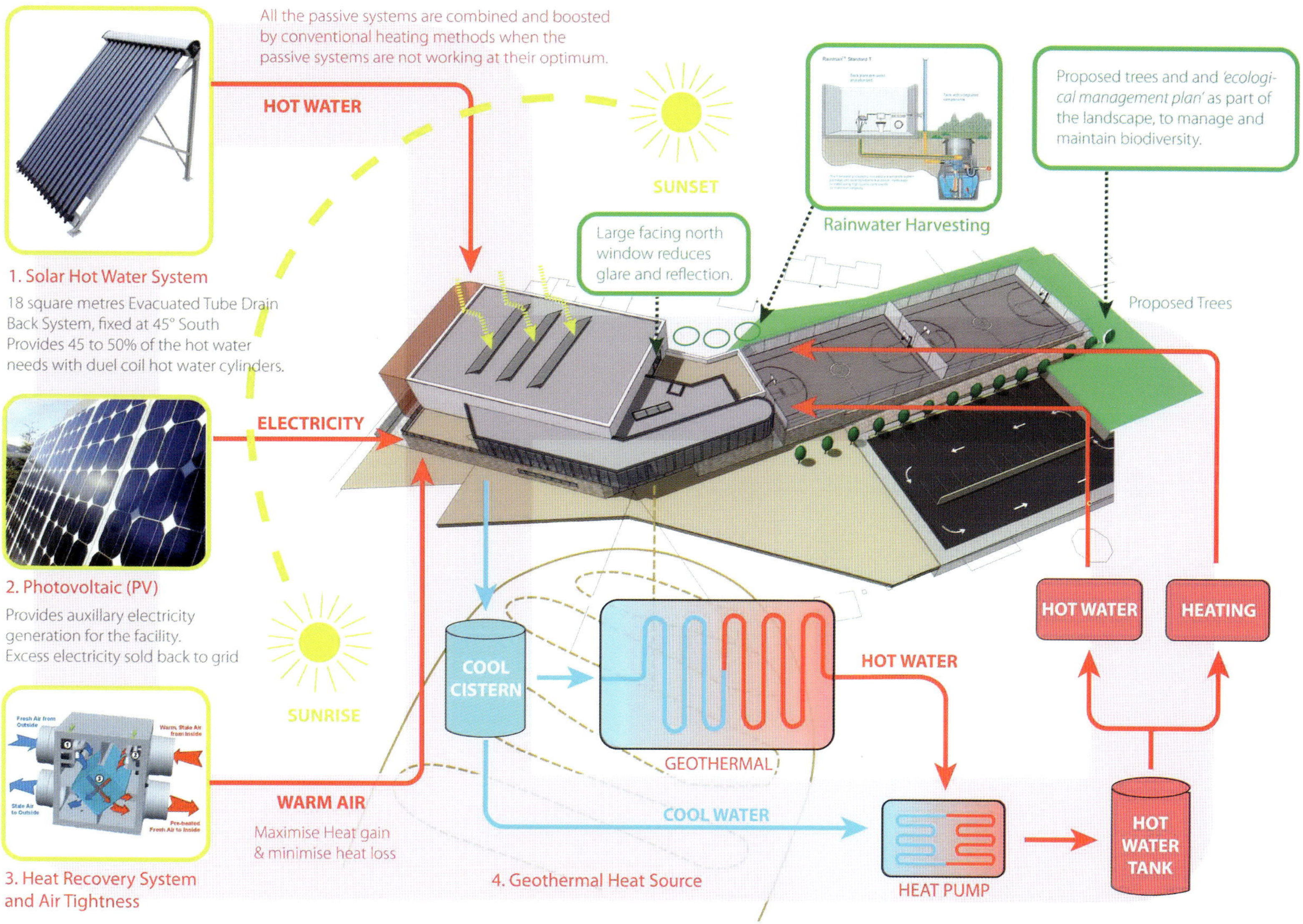

Suppose Design Office

15-1 Funairihon-machi Naka-ku
730-0843 Hiroshima, Japan
Tel.: +81 (82) 961 3000
www.suppose.jp

0901 ➤
Being situated in a small lot between two buildings, the house has no availability of natural light from normal windows. The architects made almost all of the windows on the roof.

0903
It was our intention to treat rooms and gardens as equivalent, and make the relationship between inside and out closer by creating a design featuring this garden-like room so that things normally decorating a room such as art, books, and furnishings would in a way almost be thrust into an exterior space.

0904
Using this design as a starting point, we hope that words such as garden and landscape that had only been used for exteriors can begin to take on new and varied meanings, bringing vibrant and beautiful scenery into the interior of homes as well, and make architectural aesthetics more and more diverse.

0902
Bright colors, large breakthroughs in walls, transitions without any thresholds and a garden room which extends through the entire house and, by means of skylights, provide the rooms with natural light.

0905
Rather than a design that begins to grow stale as soon as it is completed, through this design featuring the constantly changing and vibrant "garden room" we hope that the tenants daily lives will be richer than before.

0906 ➤
It is now recognized that indoor plants are able to cleanse the air and improve the chemical composition of interior environments.

0907
The surplus land from the earthwork was reused to shape the hill that acts as a garden.

0908
The site, a former field, has been incorporated into the design for bearing stratum. The leftover soil that was used for excavating the ground was employed to making the hill, which functions as the garden on the exterior and provides privacy.

0909
The banisterless central staircase has a dual function: it connects the house's different levels and it forms a volume that occupies the core space.

0910
The upper floors are composed only by the pyramid shaped roof. The main feature of the house is perhaps its skylight, which connects each floor.

Taalman Koch Architecture

1570 La Baig Ave, Unit A
Los Angeles, CA 90028, USA
Tel.: +1 213 380 1060
www.taalmankoch.com

0911

Less is less

Less clutter, less noise, less distraction, less energy, less material, less mess. Less is about stealth design and minimal spaces, letting the occupants, objects and landscape interact with the space. Strip back to the bare structural elements, leave the floor bare as exposed concrete, leave the ceiling exposed and define the space with the minimum of material.

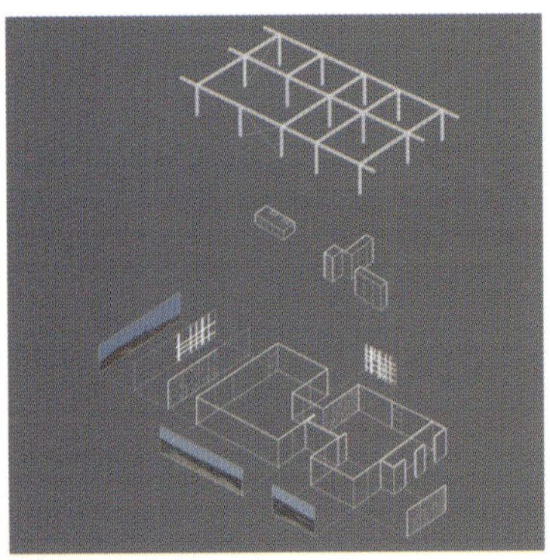

0912

Prefabricate elements and chunks, or even the whole building

Fabricating and finishing parts off site is more precise and efficient than on-site labor and is less wasteful. We minimize construction waste by pre-cutting, drilling and finishing the elements of the itHouse off site.

0913

Smaller and smarter parts = less shipping and less sitework

Construction can be messy, often requiring large equipment and temporary access. By breaking the parts of this prefabricated house down to small parts, shipping is optimized and sites can be minimally disturbed. No cranes, no temporary roads, all the parts can be brought in by small crews and assembled with few tools.

0914

Integrate the systems seamlessly

Buildings and spaces today must interface with lighting, heating, cooling systems to create, power and control their environments. We believe in seamlessly integrating technology into the design and allowing those systems to either be completely hidden from view or to become design elements. The solar panels for the off-grid itHouse double as a shade canopy for the exterior courtyards.

0915

Bring the indoors out and outdoors in

Unify the inside with the outside by bringing exterior materials indoors and opening up large views and openings to the exterior. Use material to connect the indoor and outdoor spaces.

0916

Use simple natural materials, use few materials

Keep the palette to one or two materials if possible. Use color and wallpaper to articulate space as an inexpensive way to have a big impact. We use durable and natural floor materials, such as concrete and cork, which can perform well in all types of spaces to create a unified plane.

0917

Reuse, recycle and upcycle

Reuse and recycle materials found on site, or upcycle those materials for new uses. Cut up the old slab and make a stacked concrete wall, remove old siding and create a new fence. New materials can be created from old. In the Purdy Devis House we re-purposed materials that needed to be removed from the old house and used them as landscape elements.

0918

Work with what you have

Adaptively reusing old structures makes use of existing building stock and can create new hybrid spaces and programs. The existing conditions are often taken for granted and thrown away.

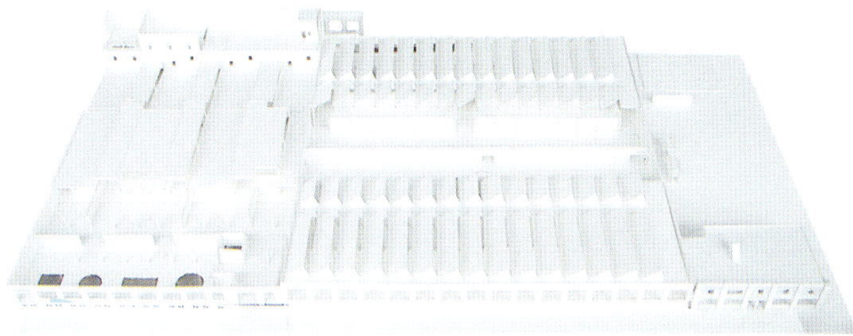

0919

Maximize and optimize spaces by creating multifunctional elements

By doubling on the function of a space new experiences emerge. In the Burns Gorman House we are creating a steel stair whose treads and risers are also the structure and form a bookcase, compressing the structural, circulation, and storage requirements into a compact and sculptural element.

0920

Use daylight as much as possible

Daylighting of spaces saves energy and allows the space to change as the natural light fluctuates. Natural light offers the best light quality to view color and detail. As the light changes the space changes, allowing the interior to reflect the exterior mood.

Theis and Khan Architects Ltd.

22 Bateman's Row
EC2A 3HH London, UK
Tel.: +44 020 7729 9329
www.theisandkhan.com

0921 ➤
Density: Bateman's Row
By densifying an area with this mixed-use project, the urban fabric is stitched back together. A more sustainable community can be established which do not rely on cars to get around. Enabling people to live in the city can create safer environments. This efficient alternative to sprawling development allows rural areas to be maintained.

0924
Solar energy: Bateman's Row
Harnessing the readily available energy of the sun, reduces the dependancy on gas and electricity in this mixed-use project. These solar panels produce the majority of hot water for the building.

0923
Green roof: Bateman's Row
A variety of planting is integrated into this inner city project to enhance the biodiversity of the area, provide solar shading and improve the privacy of the family areas. By reducing hard surfaces, water run-off can be dealt with without overloading the public system.

0922
Reuse: Lumen URC
An existing church is reconfigured and extended rather than rebuilt to give it a new lease of life. The structure is highly insulated to reduce heat loss and efficient new services integrated to minimize energy use and running costs. Community rooms and a cafe are incorporated to provide a valuable resource within walking distance for the local community.

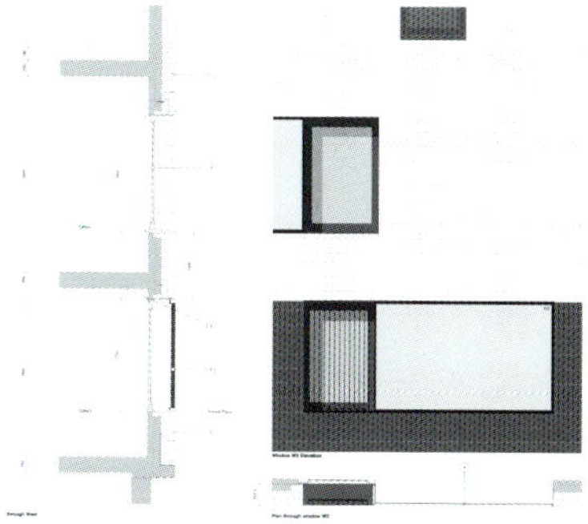

◄ 0925
Façade design: Bateman's Row
The detailed design of façades and the selection of materials ensure the building is as efficient as possible. The proportion of glazed to solid areas is carefully considered to provide optimal thermal, ventilation, light and aesthetic results.

◄ 0926
Natural ventilation: Lumen URC
A former car park is transformed into a garden, providing herbs and vegetables for the community cafe, a quiet sanctuary for locals as well as encouraging biodiversity. Community rooms are naturally ventilated with a combination of low level vents in the glazing and opening rooflights at therear of the room, which also provide natural light deep into the plan.

0927 ▼
Thermal mass: Bateman's Row
The temperature in these south-facing spaces is regulated by the thermal mass of the exposed concrete slabs. A comfortable environment is maintained throughout the year, without the need for artificial ventilation and with minimal low-temperature underfloor heating.

0928 ▲
Off-site construction: Lumen URC
Extensions are constructed from cross laminated timber panels as a truly sustainable alternative to traditional materials. As well as having the lowest energy consumption of any building material across its lifecycle, this off-site production approach reduced the overall building program and project cost whilst increasing precision and build quality.

◄ 0929
Materials: Friends House
In line with the clients' Quaker values, the approach for this project had sustainability at the core using simple, economic materials from renewable sources, such as the spruce plywood for all of the joinery.

0930 ▲
Lighting design: Lumen URC
Natural light is celebrated and combined with artificial lighting to allow a variety of uses and atmospheres in the space. Concealed low-energy linear lighting is both economic and elegant. By switching the up and down lighting separately, as well as controlling each bay, flexibility of light levels and character is integrated with minimum fittings and energy use.

TYIN Tegnestue Architects

Kjøpmanssgata 51
7011 Trondheim, Norway
Tel.: +47 452 55 502
www.tyintegnestue.no

0931
An existing boat house from the 19th century became not only the mould for the new structure, but parts of the materials from the old structure were used as cladding in the new. The rusty, old corrugated steel sheets became beautiful doors in the new façade.

0932
A crucial part of reuse is the aspect of adding value. Old, dusty timber can become a valuable asset for communities where resources are scarce, but only when some precision and care are put into the work. A dab of fresh paint over some old plywood boxes accentuates the new and sets this wall apart from any other wall.

0933
In hot, humid areas where electricity is limited and expensive, natural ventilation is a obvious choice. The large roof covers the heavy brick structures, keeping the courtyard and spaces colder in the day and warmer in the night. Woven mats of bamboo prevent radiation of heat from the corrugated metal roof.

0934

When working in the rural areas of Thailand, transport of materials is a big obstacle. The natural choice was to use locally-grown bamboo found near the building site. The material is free, grows back rapidly and is in tune with local tradition and skill.

0935

Involving people from the local community is crucial for ensuring that the project is socially viable. Through conversations, drawing workshops and model making, anyone of all ages can join in the discussion of plan for the community. Involvement creates a sense of ownership and pride in the people involved.

0936

During the process of creating architecture, surprises will arise. When the bedrock was exposed under mud and grass, the best choice was to incorporate the beautiful surface in the space itself. Being aware of opportunity during all the parts of the process usually strengthens the project.

0937

Strategical use of durable materials, such as concrete and steel, can improve the longevity of any design. The low bench gives a place to rest after the ball game, while also strengthening the the existing brick wall.

0938

Old windows found near the building site was used to create the openings in the back façade. The size of the frames determined the main axis for the structure. Combined with new construction timber treated with eco-friendly oils, old materials get a new value.

0939

Simple solutions to basic challenges. By combining plastic piping, ready-made concrete tubes and locally harvested timber, an open air bathhouse is made for Tasanee and one of her orphaned children.

0940

One of our most used tools on the building site is a white board. To explain ideas and solutions, it is very useful to make a quick sketch as you go. The white board enables rapid changes and has deemed to be a very a pliable design tool.

UCARCHITECT

283 Lisgar Street
Toronto, ON M6J 3H1, Canada
Tel.: +1 416 536 4977
www.ucarchitect.ca

◄ 0941

Site sensitivity and storm water management

Existing heavily treed ravine forest, (contours rising 85 ft in height) and drainage patterns influence the building's proportions, orientation and location. The building is embedded into the hillside and, despite its large floor plate, it blends in with its surroundings due to its extensive green roof vegetation and its one-to-two storey appearance from three sides.

0942 ►

Improvement of existing contextual conditions

Located within suburban context and yet physically surrounded by heavy vegetation on nearly all sides, the building's natural finishes and calm colors integrate it with its setting. Translucent glazing at entrance allows for natural light to enter and yet affords privacy. The building is a pleasure for the eye from many angles.

◄ 0943

Interior-exterior link

The edge separating the inside from the outside is intentionally blurred with tall glass sliding doors. The easily accessible outdoor decks encourage outdoor living in a country known for long winters as well as utilize otherwise unused roof areas.

0945 ▲

Passive daylighting

Large glazed openings and skylights make artificial lighting unnecessary during the day. Natural daylight penetrates all spaces deep within the building. South-facing elevations provide optimal daylight while interior and exterior shading devices offer additional solar control.

◄ 0944

Highly insulated exterior walls, roof, windows, and doors

The building uses wood, both as structural and finishing element, to complement the austerity of the light floors and walls.

◄ 0946

Land -se efficiency

Half perched, half nestled into its site, the building extends across the site with a light footprint, fully visible from the narrow access road but hidden from the lakeside. A generously sized wrap-around deck creates a close link between the interior and exterior.

0947 ▼

Passive ventilation

Interconnected spaces spanning all floors allow for natural cross ventilation by creating unimpeded air flow through the building. Open views are maintained throughout.

◄ 0948

Radiant floor heating embedded within pigmented poured concrete

Thermal mass provides even temperature comfort throughout all seasons.

0949

Compact and yet spacious

A modest building with a floor plate of only1 ,238 sq ft, yet spacious due to its enlarged angled volume, interconnected spaces, eliminated hallways, dual use of spaces, and well-placed views and vistas.

0950

Low environmental impact over the building's life cycle

The exterior is composed of durable weather-resistant and maintenance-free materials (unfinished red western cedar and sheets of light-coloured metal). The interior is void of unnecessary accents, baseboards, or mouldings – basic elements and varied textures take precedence.

UdA, Architetti Associati

Via Valprato, 68
10155 Torino, Italy
Tel.: +39/0112489489 int. 201
www.uda.it

0951 ▲
Surround yourself lightheartedly with things you are fond of, bearing in mind that their simplicity will always be a source of pleasure.

0952 ▼
Coherence also lies in never hide the past – better to change it into a challenge for innovation.

0953 ►
Sustainability of a building may be understood in many ways. We like to think that this term can also embrace the ability of an architecture to talk with its context, with coherence but everyone into its own extent.

0954 ▲
Never lose touch with the land, particularly when this may become a refined, aesthetic enjoyment and, in any case, a contact with life.

0955 ▼
Look upon workplaces, be they factories or offices, as often the scenes wherein the best of human talent is applied. For this reason, they must always be accompanied by nature and its elements: light, greenery, air.

© Gariglio

0958

In certain contexts, respect for a locality and its traditions must not take the form of mindless imitation of ancient forms. What is required is renovation with embodiment of the spirit of things and the traces of human endeavours.

0956

Use the more unusual or commonplace spaces and street furniture as instruments of a consciousness of our senses, bodies and everyday actions.

© Carola Ripamonti

0957

Go back to a certain friendship spirit, not at the beck of fashion or some ephemeral trend, but as an aid in rediscovering the human component that lives in houses, offices and factories. A coffee and snack corner in an office may become a new cenacle for a meeting with colleagues.

© Cane

© Carola Ripamonti

0960

Think of benches, seats and other facilities provided in public spaces as places of emotional experience for physical and psychological well-being (something children do not need to be told!)

© Gariglio

0959

A city must be the recipient of gentle grafts that serve to upgrade its existing buildings. New parts embodying better technologies improve the performance of already built-up spaces.

Vincent Snyder Architects

1711 Briar Street
Austin, TX 78704, USA
Tel.: +1 512 2289245
snyder@mail.utexas.edu

0961 ➤
Place windows to induce natural ventilation.

0962 ▼
Control heat gain during the summertime and heat loss during the winter.

0963 ➤
Low-VOC paint is less toxic for the environment.

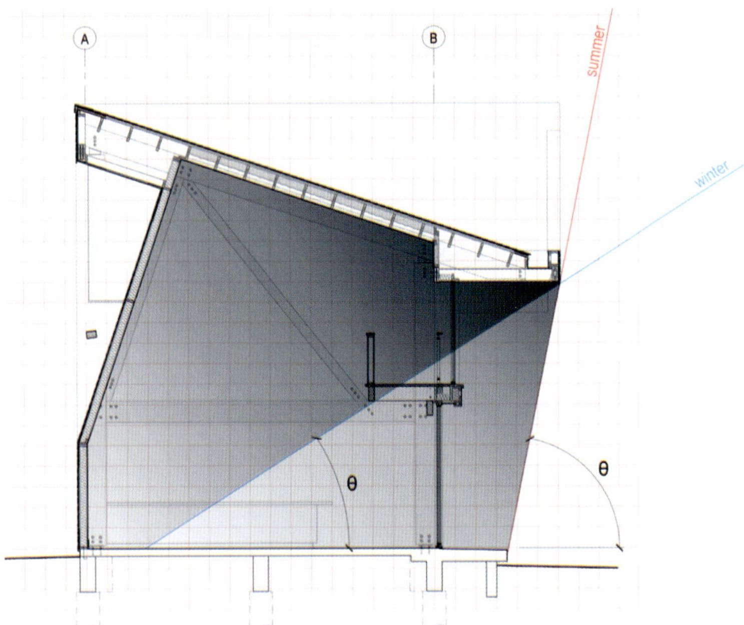

0964 ▼
Low-maintenance durable cladding gives buildings longer life, whether using an expensive material like slate or an inexpensive material like corrugated metal.

0967 ➤
Shaded openings on the north and south façades bring in light and views but diminish direct sun exposure

0968 ▼
Repeated structure, simple roof slope and repeated windows create efficiencies in construction.

0965 ▲
Use concrete slab for thermal mass.

0969 ➤
Create covered exterior spaces that double as buffer zones for indoor heat-gain.

0966 ➤
Solid massing on east and west façades mitigates early morning and late afternoon sun intrusion.

0970 ▼
Use light color finish for reflection to lower heat gain.

WD Architects

30 King St.
Cooran, 4569 QLD, Australia
Tel.: +61 485 2720
www.wdarchitects.com.au

0971

Land use and ecology

Projects are designed as an adaptation to their immediate environment. Working predominantly in the subtropics, the climate is wet and humid during the summer with a short cold dry winter and a mild spring and autumn. The pattern of living in this region favors the outdoors, with the connection between indoors and outdoors being always important.

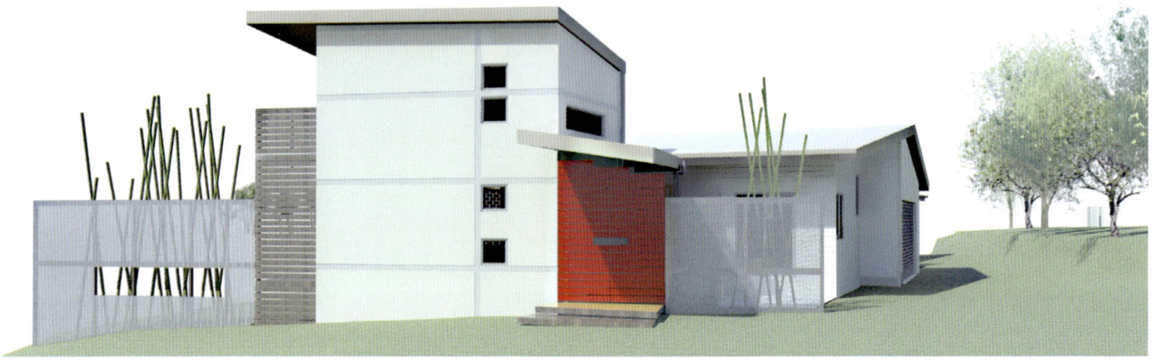

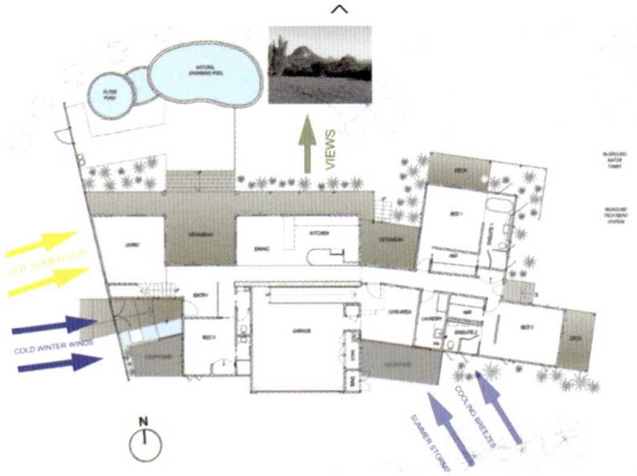

0972

Water

Australia is one of the driest continents on the planet so every project collects all its own water for internal and landscape use. Waste water is either recycled for internal reuse or recycled for landscape use. Hot water is heated via solar systems mounted on the roof and all plumbing fittings and appliances are selected for their high energy and water efficiency.

0973
Materials
Materials are chosen for their low toxicity, emissions, and embodied energy, high level insulation or thermal capacity. They are also selected for their low impact on ecosystems and biodiversity when grown, harvested or manufactured. Their ability to be reused, recycled or composted at the end of the life of the building is another consideration, as are local materials where they are available.

0974
Energy
Buildings are designed to be low users of energy and to heat and cool themselves, reducing and eliminating mechanical systems. Solar orientation, passive heating and cooling, cross and stack ventilation, and insulation are fundamental methods of reducing energy consumption employed in in all WD Architects projects, as shown in the design of the Maleny Sports Club.

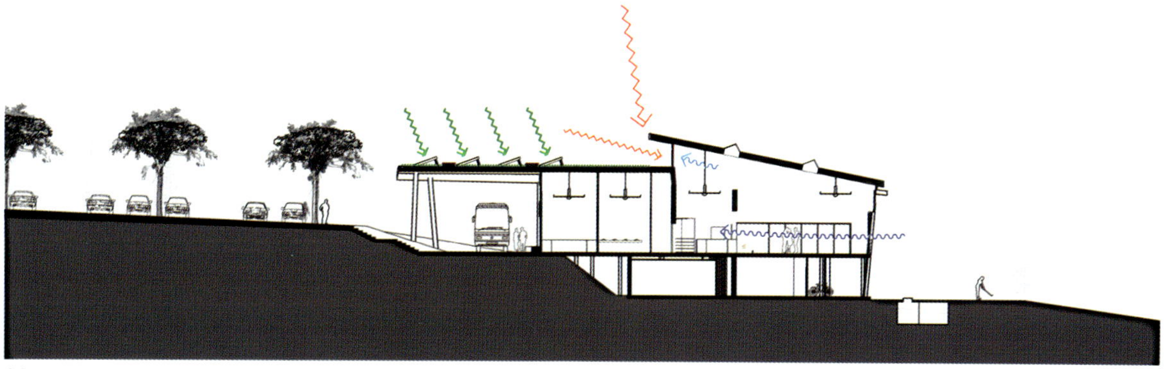

0975 ➤

Air quality

Natural ventilation is an essential part of every design for cooling and air quality. The Noosa Pengari Steiner School Hall uses cross and stack ventilation, as well as a large diameter low speed fan, to move air through the building. Air is also drawn across the lawn and from garden plants nearby, adding further cooling and filtering effects to maintain a consistently high internal air quality regardless of the weather conditions.

0976 ▼

Emissions

Designing for less energy and water consumption means less emissions into the environment and atmosphere. Composting toilets are used at the Noosa Pengari Steiner School to minimize water consumption and use composted waste for re-vegetating the school site. Minimizing the light emission from a project is another important issue to reduce the impact on local ecology at night.

0977 ▼

Size

Size affects everything so building less means less cost and impact on the environment. Buildings are conceived with less material, and materials are finished in their raw state where possible. Smaller buildings mean less energy and water consumed in their construction and over their life span. Internal space are made to feel bigger by including the outside as part of the inside and extending the landscape into the building.

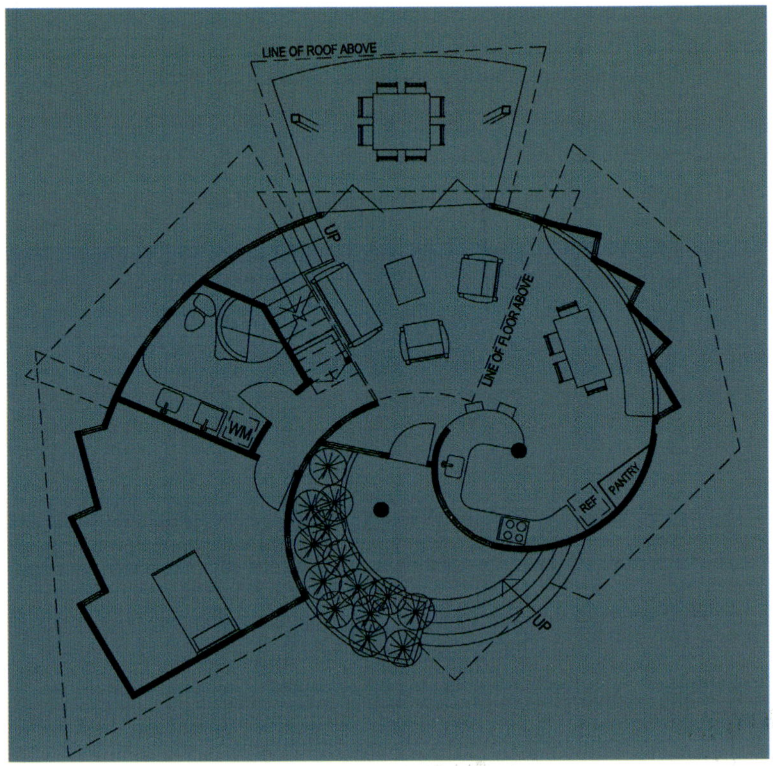

0978 ▲

Innovation

Every project is a new investigation of how to do things better, often using innovative strategies and technologies that achieve improved sustainable outcomes. The mainstay, though, are time-honored low-tech methods and solutions that allow buildings to regulate themselves through passive means, with only fine-tuning required by the occupants for individual comfort levels.

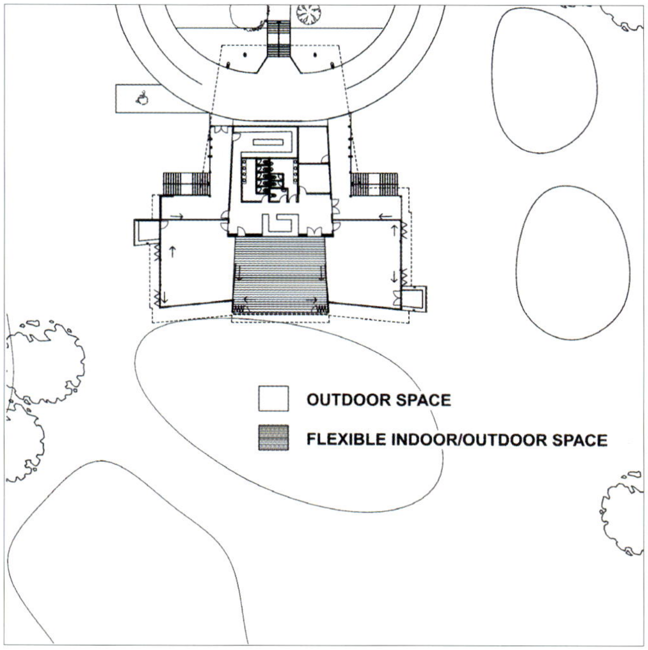

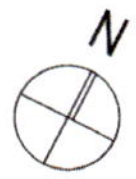

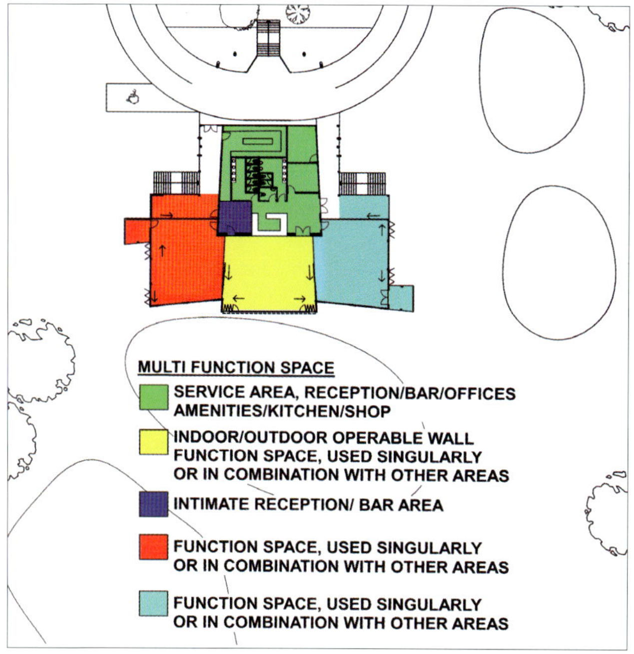

0979

Life cycle

The complete life cycle of a project is designed in its inception. Not only the cost of construction but the cost of operating the building needs to be considered, along with flexibility for future changed use, reuseability and recyclability at the end of its life span.

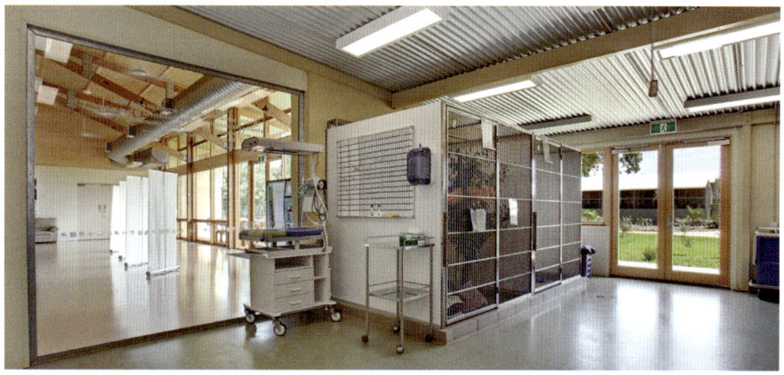

0980

Education and community

There is an education component to every project WD Architects delivers. They demonstrate the effectiveness and beauty of sustainable design and give greater a understanding of the issues and possibilities. This is especially true in a school context such as the Noosa Pengari Steiner School and in the Wildlife Warriors Veterinary Hospital.

Werner Sobek Stuttgart GmbH & Co. KG

Albstraße 14
70597 Stuttgart, Germany
Tel.: +49 711 76750 38
www.wernersobek.com

0981

The sum is greater than the sum of its parts: holistic design and interdisciplinary planning
Visions are developed in-house by a tightly knitted team of experts, who develop both individual and universal strategies and systems.

0982

Triple zero®: zero energy
Our proof-of-concept buildings generate all energy required during operation on-site.

0983

Proof of concept
Our buildings demonstrate the state of the art in both research and design. They are prototypes of building solutions for sustainable architecture in the 21st century.

0984

Triple zero®: zero emissions
Energy generation is exclusively by renewable energy sources. No fossil fuels are used on-site.

0985

Continuous exploration
Research is an integral part of our work and design. New materials and technology are incorporated when they support the overall goals of the design. Simulations support the design process and monitoring can verify assumptions and create the base for future predictions.

0986 ➤
Design for disassembly
The end-of-life phase of a building is taken into account at all stages of the design and building process.

0987 ▼
Beauty
Essential and deeply human, breathtaking beauty creates affection and a deep bond with our built environment.

0988 ▲
Triple zero®: zero waste
Our buildings are fully recyclable. Thus they don't deplete natural resources, but supply valuable resources for future generations.

0990 ▼
Urbanism
Individual buildings form the fabric of our built environment and can incorporate alternative solutions to urban issues - for example, by integrating E-mobility into the architecture and technology of the house.

0989 ➤
High hech at its best: cutting edge technology
The latest technology and software is employed for the design and operation process of our buildings. Technology is fully integrated into the design, but never a means on its own.

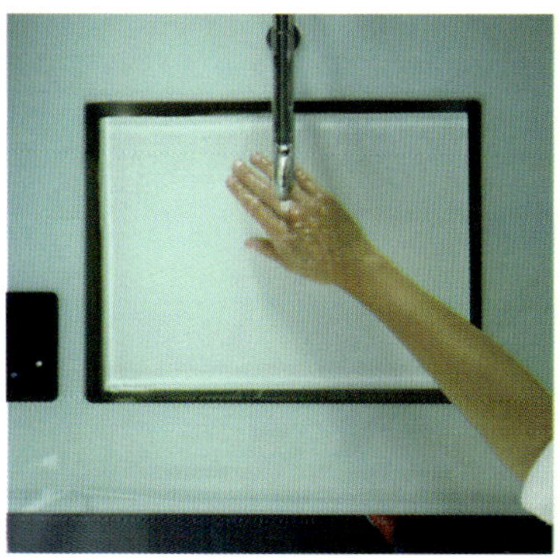

ZeroEnergy Design

156 Milk Street, Suite 3
Boston, MA 02109, USA
Tel.: +1 617 720 5002
www.zeroenergy.com

0991 ➤
Take your shoes off!
Your shoes track in chemicals and contaminants that you don't want in your healthy home. Create a mudroom or mud area near the entry door so it's convenient for family and visitors to remove shoes when entering your house.

© Michael J Lee

0992 ▼
Borrowed light
Interior glazing can transfer light to spaces that don't have direct access to daylight, minimizing the need for artificial light.

© Eric Roth

◄ 0993
Thermal mass is often over rated
Check with your energy professional before adding unnecessary concrete to your floor assembly or using a high-mass/reduced R-value wall system. Unless you live in a climate with big daily temperature swings (like the desert), a simple tile will probably provide the benefit you're looking for.

0994
Prioritize south-facing glazing
In cold climates in the northern hemisphere, high performance south-facing windows will offer a net gain over the heating season – the passive solar heat gained through the windows will exceed the heat lost. East, west, and north-facing windows, however, will be a net loss.

0995
Scenarios for living
In planning a new home, think about how you will use each space on a day-to-day basis and for the unique scenarios it will accommodate – like Thanksgiving dinner for twenty. By planning for multifunctional space, you can minimize square footage – the easiest way to conserve cost, energy, and material resources.

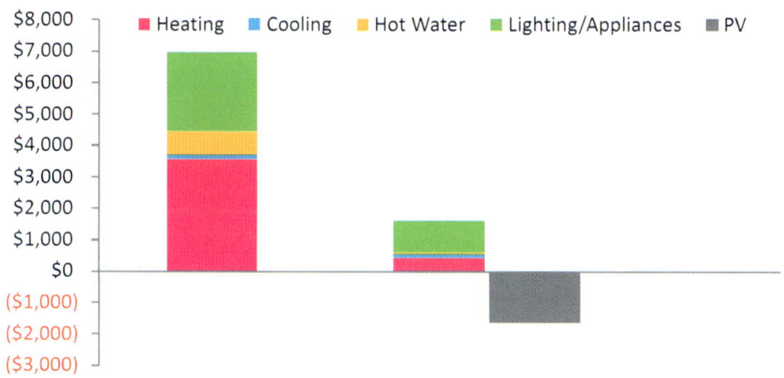

0996
Crunch the numbers and design the mechanical system
Work with a professional knowledgeable in the field of energy modeling and mechanical design to ensure that your house meets both your energy performance and thermal comfort expectations. Not sure where to find one? A Certified Passive House Consultant should have the right skill set.

0997 ➤
Avoid carpet
Carpet will trap dust, dirt, mold spores, and other allergens and contaminants. Solid surface flooring is easy to clean and a great fit for radiant heat. As a budget friendly and unique alternative to stained hardwood, consider a more economical wood floor (or even a plywood subfloor) paired will a no-VOC floor paint.

© Eric Roth

0998 ▼
Mechanical ventilation with energy recovery
Build your home as air tight as possible. Incorporate whole-house mechanical ventilation with an energy or heat recovery ventilator (ERV/HRV) to maintain excellent indoor air quality. A whole house HEPA filter can also be added to reduce common allergens.

© Jerome Eno

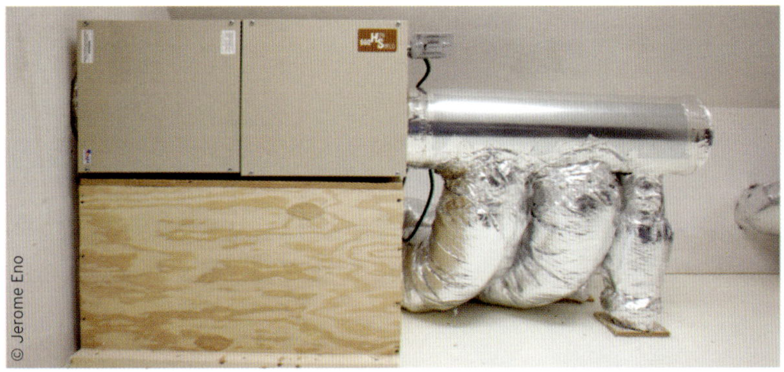

© Jerome Eno

© Jerome Eno

0999

Plan for solar

Even if it's not in the budget on day one, if your site allows, plan for solar. Decide if you'd like to see the panels on the roof or conceal them. By making the requisite roof penetrations during the initial home construction you can proper flash them and avoid future leaks that are often a result of cutting holes in your roof after the fact.

1000

Indirect lighting

Using an indirect light source is a great way to light a space. Warm up a cool light source, like a linear fluorescent lamp, by bouncing light off a wood or plywood ceiling. The thin aluminum bar in this photo is a fluorescent light fixture. An alternative detail is to create a cove with a more economical fluorescent strip light.